The Anxiety Disorders

Specific Phobias: A persistent, irrational fear and avoidance of some particular object or situation, such as flying, heights, animals, and enclosed spaces, which can emerge in early childhood.

Agoraphobia: The fear of open spaces and of being in places or situations from which escape might be difficult or embarrassing, and in which help may not be available.

Social Phobia: A persistent fear of one of more situations in which the person is exposed to possible scrutiny by others and worries about doing something or acting in a way that will be humiliating or embarrassing. It often emerges during adolescence.

Panic Disorder: An experience of minutes long episodes of intense dread, accompanied by intense autonomic overarousal such as chest palpitations or pain, breathlessness, choking, or other frightening sensations. Panic attacks can begin during adolescence.

Generalized Anxiety Disorder (GAD): Persistent tension, apprehension, irritability and worry that is unaccompanied by panic attacks, phobias or obsessions and which can surface in adolescence.

Obsessive-Compulsive Disorder (OCD): Person is plagued by unwanted repetitive thoughts (obsessions) and/or actions (compulsions). OCD can emerge during childhood.

Post-Traumatic Stress Disorder (PTSD): Development of symptoms in response to a highly traumatic event, including chronic anxiety, emotional numbness, nightmares and flashbacks of the event. Children, as well as adults, are subject to PTSD.

Separation Anxiety Disorder (SAD): prolonged worry about separating from attachment figures that is specific to childhood and characterized by incessant clinging, refusal to go to sleep, to school, to babysitters, or to be alone.

alpha
books

Recovery: The Adult

Body

- Breathing exercises
- Daily deep relaxation practice
- Regular aerobic exercise
- Eliminating caffeine, smoking, recreational drugs
- Healthy Diet
- Vitamin and mineral supplements
- Herbal relaxants and serotonin boosters
- Detoxifying the environment
- Body work
- Recognizing bodily tension

Mind

- Identifying maladaptive thinking
- Replacing destructive thoughts with constructive ones

Action

- Avoiding avoidance
- Practicing self-assertion

Whole Self

- Boosting self-esteem
- Enhancing self-efficacy and inner control
- Seeking meaning
- Taking time for self-nurturing

Recovery: The Child

To exorcise your child's demons, work to increase the following:

Self-Efficacy—The feeling that your child's actions have the power to get her needs met, that she has the ability to create a favorable outcome for herself.

Inner Control—The capacity to organize events and to reasonably predict a favorable outcome.

Trust—The perception that he can depend on you to safeguard him from harm, both physical and psychological, and to not abandon him.

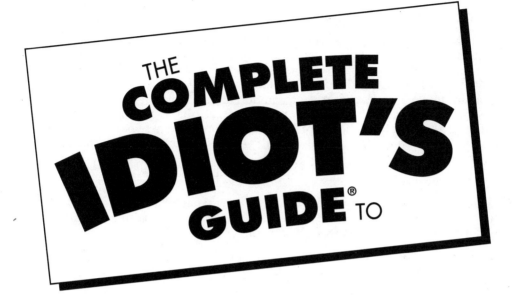

THE COMPLETE IDIOT'S GUIDE® TO

Conquering
Fear and Anxiety

by Sharon Heller, Ph.D.

alpha
books

A Division of Macmillan General Reference
A Pearson Education Macmillan Company
1633 Broadway, New York, NY 10019-6785

Macmillan General Reference books may be purchased for business or sales promotional use. For information, please write: Special Markets Department, Macmillan Publishing USA, 1633 Broadway, New York, NY 10019.

International Standard Book Number: 0-02-862727-X
Library of Congress Catalog Card Number: 98-85977

01 00 99   8 7 6 5 4 3 2 1

Interpretation of the printing code: the rightmost number of the first series of numbers is the year of the book's printing; the rightmost number of the second series of numbers is the number of the book's printing. For example, a printing code of 99-1 shows that the first printing occurred in 1999.

Printed in the United States of America

Note: This publication contains the opinions and ideas of its author. It is intended to provide helpful and informative material on the subject matter covered. It is sold with the understanding that the author and publisher are not engaged in rendering professional services in the book. If the reader requires personal assistance or advice, a competent professional should be consulted.

Alpha Development Team

Publisher
Kathy Nebenhaus

Editorial Director
Gary M. Krebs

Managing Editor
Bob Shuman

Marketing Brand Manager
Felice Primeau

Acquisitions Editor
Jessica Faust

Development Editors
Phil Kitchel
Amy Zavatto

Assistant Editor
Georgette Blau

Production Team

Development Editor
Al McDermid

Production Editor
Mark Enochs

Cover Designer
Mike Freeland

Photo Editor
Richard H. Fox

Illustrator
Jody P. Schaeffer

Book Designers
Scott Cook and Amy Adams of DesignLab

Indexer
Nadia Ibrahim

Layout/Proofreading
Marie Kristine Parial-Leonardo
John Bitter

Contents at a Glance

Contents

Part 4: Anxiety...Panic...Obsessions...Trauma...   211

15 Preventing Sudden Terror   213

16 First Aid for Nervous Wrecks   227

Foreword

I am pleased to write this foreword to *The Complete Idiot's Guide to Conquering Fear and Anxiety*. This book will go a long way in making this often confusing and sometimes complicated information easily understandable. The style of the book is interesting and engaging and clearly explains the roots, causes, and significance of everyday fears and phobias. The author makes use of individual examples that help to simplify and clarify useful lessons in understanding and conquering fears. Examples of fears and phobias from many well-known individuals and television personalities are effectively shown to help readers understand that they are not alone in experiencing their fears.

Anxiety disorders, the most common mental illnesses, are a significant and costly problem. In the United States alone, 23 million people suffer from an anxiety disorder, with anxiety disorders being the fifth most common diagnosis in primary care and the most common psychiatric diagnosis made by primary care physicians. Specific phobias, which are one type of anxiety disorder, are the most prevalent mental health disorder, more common than alcohol abuse, alcohol dependence, or major depression. Moreover, 33 percent of patients who describe their symptoms as chest pains, abdominal pains, or insomnia actually have an anxiety disorder, as do 25 percent of those with fatigue, headache, or joint pain. The average person with an anxiety disorder has ten encounters with the health-care system before being correctly diagnosed, increasing healthcare costs and causing frustration on the part of both the patient and physician.

In 1990, 147.8 billion mental health dollars were spent in the United States. Of this amount, $46.6 billion (32 percent) was spent on the treatment of anxiety disorders. The cost of treatment of all other mental health disorders was $101.2 billion. In a more recent study, $15 billion in direct costs and $50 billion in indirect costs were the amounts estimated for anxiety disorders.

Anxiety disorders have long been viewed by most clinicians as particularly challenging to treat, requiring extensive long-term therapy. However, given the advent of managed care and healthcare reform, clinicians are being pressured to become more efficient in their treatment of these clients.

In my experience in treating patients with anxiety disorders at the Center for Advanced Multimedia Psychotherapy, I have found that treatment often requires a variety of interrelated techniques and disciplines. Clearly however, educating patients about the nature of their fears is an important first step for everyone. Relaxation techniques combined with some type of exposure therapy is also useful. Cognitive-behavioral techniques that include coping strategies, thought stopping, and anxiety management, are additional adjuncts to treatment. It is often necessary to individualize treatment for each patient's individual circumstances.

The Complete Idiot's Guide to Conquering Fear and Anxiety is an important contribution because it approaches this significant problem in a clear and concise style without oversimplifying or minimizing the seriousness of these conditions. Making easy-to-understand information widely available is necessary to help individuals so they can effectively participate in their own recovery.

Brenda K. Wiederhold, Ph.D., MBA
Director
Center for Advanced Multimedia Psychotherapy
California School of Professional Psychology
Research and Service Foundation
San Diego, California 92121

Brenda K. Wiederhold, Ph.D., MBA is the Director of the Center for Advanced Multimedia Psychotherapy (CAMP) at the California School of Professional Psychology in San Diego, California. She is nationally certified in both biofeedback and neurofeedback by the Biofeedback Certification Institute of America and serves on the editorial board of CyberPsychology and Behavior Journal. Dr. Wiederhold is recognized as a national and international leader in the treatment of anxiety and phobias with virtual reality and has completed over 500 VR therapy sessions with patients. The Center for Advanced Multimedia Psychotherapy has comprehensive programs to treat fear of flying, fear of driving, anxiety disorders, psychophysiological disorders and uses a combination of cognitive-behavioral techniques, including relaxation training, coping strategies, and real-life exposure to help individuals overcome their fears.

Introduction

For most, fear is a friend not foe, a normal emotion that forces us to take action to protect ourselves. But when unreasonable fears—of rejection, of failure, of loss, of being hurt, of change—take possession of our bodies, minds, and souls, they need to be exorcised.

This isn't easy. Our fears have been trailing us since childhood and can be stubborn to conquer. They have voices like, "Who said you can? You know you're stupid and clumsy." or "I'll panic if I get in that elevator." But if we come face to face with these psychic invaders, we can scare them away. Not overnight. It takes time, perseverance, and a belief that you can defeat them. Many people can. Change may be slow, but every step that makes you less vulnerable to fear and more in control of your life's path is a step well worth taking.

What You'll Find in This Book

The Complete Idiot's Guide to Conquering Fear and Anxiety is divided into five parts. You can read the book from start to finish, or you can browse through the Table of Contents to find the chapters that cover your personal fears and anxieties.

Here's how the book is organized:

Part 1, "The Heart of Your Fears," introduces the basics: why we fear; how to distinguish normal from abnormal fears in you and in your child; and what triggers anxiety and panic.

Part 2, "Making It All Better," explores all the ways to scare your internal demons away.

Part 3, "Overcoming Phobias" looks at the common phobias—agoraphobia, fear of flying, social phobia, stage fright, and fear of failure or success—and what you can do to reduce or even eliminate their control over your life.

Part 4, "Anxiety... Panic... Obsessions...Trauma...," investigates panic disorder, Generalized Anxiety Disorder, Obsessive-Compulsive Disorder and Post-Traumatic Stress Disorder and ways to help you come to grips with them.

Part 5, "Childhood Fears," explores how to distinguish normal from abnormal childhood fears and how to bust those ghosts and prevent them from haunting your child later on.

A Little Help from the Side Lines

Scattered throughout are little boxes of information to bolster the material, offer suggestions, provide insight, add a bit of humor, and to warn against potential pitfalls.

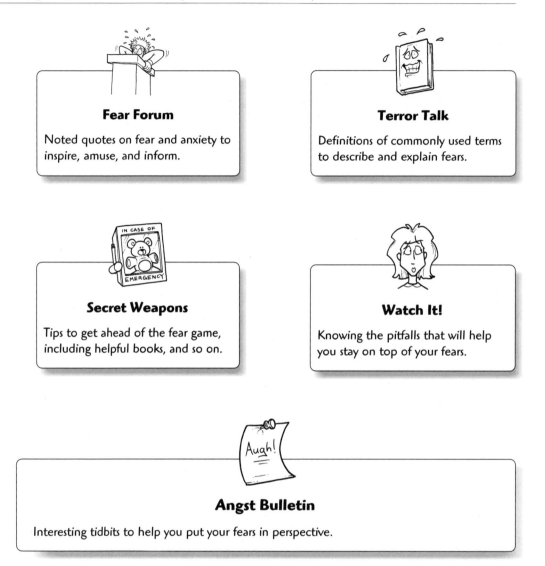

Fear Forum

Noted quotes on fear and anxiety to inspire, amuse, and inform.

Terror Talk

Definitions of commonly used terms to describe and explain fears.

Secret Weapons

Tips to get ahead of the fear game, including helpful books, and so on.

Watch It!

Knowing the pitfalls that will help you stay on top of your fears.

Angst Bulletin

Interesting tidbits to help you put your fears in perspective.

Acknowledgments

Heartfelt thanks to good friends Robert Rock and Carolyn Singer for their insightful and clever suggestions, which I happily incorporated into this book. Special thanks to my agent, Mary Ann Naples from Creative Culture, a warm, upbeat, diligent, and meticulous person, who patiently nudges me toward my personal best.

At Alpha Books, I am grateful to my acquisition editor, Jessica Faust, for her patience and support and to my development editor, Al McDermid, for championing this book with ongoing encouragement and for pulling no punches in the editing.

I wish to thank my technical editor, Manuel Tancer, M.D., Associate Professor of Psychiatry and Behavioral Neurosciences and Pharmacology at Wayne State University School of Medicine, for his careful review of the manuscript. I also wish to thank psychologist Mitch Spero of Child and Family Psychologists in Plantation, Florida for his helpful input.

Part 1
The Heart of Your Fears

"Fear lent wings to his feet."—Virgil, Aeneid

Who doesn't have strong fears? Of thunderstorms, of snakes, of heights, of the dentist, of the future, of failing, of dying. Fear is an internal alarm system to alert us to harm's way so we can take self-protection. But some people have powerful fears and anxiety of things or situations that are not immediately dangerous and which take possession of the person's body, mind, feelings and actions.

Part 1 identifies fears, both normal and abnormal, what triggers them and how to know if you or your child has crippling fears that take control of your life.

Chapter 1

Why We Fear

In This Chapter

➤ What is fear?

➤ When are fears unreasonable and irrational?

➤ How common are uncontrollable fears?

➤ How can we explain fears?

Fears are just for kids, right? Wrong. Everyone feels fear when faced with perceived danger. It helps us to avoid potential peril. Some people are relatively intrepid, others are quickly terrified and sometimes unreasonably so—even those thought to be most courageous.

Napoleon Bonaparte set out to conquer the world, but he couldn't conquer his obsession to stop in front of tall buildings and count the windows one by one, a ritual he needed to quell undue anxiety.

Edgar Allen Poe was a famous claustrophobic who used his real life fear of closed spaces in such classic tales as "The Premature Burial" and "The Black Cat."

Frederick the Great, King of Prussia, was so afraid of water that he wouldn't wash, and instead forced his servants to wipe his face clean with a dry towel.

Today there's John Madden—a six foot, four inch, 240-pound former football player and head coach of the Oakland Raiders professional football team and, today, a well-known TV sports personality. Once while flying, he experienced a panic attack. He got

Terror Talk

Anxiety comes from a Latin word meaning, "worried about the unknown." It is also related to a Greek word meaning "compress or strangle."

off the plane at a stop halfway to his destination, and has never flown since. Instead, he travels the country turtle style in his specially equipped luxury bus, donated for his use by Greyhound.

Napoleon Bonaparte was obsessive-compulsive, Edgar Allen Poe and Frederick the Great were both phobic. John Madden is phobic as well. He has *aviophobia*, better known as fear of flying.

He is not alone in feeling uncontrollable and incapacitating panic, anxiety, and abnormal fear at some time. In fact, *anxiety disorders* are considered the number one mental health problem in America; thirteen percent of the general population alone suffer from some kind of *phobia*, the most common anxiety disorder.

Age of Anxiety

Why is our society so fearful? We live in extremely stressful times; times that have been called the "Age of Anxiety." And as such, stress plays a key role in the development of our fears.

When we lived in caves, real dangers, like hungry sabre-toothed tigers, were all around. Upon perceiving danger, the brain activated the *sympathetic nervous system* (SNS), which is part of our involuntary autonomic nervous system, to give us the energy we need to fight the danger or to flee from it. In this "fight-or-flight" response, which you may recognize from your own experience, hormones are released and the SNS sends signals to various parts of the body to produce the following changes:

➤ The heart starts pumping, which rushes fuel (oxygen-laden blood) to every cell.

➤ Breathing comes in quick spurts. Nostrils and air passages in the lungs open wider to get air more quickly.

➤ Blood rushes away from the abdomen to the legs to allow us to run faster (thus the sinking feeling in our stomach when we are afraid).

➤ We begin to sweat to cool ourselves down.

➤ Blood clotting ability increases, to prepare us for possible injury.

➤ To conserve energy, digestion and other bodily functions grind to a halt.

➤ The liver releases sugar to provide quick energy.

➤ Pupils dilate to increase visual acuity.

➤ Saliva production decreases, causing a dry mouth.

➤ Sphincter muscles contract to close the openings of the bowel and bladder.

➤ Immune responses decrease, which is useful in the short term to allow massive response to immediate threat, but can become harmful over a long period.

Once the danger passes, the parasympathetic nervous system takes over to prepare the body for rest and restoration of bodily needs:

➤ Blood pressure drops

➤ Heart rate and breathing slow

➤ Sweating stops

➤ Blood returns to the abdomen.

For our early ancestors, this meant they could now relax and enjoy a peaceful dinner around the fire with the rest of the clan. If there was no roar, no growl, no hiss, boom, or scream, there was no fear and life consisted of the business of searching for food and water.

Terror Talk

The **Autonomic Nervous System** controls all involuntary muscles, including our heart, our lungs and other internal organs, and is modified by our emotions: anger raises blood pressure and heart rate; fear makes your stomach do somersaults.

This flight-fight response, which upped the chances our distant ancestors would survive to the next generation, worked well when running from real life-threatening dangers like charging bulls or spear-carrying rival tribesmen. However, it is also the basis of our anxiety. In today's world, we confront daily non-life-threatening events that build up and elicit a false flight-fight response. Unable to either flee or fight paying the bills, loud noise, rush-hour traffic, unruly children and a rising crime rate, to say nothing of acid rain and the greenhouse effect, we are like cornered animals who cannot switch off this no-longer-needed extra energy. Instead, we remain charged up and stress builds up. When it reaches the boiling point, our brain registers "alarm" and the hormone adrenaline surges through our bloodstream: within seconds the sympathetic nervous system goes into overdrive.

This is what happens when you have a *panic attack*. While driving over a bridge, entering a crowded subway, or giving a speech, something miscues your brain into "red alert—run!" and your body goes on maximum defense: Your heart pounds and your breath comes in quick spurts. In fact, if you've had a panic attack, you may have felt as if you were having a heart attack. When this happens, your body is telling you that you should be frightened out of your wits, so you flee and avoid the situation in the future. You respond exactly how your brain is programmed to respond, except your response is out of proportion to the actual danger of the situation.

The Devil You Know and the Devil You Don't

What is the difference between fear and anxiety? Fear is something tangible, and commonly accepted: a fear of spiders, of failing an exam, forgetting your speech or becoming tongue-tied when asking someone for a date. The source of anxiety, on the other hand, is internal and hard to put your finger on—"free floating" as Freud described it. The danger does not represent an objective source of bodily danger, such as a predator or a fire, but appears vague and distant. You may feel anxious about losing control, not measuring up to your boss's expectations, or of something bad happening to you.

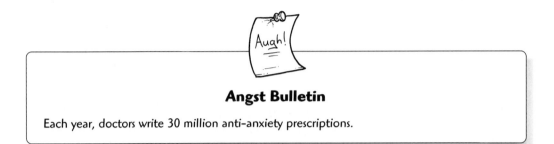

Angst Bulletin

Each year, doctors write 30 million anti-anxiety prescriptions.

In people with anxiety disorders, the subjective feeling of fear and anxiety get easily blurred. In situations that few would consider realistically dangerous, you react with the flight-fight response so that both fear and anxiety cause the same physical reaction—a pumping heart, sweaty palms, tense muscles and so on. You tend to feel both fear and anxiety regarding any given event. For instance, days before going to the dreaded dentist, taking an exam or giving a speech, you may experience unfocused apprehension that you don't directly associate with the event. Consequently, in this book I will use the two terms interchangeably.

Fear Forum

"We are largely the playthings of our fears. In one, fear of the dark; to another, of physical pain; to a third, of public ridicule; to a fourth, of poverty; to a fifth, of loneliness—for all of us our particular creature awaits us in ambush."
—Horace Walpole

Let's look closely at the difference between normal and abnormal fear responses:

➤ **Normal Fear:** A state of alarm or dread to prepare you to flee, fight, or freeze. Necessary for survival, it mobilizes you to take action to protect yourself from threats. If you can flee the snarling dog, you do so. If the dog has you by your pants and is dragging you down the street, you may try to kick the dog somehow. If someone is around, you scream for help and hope this person can either fight off the dog or get help from someone who can. If the dog has you pinned as it growls in your face and you feel either running or attacking him would incite him more, you freeze in your tracks to calm him into submission—a tactic taken by

battered wives and abused children to dispel the spouse or parent's anger. Freezing gives you time to assess the danger of the situation and prevent impulsive actions that might provoke an attack.

➤ **Irrational Fear:** A powerful feeling of peril when little or no real danger threatens. For example, the dog is safely across the street chained and you're trembling in your boots.

➤ **Anxiety:** A vague feeling of fear and apprehension that creates unease. Though feeling agitated, you may be unable to put into words what actually threatens you. On the way to your best friend's birthday party, you feel unexplained disquiet.

➤ **Phobia:** A disrupting and persistent fear of an object or an idea that is out of proportion to any proposed danger. You know it's ridiculous to fear bees but feel helpless to control the fear.

➤ **Panic:** A sudden surge of acute terror, as John Madden feels while flying in an airplane.

Imagining the Bark as the Bite

Sometimes our imagination can run wild with all of the possible things that could happen to us: cancer, a cheating spouse, failing an exam, or getting hit by lightning. Getting in a tizzy over "coulds" is called *anticipatory anxiety* or, when mild, worry. But in some people, even just worrying about going to the dentist creates *anticipatory panic*.

These coulds, or imagined fears, are a cover for the archaic threats to our existence that lie deep within our psyche: abandonment, helplessness, dependency, failing, losing control.

We all share in this existential angst. And it can be useful. As Freud first noted, it serves as mental rehearsal to prepare us should we fail that exam or should our spouse ask for a divorce. What makes for an anxiety disorder is when your felt experience is intense, persistent, or leads to a phobic reaction like avoidance. For example, quitting a class rather than take an exam, or passing up a free trip to Paris for fear of flying. If it interferes with function, it is an anxiety disorder.

The Face of Fear

Running scared takes different forms. You may:

➤ Feel trapped in an elevator

➤ Get dizzy when taking an escalator

➤ Blush bright red when approaching a potential date

➤ Shake in your boots when speaking in public

Fear Forum

"The man who fears suffering is already suffering from what he fears."
—Michel de Montaigne

➤ Drive miles out of your way to avoid a bridge or a tunnel

➤ Break out into a sweat and shakes for no apparent reason

And this list is only a start. If you experience any of the following symptoms on a frequent basis, you live with a larger than normal amount of anxiety:

Irritability	Lump in throat
Jitteriness	Smothering or choking feelings
Tension	Feeling that things are unreal
Fatigue	Apprehension
Heart pounding	Sleeplessness
Dizziness	Fear of going crazy
Faintness	Difficulty in concentrating
Breathlessness	Unwanted thoughts
Sweating	Fear of losing control
Trembling	Fear of dying
Eyelid or facial twitch	Vigilance
Frequent urination	Worry
Frequent upset stomach	

If any of the above incapacitates you, fear not. Many people have felt as terrified as you do and have overcome their fears. There are many ways to do this. The first step is to identify your fears. Of course, some of you are already too aware. But some of you may be living in denial of your fears. In Chapter 4, a self-test will help you identify what frightens you, and in Chapter 5, a fear test for children will help you pinpoint your child's fears.

Terror Talk

Angst is a Danish and German word meaning anxiety, apprehension or insecurity.

Fear as Friend/Foe

All of us feel fear. And fear, in and of itself, is useful. Whose stomach would not flutter and heart race when confronted with an ominous looking stranger in a dark alley, a car racing directly toward us, or the sound of a hissing snake? In fact, it would be strange and dangerous to not feel scared in situations that could put us in harm's way.

Some fears, such as the fear of snakes or mice, are learned. Other fears are innate—pre-programmed by biological evolution to prepare us to react defensively to potential danger. These are:

➤ Darkness, which makes us less aware of danger

➤ Being alone, because we lose the protection of others

➤ Loud, close, and sudden noises, which indicate possible predators

➤ Loss of physical support, leaving us vulnerable to falling

➤ Strangers, who might harm us

➤ Heights, from which we could fall

Your brain automatically interprets any of these conditions as a potential disaster waiting to happen and then evaluates the situation as either "safe" or "dangerous." If evaluated as dangerous, you feel apprehensive or fearful. The more clustered these conditions, the more unsafe and anxious you feel. Children, for instance, dislike sleeping in their own room because that summons two innate fears: the dark and being alone. Add noise from a thunderstorm, a parental fight, gunshots or the neighbor's car alarm, and all their protective responses get jostled. Nor, at a gut level, does this change except in degree.

In most people, the degree of autonomic arousal you experience matches the degree of threat you encounter. When mildly threatened, say by an impending visit from your mother-in-law, you feel slight agitation. In situations that could be perceived as more dangerous, like when your BMW runs out of gas and rolls to a stop in front of a biker bar, your heart rate and respiration intensify, along with the tightening of your gut and the tensing of your muscles. If the situation becomes imminently dangerous—someone is pointing a gun in our face—you feel sheer terror and an overwhelming need to escape. This is normal and helps you to take necessary action to flee a potential foe or perilous situation.

But sometimes your level of agitation is exaggerated. Remember a frightened Woody Allen trying to pummel two spiders in the bathtub with a tennis racket in the movie *Annie Hall*. When your response is magnified beyond reason, fear becomes no longer useful but potentially debilitating.

Master or Slave to Fear

When real fears match the perceived danger of any particular situation, and imagined fears are kept neatly in check, you are able to meet life head on.

But when the actual becomes unrealistically terrifying and (or) the imagined becomes the dreaded, your fears take command of your will

Terror Talk

Phobia originates from the Greek word phobos, meaning flight. Phobos, the Greek god of fear, provoked fear and panic in his enemies.

power. You may not know your enemy's name or face, but walk around shadowed by a vague uneasiness and sense of impending doom. Or you recognize your enemy—lizards, public speaking, elevators, thunderstorms—but seem powerless to conquer it. Sitting back helplessly, as the fears take command of your relationships, your decisions, your actions, you sidestep through life to avoid bumping into a spider, an elevator, a math test, a boss, or a romantic interlude. You have something beyond reasonable fear. You have a *phobia*.

You may feel shame and embarrassment at being so "weak," as if something is profoundly wrong with you, and wonder why you can't just pull yourself up by your bootstraps. But overwhelming fears don't discriminate weak from strong personalities, as John Madden and others illustrate.

Like many, you might find it hard to share feelings so frightening and irrational, which is why less than one fourth of people receive treatment for crippling fears. Unfortunately, this can begin a downward spiral leading to a string of failures that can rob you of your health, livelihood and personal life.

Yet, if you're one of those who did seek help, you may not have found it helpful. Going from doctor to doctor, you may have been one of those misdiagnosed as the "worried well," a hypochondriac or malingerer whose symptoms are "all in your head."

Angst Bulletin

If you are unable to flee, the extra energy may be released in vomiting or losing control of your bowels—as in "scared shitless"—likely a primitive mechanism to lighten the body, equipping it to run faster.

In Your Head, Your Face, Your Tummy

Nothing is all in your head. This is splitting the mind and the body into two separate entities—as if the mind were something "out there." Thoughts, feelings, bodily reaction, outward expression and action intertwine. At any one time, fears comprise:

Feelings:

➤ Fear, anxiety, worry or terror

➤ Depression or other disturbing emotions

Thoughts:

> ➤ "I'm crazy"
> ➤ "I'm weak"
> ➤ "I'm numb"

Bodily experience:

> ➤ Pounding heart
> ➤ Quick, shallow breathing
> ➤ Tense muscles
> ➤ Sweating
> ➤ Shaking limbs
> ➤ Dizziness
> ➤ Weakness
> ➤ Butterflies in stomach
> ➤ Nausea or cramps
> ➤ Constricted or dry throat

Outward expressions:

> ➤ **Appearance:** Eyes and mouth open wide; white of eyes seen; lips tense, brows raised and drawn together; neck and shoulders rigid; hands tightly clenched.
> ➤ **Actions:** Pacing; wringing of, and/or vague gestures with the hands; wiping the brow; touching hair or face; cringing; hands and lips tremble; voice quivers or becomes hoarse.

This is an expression of fear from the lab of Dr. Carroll Izard of the University of Delaware.

Responses:

➤ Flee from danger by running, climbing or hiding

➤ Fight by warding off the danger and, if possible, seek aid or reassurance from a powerful figure, who can protect you, soothe you, or both

➤ Freeze—turn all one's energy inward

What's more, fears may not originate in your head at all but in last night's dinner, inside your ear, or in something in the air that's making you sick.

Fear Fighters

Until recently, abnormal fears such as panic attacks and phobias, were believed to exist purely in the psyche and so were only treated psychologically. But sometimes non-psychological causes, such as disease or chemicals in the environment, can create anxiety and mimic panic like symptoms. Proper treatment relies on an accurate diagnosis. So, if you suffer from panic attacks or phobias, you may consider seeing your physician and get a medical examination to rule out a potential medical cause of anxiety symptoms. Generally, though, it's hard to pinpoint a single cause of anxiety; the psyche and the body are one and in collusion. In the very least, medical problems can contribute to and exacerbate anxiety symptoms. For instance, though a panic attack may be triggered by an allergy, the allergy itself may be influenced by stress that results from negative thought processes and poor coping skills. This book will discuss the different triggers of fears and the various treatment approaches that allow you to master them.

Roots of Fear

We don't know if our cave-dwelling ancestors also suffered panic attacks and phobias: They, after all, had to worry about real demons of the night. But we do know that phobias have been around as long as recorded human history.

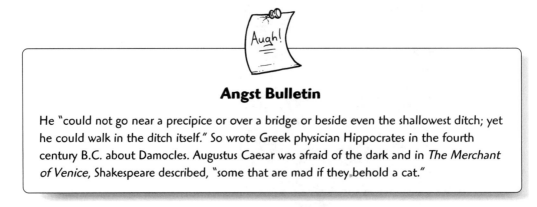

Angst Bulletin

He "could not go near a precipice or over a bridge or beside even the shallowest ditch; yet he could walk in the ditch itself." So wrote Greek physician Hippocrates in the fourth century B.C. about Damocles. Augustus Caesar was afraid of the dark and in *The Merchant of Venice*, Shakespeare described, "some that are mad if they behold a cat."

Yet, it wasn't until Sigmund Freud began pondering the unconscious that phobias were placed in the psychic terrain.

Freud's Legacy

According to Sigmund Freud, we all possess unconscious fears that stem from unresolved childhood conflicts. When these fears threaten to seep into conscious awareness, we protect ourselves by camouflaging them as "free floating" anxiety, or displacing them onto a fear of an object or a situation. In the extreme, they become a phobia. For instance, if a child fears his father, whom he cannot escape or defend himself against, he may displace his fear onto that of dogs, from whom he can run or avoid. Fear of a dog's bark is safer than fear of your father's bark.

Fear Forum

"Fear is a kind of a bell. ...it is the soul's signal for rallying."
—Henry Ward Beecher

In Freud's famous case study, a five-year-old boy known as Little Hans refused to venture outside because he was afraid a horse might bite him. Hans described black things around the horse's mouths and things in front of the eyes, leading Freud to speculate that the horse represented the boy's father, who wore glasses and had a mustache.

According to psychoanalytic theory, forbidden fears may also break through as thoughts. To suppress the resulting anxiety, we take action in the form of obsessions and compulsions. Repetitive hand washing, for instance, may help suppress anxiety over your "dirty" urges.

Fears Are Learned

Around the turn of the century, another school of thought emerged along with Freud's psychoanalytic theory. This was behaviorism. The behaviorists didn't buy into Freud's notion that the unconscious was the culprit behind feelings of fear. To them, fear was a learned reaction that could also be unlearned. The fear's origins mattered little.

You learn to be afraid because you associate a particular situation with something unpleasant. Let's say you dined at a restaurant and got food poisoning from eating lobster. Thereafter, the sight of those red claws alone may create some queasiness. After falling down stairs and landing on my head, I received a wound that required stitches and a night in the emergency room. Fifteen years later, I still walk carefully down stairs and hold onto the railing. In some people, these fears spread so that an initial fear of heights mushrooms into a fear of flying. To reduce your fear, you avoid or escape the situation, thus reinforcing the phobia.

Fears are also catchy, particularly between parent and child. If a child sees her mother on top of the dining room table screaming "Help!" while staring at a little mouse scurrying across the floor, the child too might scream and seek higher ground. On the other hand, though parental reactions can teach children to be unduly fearful, later phobias don't necessarily replicate parental phobias. We also learn from our thoughts. If you watch a scary story and perseverate on it, you may talk yourself into becoming afraid of ghosts.

Fear Is in Our Genes

But fears are more than just learned behaviors and unconscious protection against threatening feelings. They are deep within our genes and biochemistry. As you've seen, biological evolution has pre-programmed us to fear that which can potentially harm us. This is why many fear snakes but not flowers which, unless you have an allergy, are unlikely to harm you. Anxiety disorders, which are typified by autonomic over-arousal, are merely an exaggeration of behaviors that contribute to our survival. For instance, in obsessive-compulsive disorder, washing ourselves becomes ritual hand washing and checking territorial boundaries becomes checking and rechecking a door known to be locked. In other words, fears are at the same time pre-wired in our brain, transmitted genetically and learned.

The Least You Need to Know

➤ Everyone feels fear and anxiety.

➤ Fears don't become phobic until you start avoiding them.

➤ Fears have different causes and different treatments.

➤ Fears are never all in your head.

ARACHNOPHOBIA

Chapter 2

Fear and Trembling

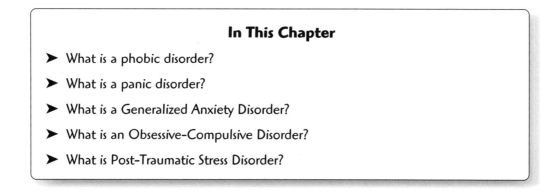

In This Chapter

➤ What is a phobic disorder?

➤ What is a panic disorder?

➤ What is a Generalized Anxiety Disorder?

➤ What is an Obsessive-Compulsive Disorder?

➤ What is Post-Traumatic Stress Disorder?

Do any of the following anxiety disorders sound familiar to you?

At any time, Susan feels tense and jumpy. Everything gets her into a tizzy—forgetting her keys, someone cutting in front of her in line, even a ringing telephone. She worries about catching the Ebola virus or AIDS from public toilets, and fears that an asteroid might soon smash the earth to smithereens.

Without warning, Omar will suddenly feel overwhelmed with terror. He can't catch his breath, sometimes the ground seems as if it is slipping from under him, and his heart is pounding so he is sure he is having a heart attack.

Germaine experiences similar symptoms whenever he encounters a cockroach. He can't tell you why he's terrified of them, but even when he sees one from afar, his heart races and his brain yells, "Run!" To make sure that he never finds one in any food he eats, he examines each morsel carefully. While walking down the street, his face is glued to the ground to avoid even stepping on one.

Dahlia arranges all of her packaged food alphabetically and by date of purchase. If her husband places a can of tuna ahead of a can of crushed pineapple, upsetting her order, she becomes furious and takes out all the cans and begins to arrange them anew in the proper order. She can spend hours a day rearranging her house to insure that the correct order is preserved.

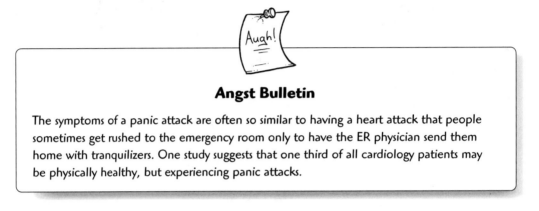

Angst Bulletin

The symptoms of a panic attack are often so similar to having a heart attack that people sometimes get rushed to the emergency room only to have the ER physician send them home with tranquilizers. One study suggests that one third of all cardiology patients may be physically healthy, but experiencing panic attacks.

Marilee was a victim of rape by a complete stranger. After the incident, she found herself beset with trembling, uncontrollable crying, nightmares, and terror of being alone. Though pleasant and relatively easy-going before, she is now often ill-tempered, and snaps and yells easily at her friends about nothing.

Do you recognize any of these problems by name?

➤ Susan suffers from Generalized Anxiety Disorder (GAD)

➤ Omar from Panic Disorder

➤ Germaine from a specific Phobia

➤ Dahlia from Obsessive-Compulsive Disorder (OCD)

➤ Marilee from Post-Traumatic Stress Disorder

Although each one manifests itself differently, at the core, all these syndromes serve the same purpose—to alert you to take self-protection from a real or perceived threat that makes you feel horrifically unsafe in the world.

In this chapter, I will discuss each of these anxiety disorders in brief and in Parts 3 and 4, I will discuss each in detail.

Sudden Panic: Panic Disorder

Willard Scott, NBC-TV's national weatherman, frequently suffers from symptoms of panic attack before going on air. If he has a full-blown one and still gets himself in front of the camera, he is amazingly brave, because a panic attack is the flight-fight response at its most extreme, and therefore, the immediate response is an almost overwhelming urge to flee that real or imagined tiger.

A panic attack is defined as a sudden and inexplicable onset of terror, and is characterized by both somatic and psychological symptoms:

Somatic Symptoms:

➤ Labored breathing

➤ Racing heart

➤ Chest pain or discomfort

➤ Feelings of choking and smothering

➤ Nausea, dizziness, sweating, trembling

➤ Numbness or tingling in hands or feet

➤ Hot and cold flashes

Psychological Symptoms:

➤ Intense apprehension, feelings of terror

➤ Feelings of impending doom

➤ Fear of going crazy or losing control

➤ Feelings of depersonalization like being outside one's body and of the world not being real

➤ Fear of dying

Attacking men and women alike, the first panic attack generally begins in early adulthood.

> **Fear Forum**
>
> "Fear of disease killed more men than disease itself."
> —Mohandas Gandhi (1869–1948)

Are All Panic Attacks the Same?

No. Storming in out of the blue and without a set pattern, panic attacks run from mild to severe. In some cases, you may experience mainly the bodily discomfort of intense anxiety. Or you may experience a full-blown panic attack, in which psychological symptoms, including depersonalization, an overwhelming sense of dread, and the terror of imminent death, accompany the terrifying physiologic symptoms.

How Often Do They Occur?

You may experience one panic attack and, if you're lucky, never again. Or you may experience panic attacks several times a week, even daily. Sometimes they may come in a bunch and then disappear for months or years.

How Long Do They Last?

The terror itself lasts intensely for seconds, minutes or, more rarely, in "waves" for up to two hours and leaves you emotionally spent and physically exhausted.

Panic can be predisposed or spontaneous:

➤ Spontaneous panic comes from nowhere, hits hard and then winds down gradually. The peak is usually reached within five minutes and then tapers off usually within 30–40 minutes.

➤ Predisposed panic can come from merely thinking about a dreaded situation. It tends to build slowly and wind down slowly as you get preoccupied with something else.

What Causes Them?

The culprit in most panic attacks is good old stress, which generally begins in early adulthood and attacks men and women alike. I will discuss medical conditions that mimic anxiety in the next chapter.

Terror Talk

Phobic disorder is a state of fear or anxiety of an irrational, excessive quality, induced by specific types of situations (heights), animals (snakes), or objects (open drawers).

The Terror of the Next Terror

Panic attacks fill you with dread not only during the attack, but after your body quiets, since their unpredictability leaves you in horror of the next strike. You may chastise yourself for being unable to control such "childish" dread, but you can't control something that appears without warning, overwhelming you in seconds.

If the attacks themselves continue, along with the fear of having one, you may become agoraphobic and afraid to leave the safety of your house, or you may develop some other specific phobia.

What Flying, Spiders, and Elevators Have in Common: Phobias

The easiest fears to pinpoint are the phobias, an inordinate fear of a situation or a thing. Drawing their energy from our primal need for survival that is buried deep in the most primitive region of our brain, they span the alphabet from A to Z, from acrophobia (heights) to zelophobia (jealousy), and number into the hundreds. We all have at least one—even the most intrepid fear something: snakes, rats, bats and spiders are a few of the most commonly feared creature-discomforts.

Some common phobias:

➤ Animal phobias: snakes, rats, bees, spiders, bats, even cats or dogs. I have a friend who, after viewing a news story about a woman who found a boa constrictor in her toilet, did her business, all of it, standing up over the toilet for a week. She also had regular nightmares about her private parts being ambushed.

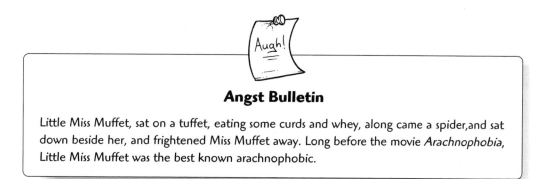

Angst Bulletin

Little Miss Muffet, sat on a tuffet, eating some curds and whey, along came a spider, and sat down beside her, and frightened Miss Muffet away. Long before the movie *Arachnophobia*, Little Miss Muffet was the best known arachnophobic.

➤ Acrophobia (fear of heights): You avoid high floors of buildings, ledges, airplanes, hills, mountain treks, or even a highway bridge. If stuck in such situations, you may experience vertigo (dizziness)—remember how James Stewart in the movie "Vertigo?" was continually a victim of this personal fear—and a feeling that you might accidentally slip and fall. Sometimes people feel as if some external force were pulling them to the edge.

"Cornice" by George Tooker captures the sense of a fear of heights. Columbus Museum of Art, Ohio.

19

Secret Weapons

If you fear heights, you probably won't go rock climbing to help you overcome your acrophobia. Leave that to the fearless duo in "Climber," the extreme screensaver that challenges a pair of animated rock climbers to successfully scale a random, computer-generated rock face. You get to watch as the climbers progress up the cliff, with each step carefully planned and executed in real-time decisions.

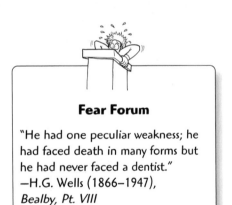

Fear Forum

"He had one peculiar weakness; he had faced death in many forms but he had never faced a dentist."
—H.G. Wells (1866–1947), *Bealby, Pt. VIII*

➤ Claustrophobia (fear of enclosed spaces): You begin to panic when in confined spaces, like an elevator, in which there's no ready exit. Claustrophobia is common to patients who undergo an MRI (Magnetic Resonance Imaging) scan, in which, until recent improvements you would have to lay completely still inside a narrow chamber for as long as 45 minutes. If you wonder if you might be at all claustrophobic, imagine yourself buried in the sand with only your head sticking up and see if you get the heebie-jeebies!

➤ Doctor/Dentist Phobia: This fear often begins after an event of excruciating pain and generalizes to avoiding doctors and dentists altogether.

➤ Blood Phobia: Ever know anyone to faint at the sight of blood? When I watched cardiac bypass surgery one time out of academic curiosity, the cardiac surgeon commended my ease at viewing the procedure. "Last week two guys from ABC News were here taping," he said, "and fainted one by one before I finished cutting the patient's chest open."

➤ Illness Phobia: You dread getting sick and spend much time visiting doctors for every ache and pain. It differs from hypochondria in that you imagine getting one specific disease (cancer, AIDS) rather than a slew of diseases. You worry that every minor disorder means cancer, for instance. You may fear dying, or focus on the pain, helplessness and possible disfigurement, a common dread in women who ruminate about getting breast cancer.

Are these fears a problem? Most of the time, no. In fact, some are common sense: snakes can be lethal. They become a problem when avoiding them disrupts your life, when fear becomes terror. Here are some examples of fears that are out of control:

1. A student, preparing for her classroom presentation for her management class, spends the night vomiting and misses her class.

2. A writer steps outside the safety of his home and begins to tremble and hyperventilate.

3. A schoolteacher walks up twenty flights of stairs rather than taking the elevator to attend her best friend's prenuptial party.

4. A secretary trembles as she types and makes the same mistakes three times because she fears her co-workers are secretly staring at her.

5. A middle-aged divorcé, fearful of being alone, stays out all night partying to avoid going home to her empty apartment.

6. A young mother doesn't allow her four-year-old to play in another child's house because she worries that he might get hit by his playmate, or fall down the stairs at the other child's house.

7. A man with advanced symptoms of pneumonia delays going to the hospital and almost dies because of his lifelong fear of doctors.

If you recognize yourself or anyone you might know in any of these examples, don't be surprised. One in nine adults in this country suffer from phobias, to the point of seeking psychiatric help. Often these fears begin in early childhood and we rarely outgrow them. Or we develop a fear after a single experience, like a dentist hitting a raw nerve, or a trauma, like getting knocked about by an Atlantic coastal hurricane, a Texas twister, or a West coast earthquake. But occasionally they pop up out of nowhere: one day you get on an airplane for an otherwise routine trip and wham!—you have a panic attack.

Fear Forum

"Fear is a noose that binds until it strangles."
—Jean Toomer

Don't you love it when people tell you that your fears are unreasonable: "Just keep a stiff upper lip." You'd like to give them a fat lip. You know your fears are ridiculous, but just knowing that doesn't stop the immediate and compelling "run for your life" gut response you get when they come upon you. This is especially so in agoraphobia, when phobias multiply to the point where you fear so many things and situations that you become housebound, and where your fear broadens to "fear of fear."

Locked Up in Fear: Agoraphobia

Imagine standing in line at the bank, riding up an elevator, or driving over a bridge and suddenly experiencing mortal terror, as if the sky were about to fall and collapse on you. Soon, your panic spreads so that any situation in which you feel escape is difficult or where there's no one there to protect you elicits terror.

Fearing the shaking, the thumping heart, the knot in the gut, and the dread that overcomes you, you live in chronic anxiety, waiting for the next attack. The only time you seem to feel safe is when accompanied by someone close to you, who can guard you, or when near to or inside your home. The more the terror escalates in public places and the more helpless you feel to control it, the more you cope by locking yourself inside the safe four walls of home. Such is the fate of the *agoraphobic*.

Agoraphobia, the most common phobia, means fear of open places. One in twenty people, eighty percent of whom are women, suffer it to some degree: The only other disorder more prevalent in this country is alcoholism.

Agoraphobics commonly avoid:

➤ Being in a crowd or standing in a line, such as supermarkets, department stores, restaurants

➤ Traveling in a bus, train, car, subway, plane

➤ Being in enclosed or confined places such as tunnels, bridges, elevators

➤ Being at home alone

The good news is that it is quite treatable, as we'll see in Chapter 10. Social phobias, a somewhat different syndrome that can also keep you somewhat housebound, are also often successfully overcome.

Allergic to People: Social Phobias

➤ Do you fear that you blush easily in public?

➤ Do you feel apprehensive about taking tests or examinations?

➤ Do you avoid crowded places?

➤ Do you worry about choking on, dropping or spilling food while eating in a restaurant?

➤ Do you shun using public toilets to the point of discomfort?

➤ Do you feel panicky when speaking or performing in front of an audience?

Angst Bulletin

After years of starring in famous roles, stage fright suddenly hit the famous British actor, Sir Laurence Olivier.

Many people will answer yes to one of the above, most of which are routine concerns. But if your fear of making a fool of yourself is strong enough for you to stay home rather than chance any public mishap, you may have a social phobia—a persistent irrational fear of doing or saying something inappropriate in the presence of others that will embarrass and even humiliate you.

Topping the list of social fears is public speaking. It crosses gender lines, social class, race and popularity, as it strikes performers, speakers, and students alike. Nor does it care how much the public adores you: Barbra Streisand and Carly Simon are among a surprising list of entertainers who temporarily gave up performing for years because of stage fright.

If you are shy, you are more vulnerable to social phobia, and especially so if you possess poor social skills. You may compensate just fine if you have an understanding spouse or person with whom to share your life, especially if this person is more outgoing. But if not, an otherwise stable person can become socially phobic. Norman, a quiet man, was quite content until his wife died of cancer. Feeling awkward about going out and dating, he felt lost and alone and became a recluse.

If you are social phobic, there's a good chance you've been this way since adolescence. There's an equally good chance that this is not your only symptom, that you also have a specific phobia or that you've experienced panic attacks or chronic anxiety. It's important to not blame yourself. You may have been, as we'll see in Chapter 4, born fear-prone.

High Anxiety: Generalized Anxiety Disorder

"The sky is falling! The sky is falling!" yelled Chicken Little. Today, his unrealistic doomsaying might get him diagnosed as suffering from *Generalized Anxiety Disorder (GAD)*. If you also experience chronic, uncontrolled worry about neutral things and are persistently anxious about all the bad things that "might" happen, you too may fall into that category. Perhaps you worry that your child, who's always been healthy, will catch a serious illness from a schoolmate. Or fret that your husband, who is a half-hour late coming home, is pinned under a huge truck.

Terror Talk

Generalized Anxiety Disorder is a prolonged, vague, unexplained, but intense fear that is chronic and felt in many different situations.

But worrying is only the half of it. When chronically anxious, you live daily in a keyed-up, agitated state and everything gets sped up. Thoughts rush through your head, you feel jumpy and may be unable to sit still, your heart thumps, and your stomach jumps, sending you to the bathroom frequently.

True GAD lacks the full punch of a panic attack. But relentless tension, which wearies you emotionally and physically and affects your overall health, is also no joy ride. If you experience at least three of the following symptoms more days than not, and have been like this for six months or more, you can be clinically diagnosed with GAD:

➤ Muscle tension

➤ Fidgeting and restlessness

➤ Irritability and perhaps angry outbursts

➤ Sleep difficulties

➤ Concentration difficulties

➤ Easily fatigued

➤ Persistent worry

GAD, which affects about four percent of the population, women somewhat more than men, can begin at any age—in other words, you're never too young to be anxious. If you are depressed, have a social phobia, or have been diagnosed with obsessive-compulsive disorder, there's a good chance that you also suffer from GAD.

Angst Bulletin

Sigmund Freud called generalized anxiety "free-floating" anxiety.

Ziggy, by Tom Wilson; ©1994, Ziggy and Friends, Inc. Distributed by Universal Press Syndicate.

Repeating Ad Infinitum: Obsessive-Compulsive Disorder

June obsesses about gaining weight. Dotty is a compulsive gambler. Sandy is an "anal-fixated" neat freak. But there's a heap of difference between these people and the extreme and irrational behavior of the character Melvin Udall in the movie *As Good As It Gets*. Melvin, as you may recall, walks unevenly along the street to avoid every possible crack or anyone touching him. Upon returning home, he locks each lock on his door five times, turns the hallway light on and off five times, the bathroom light on and off five times and then proceeds to wash his hands under very hot water with a new bar of glycerine soap, which he throws away, replaces with another new bar, washes again and throws the second new bar away. He brings his own unopened plastic silverware to the restaurant that he frequents and wears gloves while driving a car. Melvin's rituals, or compulsions, serve the purpose of dismantling extreme anxiety that results from terrifying obsessive thoughts. Melvin is a classic obsessive-compulsive—obsessions and compulsions rule his life.

Obsessions are unwanted, repetitive, intrusive thoughts, ideas or images. Irrational and uncontrollable, their force and frequency interferes with normal functioning.

Examples of Obsessions:

1. Doubts—Did I lock the door?
2. Thinking—What will I do if I forget my toothbrush?
3. Impulses—I'd like to kill my husband.
4. Fears—What if my baby stops breathing?
5. Images—I imagine my house burning.

Angst Bulletin

Lady Macbeth washed her hands continually after the murder of Duncan (presumably to compensate for her fear of being caught).

Compulsions are repetitive behaviors that you feel compelled to perform to reduce stress and prevent a potential calamity that you obsess over: hand-washing dispels your fear of contamination; repeatedly locking the doors dispels your fear of intrusion.

Terror Talk

An **Obsessive-Compulsive Disorder (OCD)** would be thinking certain thoughts and/or neglecting to do certain things that arouse intense anxiety and concern.

Washing, checking and counting, the most common such rituals, are often repeated over and over in elaborate ceremonies. You can use up hours a day washing your hands, shampooing your hair and taking showers. Or checking and rechecking to see if your doors are still locked, the stove is turned off, the alarm system is on. Or retracing your tracks to ensure that you haven't run someone over on the way home. You *know* that the door is locked, the stove is turned off, but as soon as you walk away anxiety rises and you feel compelled to recheck the door or stove. To prevent harm for yourself or others, you may feel compelled to count to a certain number or repeat a word ad nauseum. In general, women tend to wash, men to count and check.

Though it sounds as if you would have to be nuts to engage in such bizarre behavior, obsessing and compulsing are unrelated to craziness. In fact, you feel a sense of shame at performing such repeated behaviors but feel helpless to control the urge to do so; eventually you just give in. Life exhausts you.

The line between obsessions and compulsions is not always sharp. And you can be obsessive about something—you'll drop your baby—without being compulsive.

One to three percent of the population suffer from OCD in varying degrees. It's a guy thing as well as a girl thing, though its inception generally begins earlier in men, often in childhood. It frequently begins following a depressive episode or stressful event and often co-exists with other anxiety disorders and personality disturbances.

After the Fall: Post-Traumatic Stress Disorder

During World War I, psychologists studied combat soldiers, many quite normal, who began to show bizarre symptoms of uncontrolled shaking, staring into space, crying jags and the like. They called it "shellshock." Today, we call such a psychological disturbance after a traumatic event Post-Traumatic Stress Disorder (PTSD). It is an extreme response to extreme stress that lasts more than 30 days following the trauma.

Who are the candidates for PTSD? Anyone. If you've been a victim of a horrific event, such as a plane or car crash, a natural disaster like an earthquake or tornado, or rape, assault and other violence against yourself or your immediate family, you may find yourself living an ongoing nightmare. The following are among the common symptoms suffered by trauma victims:

➤ Re-experiencing traumatic events in nightmares

➤ Re-experiencing traumatic event(s) in their waking minds

➤ Avoiding anything associated with the event

➤ A general emotional numbing

➤ Skillful avoidance (often unconsciously) of talking/thinking about it

➤ Difficulties in sleep and concentrating

➤ Hyper-vigilance

➤ Depression, suicidal thoughts

You may experience horrific flashbacks so intense that it's as if the trauma were being replayed live. Anxious and depressed, you may impulsively take off on a trip, or change jobs or residence. If others have died, particularly those close to you, you may feel guilty for having survived, something that Holocaust victims overwhelmingly report. The youngest victims begin to have nightmares about monsters and may either act out or become withdrawn.

Not everyone who suffers a trauma develops PTSD. Most people recover after a few days or a few weeks. Good social supports make a difference, as well as validation of the horrific nature of the trauma once the crisis is past—something that was lacking for Vietnam Vets and often for rape victims, among others.

The Least You Need to Know

➤ Though all people experience phobias, avoidance that disrupts your life is the mark of pathology.

➤ Panic attacks can disappear as suddenly as they come.

➤ Preservation and fastidiousness do not make an obsession.

➤ Following a trauma, anyone can experience Post-Traumatic Stress Disorder.

Chapter 3

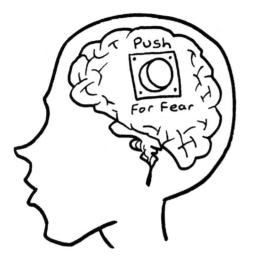

Fear Triggers

> ## In This Chapter
>
> ➤ How medical conditions mimic anxiety
>
> ➤ How food allergies and nutritional depletion mimic anxiety
>
> ➤ How environmental toxins mimic anxiety
>
> ➤ How other conditions surprisingly mimic panic attacks

What triggers anxiety? Generally it's stress. It builds and builds until our nervous system says "too much" and we become anxious, sometimes to the point of panic. Generally, we assume the psyche to be the primary driving force for anxiety. And it is in the majority of cases. But sometimes physical problems, such as hypoglycemia or mitral valve prolapse, or even chemical imbalances can cause anxiety and mimic panic-like symptoms. These biomedical triggers can join with psychophysiology to create a panic attack, but in some instances, they can provoke panic-like symptoms independent of any gross psychological markers. Yet physical problems as a cause for panic-like symptoms are often overlooked.

If you suffer from acute anxiety, how do you know if its primary cause is psychological or physical? Emotional terror is often obvious—we know we dread snakes, thunder, blood, or getting up in front of a class to speak. Non-psychological causes of anxiety are more likely to appear willy-nilly. You are laughing and eating pizza with a friend and out of nowhere comes terror and shakes. Or following a car accident, in which you suffered a minor concussion, you begin to get panic attacks, though you've never felt very fearful before.

Watch It!

Mark Gold, M.D. in *The Good News About Panic, Anxiety & Phobias* warns that anxiety mimickers "are insidious, deceptive, and almost impossible to detect without aggressive and sophisticated diagnostic testing." His book contains detailed information on triggers of anxiety and panic.

If you suffer from panic and feel you are without psychological problems, you may want to find out if your panic is medically caused. Though infrequent, purely medical causes for panic do happen. To find this out takes assertiveness, since few medical doctors will aggressively pursue a non-psychological cause for panic attacks, and psychologists and psychiatrists may assume only a psychological cause for anxiety. This chapter will go over possible non-psychological anxiety and panic triggers.

Physical

Dr. Mark Gold, Professor of Psychiatry at the University of Florida, describes James, who suffered from debilitating panic attacks. His first one hit like a bolt of lightning. James was found on a neighbor's patio screaming, "I'm dying! I'm having a heart attack!" and rushed to the nearest hospital. But the emergency room physician found nothing physically wrong with him and referred him to a psychoanalyst.

After four years in analysis, James felt understood as a person and had gained some insight into his behavior. But the panic attacks continued. Next, he saw a psychiatrist who diagnosed him as depressed and put him on antidepressants. The panic attacks continued. Finally, James was referred for electroconvulsive therapy (ECT). Before being hospitalized, he met with Dr. Gold who suggested a complete medical, neurological and endocrinological testing. His glucose-tolerance test revealed the source of James' panic attacks: non-insulin dependent diabetes. His panic attacks were apparently triggered by wild fluctuations in his blood sugar levels.

Although a case like James is rare, Dr. Gold discovered that biological problems, from brain tumors to heart problems to vitamin deficiencies, can produce symptoms identical to a panic attack. Obsessive-compulsive disorder can result from head injuries, brain tumors, strep throat, or encephalitis.

Body Dis-Ease

Consider some medical problems that can cause anxiety or mimic panic:

➤ **Hyperventilation:** Involuntary rapid, shallow breathing, or hyperventilation, leads sometimes to excessive lowering of carbon dioxide in your bloodstream. The result is light-headedness, dizziness, feelings of unreality, shortness of breath and numbness, which is not unlike having a panic attack. It's unclear whether the hyperventilation causes the panic, the panic causes the hyperventilation, or whether both occur from a common cause.

➤ **Hypoglycemia:** Are you a junk food junkie? Are you stressed out? Many people will answer yes to at least one. If so, be aware that both stress and overloading yourself with sugar can cause blood sugar levels to fall too low. This can result in hypoglycemia, which can mimic a variety of symptoms similar to a panic reaction, including anxiety, shakiness, dizziness, weakness and disorientation.

➤ **Hyperthyroidism:** Rapid heartbeat, sweating, hyperactivity, shortened attention span, fatigue and generalized anxiety are some of the side effects from excessive secretion of thyroid hormone, which raises your metabolic rate.

Watch It!

The age-old cure for hyperventilation is breathing into a paper bag, in which you re-breathe the same air, thus taking in higher levels of carbon dioxide. But if you're panic prone, this may be the worst thing to do since increased carbon dioxide can trigger a panic attack.

➤ **Mitral Valve Prolapse:** This is a common and minor heart condition. Blood moves through the mitral valve, the valve separating the upper and lower chambers on the left side of your heart, as it passes from the upper to the lower chamber. With mitral valve prolapse, there is a slight defect and the valve doesn't close completely; some of the blood can flow back from the lower to upper chamber, creating a slight heart murmur. Though not serious in most cases, the resulting rhythmic disturbance can throw you, especially when accompanied, as it sometimes is, by chest pain, palpitations, fatigue, difficulty breathing and anxiety. The majority of people with MVP, however, do not experience anxiety symptoms.

Angst Bulletin

One out of every three panic attack victims has mitral valve prolapse.

➤ **Hormonal Imbalance:** If you are anxious, this is more bad news. Even when in a non-threatening situation, you have elevated levels of hormones circulating your bloodstream. If you are a woman, notice if you experience panic-like reactions or strong anxiety around the time that you get your period—PMS (Premenstrual Syndrome) can cause anxiety and panic-like behavior.

Watch It!

Not only taking, but stopping drug use or switching to a different class of drugs can cause anxiety or panic like symptoms.

Terror Talk

Hormones are substances (like cortisol, estrogen, or testosterone) that travel through our bloodstream to tissues and organs and impact on their functions or structures.

More serious illnesses that can mimic panic symptoms include:

➤ Emphysema

➤ Cushing's syndrome

➤ Parathyroid disease

➤ Encephalitis

➤ Cardiac arrhythmia

➤ Pulmonary embolism

➤ Congestive heart failure

➤ Brain injury

Drug Side Effects

All drugs can cause potential side effects. Here are some drugs, but by no means all, that can cause anxiety or panic like symptoms.

Prescription Drugs:

➤ **Lidocaine:** Used to treat cardiac arrhythmias (irregular heartbeats), as well as for general and local anesthesia. Lidocaine can cause "doom anxiety."

➤ **Monoamine Oxidase Inhibitors:** These antidepressants can cause anxiety symptoms, nervousness, insomnia, and euphoria. If unmonitored, these side effects can mushroom into symptoms indistinguishable from panic, mania, or schizophrenia.

➤ **Prednisone:** This corticosteroid anti-inflammatory drug can cause panic attacks, depression, and mild mania.

➤ **Indomethacin:** Side effects to this non-steroidal anti-inflammatory drug include anxiety, along with hostility, disorientation, hallucinations, depression, and even psychosis.

➤ **Vinblastine:** An anti-cancer drug, 80 percent of patients report anxiety and depression within two to three days of treatment.

➤ **Nalorphine:** A pre-anesthetic given prior to the main anesthetic, this drug can mimic panic disorder, creating immediate sensations of panic, suffocation, and fear of impending doom.

➤ **Birth control pills:** All oral contraceptives can cause panic attacks.

Non-Prescription "Drugs":

➤ **Laxatives:** Some laxatives contain mercurous chloride. Overuse of these laxatives can lead to mercury poisoning which can mimic heightened anxiety and phobic behavior. There will be more on this in the section on environmental toxins.

➤ **Diet pills:** Even over-the-counter, these can create anxiety symptoms.

Watch It!

In normal people, eight cups of coffee quickly ingested can produce symptoms that mimic a panic attack.

➤ **Caffeine:** I gave up drinking coffee over 20 years ago. One day, at a friend's house, I drank two cups of supposedly decaffeinated coffee, which was actually strong regular coffee. Suddenly, my heart began to race, my hands began to shake and I felt jumpy all over. My experience was not unusual. Caffeine can produce instant panic in the panic-prone and panic-like symptoms in normal people. One possible reason is that coffee depletes vitamin B1 (thiamin), one of the anti-stress vitamins, and may also affect calcium balance.

Drug Overuse:

➤ **Yeast Infections:** Long term use of antibiotics, steroids, birth control pills, tranquilizers and sleeping pills can weaken the immune system and allow candida albicans, a normally present fungus in the bowel, to multiply and crowd out healthy intestinal bacteria. This upsets the digestive system and produces numerous chemicals, including male and female hormones, that in some people can create mood swings, anxiety and depression. Few people who suffer from candida overgrowth know it, and doctors tend to only prescribe more pills for its symptoms, which in addition to anxiety include irritable bowel syndrome, bloating, gas, allergies, arthritis and fatigue. Though rarely the sole reason for anxiety, yeast infections can be a contributing factor.

Drug Abuse

Drug abuse and panic attacks often go hand in hand, as many anxious people use substances to induce calm.

➤ **Alcohol:** When people drink, they tend to not eat, which causes nutritional problems. If you use alcohol to calm yourself, as people do since it initially acts as a depressant, you may unknowingly further your panic attacks. As the effect of the alcohol wears off, your anxiety will return more intensely and create an immediate need for more alcohol.

➤ **Marijuana:** Arianna only had one joint of marijuana, shared with two friends at a party, but the sensations were far from relaxing and pleasant. She felt estranged from her body, as if she were behind a glass wall watching people laugh and talk. This depersonalization and sense of unreality is a possible side effect of marijuana and a symptom of panic attacks.

Angst Bulletin

Anywhere from 18 to 32 percent of patients hospitalized for alcoholism may be suffering from a panic disorder, agoraphobia, or from other social phobias.

➤ **Cocaine:** Regardless whether cocaine is sniffed, injected, or smoked (as freebase or crack), it can produce anxiety-mimicking side effects, such as increased heart rate and irregular heart beat, restlessness, and high blood pressure. EEG tracings of the brain following cocaine injection show activity in the same area of the brain responsible for "flight or fight"—the exact reaction during a panic attack.

➤ **Amphetamines:** Common side effects of amphetamines, or "speed," include rapid heartbeat, elevated blood pressure, and overstimulation—in other words, some familiar symptoms of anxiety disorders.

➤ **Narcotics withdrawal:** Withdrawal from narcotics such as heroin, methadone, and codeine can result in anxiety symptoms.

Less Well Known Anxiety and Panic Mimickers

In addition to drugs, other less common conditions have been known to mimic anxiety and panic symptoms or at least exacerbate them. These include inner ear problems, nutritional imbalance, as well as environmental triggers.

Teetering on the Edge: Inner Ear Malfunction

If you have twenty people on a bus stuck in a black tunnel, or a plane full of people who experience a sudden, horrifying drop, all might feel frightened but only a handful will lose it. And only a few of those will later become phobic. Could some very basic physical problem distinguish the fear-prone from the fear-resilient? Dr. Harold Levinson, author of *Phobia Free*, believes that, in many cases, the answer is yes: the functioning of your inner ear system.

Levinson maintains that 90 percent of all phobic behavior is the result of an underlying malfunction within the inner-ear system. Though the phobia is set off by an actual trauma, this physiological malfunction predisposes the person to react excessively, and for the panic attacks and phobias to persist.

Although his contention may seem far out, many of the symptoms of panic attacks, like anxiety, dizziness, disorientation, fainting, and nausea, directly relate to functions controlled by our inner-ear or cerebellar-vestibular system (CVS). These include:

➤ Our sense of balance

➤ Our orientation in space

➤ The tuning and fine-tuning of all the sensory information entering the brain: light, sound, motion, gravity, temperature, barometric pressure, chemicals, and so on

➤ The regulation of our internal time clock, giving us a sense of time and rhythm

➤ The coordination of our movements in time and space

If your CVS is damaged in some way, one or more of these functions can be thrown off and result in any of the following:

➤ Loss of balance and coordination

➤ Problems with vision and hearing

➤ Problems with sense of direction

➤ Compromised sense of time

➤ Motion sensitivity

➤ Problems with memory and concentration

➤ Hyperactivity and overactivity

➤ Obsessions and compulsions

➤ Increased anxiety

Furthermore, anxiety gets arbitrated through the cerebellar-vestibular system (CVS), or the inner-ear system. Throw off your CVS functioning, and your anxiety-control network can misfire: mild anxiety can erupt into intense fear, or total panic.

Levinson believes that more than twenty percent of the population has some kind of inner-ear dysfunction. Not all people get phobic because dysfunction depends on the extent of the damage and many people learn to compensate by developing and strengthening mechanisms that counter or neutralize phobic symptoms. But certain things

Secret Weapons

For more information on how inner ear disturbances can cause phobias, see *Phobia Free* by Harold N. Levinson, M.D.

Secret Weapons

No More Fears, How to Free Yourself from Disabling and Unreasonable Panic with a Simple, New Program of Nutritional Supplements, by Douglas Hunt, M.D, explains how food allergies can trigger panic attacks and how to use food supplements as a preventive measure to stave off an attack.

can aggravate the problem or reduce your ability to compensate for inner-ear problems. The list is long:

➤ Severe or repeated ear infections

➤ Mononucleosis

➤ Sinus infections and various other infections known to affect the inner-ear system

➤ Concussions and/or whiplash

➤ Degenerative disorders

➤ Old age

➤ Tumors or blood clots (or other lesions that put pressure on the inner-ear system)

➤ Prolonged or turbulent air travel

➤ Surgical procedures

➤ Temporomandibular joint syndrome (TMJ)

Chemical changes in the brain due to the following can also aggravate this problem:

➤ Drug use or abuse

➤ Menopause

➤ Allergies

➤ Birth control pills

➤ Changes in diet

➤ Emotional stress

➤ Pregnancy

➤ Fluctuating hormone levels

➤ Menstruation

➤ Anesthesia

If your experience of anxiety, panic attacks, or phobias includes dizziness, light-headedness, or balance problems, you may wish to consult an otolaryngologist (ENT) for an inner ear examination.

Food and You

Are you careful about the kind of fuel you put into your car to insure it runs efficiently? If so, are you as careful about the kind of fuel you put into your body to ensure it runs efficiently? Probably not, if you are the average person. Yet, if we lack proper nutrition, our whole nervous system can be thrown out of whack.

It's well known that what you eat directly and importantly impacts your body's functioning and your subsequent experience of well being. In fact, some people refer to food as a drug. When you are allergic to a food, fighting off the allergy puts stress on your immune system. If your anxiety level is high, your immune system is already stressed; your weakened immune in turn induces more stress, which also increases the likelihood that you have food allergies of which you are perhaps unaware. According to Douglas Hunt (*No More Fears,* Warner, 1988), in some cases, food allergies can trigger panic like symptoms. He describes one woman who panicked after eating tomatoes, another after eating peanuts.

If you are a junk food addict, or if chronic stress and anxiety leave you forever prepped to flee, not allowing you to properly absorb the nutrients in the foods that you do eat, you may be missing out on essential nutrients necessary to master your fears. Moreover, when under stress, your need for vitamins and minerals increases.

Fear Forum

"The combined assault of chemicals, excessive pollens, dusts, and molds with excessive intake of sugar, milk, yeast, or wheat can overload one's body to the breaking point."
—Douglas Hunt, M.D. in *No More Fears.*

He suggests that food allergies can trigger panic like symptoms and that food supplements can bring fast relief from frightening panic attacks and even stave off an attack.

According to Dr. Douglas Hunt, the following are essential anxiety smashers:

➤ B vitamins and Vitamin C

➤ The mineral calcium

➤ The amino acids gamma-aminobutyric acid (GABA) and glutamine

Take just one of these nutrients, vitamin B1, on which the efficiency of your hypothalamus depends. When stress overloads the hypothalamus, for example, in the case of a prolonged infection like mononucleosis or hepatitis, a serious fever, heavy anesthesia during surgery, or extended grief, B1 gets depleted. The normal person, explains Hunt, will eventually bounce back, though it takes time. But if you are fear-prone and easily overwhelmed by stress, thiamine metabolism in the hypothalamus may never catch up. If you also smoke, drink alcohol, or eat excessive carbohydrates, essential vitamin and minerals are further exhausted.

Environment

Our bodies absorb more than that which we swallow. We take in the whole of our environment through our senses—smells, sound waves, light waves, sensations of heat and cold. As such, things like chemicals in the environment, the way we light our lives, and ambient temperature can affect our body's functioning.

Toxin Exposure

Jack, a 52-year-old housepainter, suffers from "brain fog," fatigue, heart palpitations, shortness of breath, numbness, stomachaches, and leg cramps. Years of toxic fumes from paint chemicals have taken their toll: Jack is chemically sensitive, a syndrome called MCS (multiple chemical sensitivity).

Sniff around you—if you dare. Over 150 different chemicals pervade the air in our perfumes, make-up, clothing (especially when dry-cleaned), food, carpets, paint and the air that comes through our heating and air conditioning ducts. And that's just a start of the toxins invading our lungs. Even small levels of toxic elements in our bloodstream can upset brain chemistry, and in some cases, although it's rare, trigger panic or anxiety:

➤ **Mercury:** Inhaling mercury vapors from industrial settings, mercury-tainted food or water (remember the ban against canned tuna fish from Japan several years ago) or from the use of mercury-based products such as skin creams, laxatives, and douches can cause mercury poisoning. Xenophobia (an abnormal fear of strangers) is one symptom, along with anxiety, depression, mood swings, and severe irritability.

➤ **Bismuth:** A major ingredient in skin-lightening creams, and popular stomach medications made in Europe and Australia, bismuth toxicity begins with anxiety symptoms, apathy, depression and delusions. If the condition progresses, it leads to terrifying hallucinations, fluctuating states of consciousness, and language reduced to babbling.

➤ **Carbon Dioxide:** Inhaling carbon dioxide could induce anxiety symptoms, sometimes even in subjects with no history of panic disorder.

➤ **Volatile substances:** Volatile hydrocarbons, such as those found in glue, paint, gasoline, and nitrous oxide, can cause anxiety, panic, depression, personality changes, and other psychiatric symptoms and in high doses disorientation, confusion and coma. At special risk are those exposed daily to inhalation of volatile fumes—painters, refinery workers, and members of airport crews who refuel aircraft, for instance—as well as people who sniff glue, gasoline, nitrous oxide, and other agents to get high.

➤ **Insecticides:** Bug-killing chemicals containing organophosphates block the production of an essential brain enzyme. Anxiety, irritability, depression, restlessness, drowsiness, and decreased memory and attention span can result.

Over-Lighting Our Lives

Did you ever feel wiped out after working all day under fluorescent lights? If so, it's not surprising. Fluorescent lights flicker and this can be annoying. The effort of trying to tune it out can exhaust you.

If you're fear-prone, little annoyances like this grate that much more on your nerves, escalating your anxiety level. Agoraphobic patients are often light defensive and avoid well-lit places. When forced to be in a bright environment like a mall or a market, their uneasiness about being out in public escalates, compelling them to leave.

We're Having a Heat Wave

Do you get more hot-tempered in the heat, and especially when it's hot and humid? Many people do. Assaults and murders rise in summer, as does wife beating. Suicide rates peak in May and June.

Secret Weapons

For detailed information on the biological basis of fears, pick up *The Good News about Panic, Anxiety & Phobias* by Dr. Mark Gold.

Weather affects our state of mind. Many people feel a drop in spirit in October, as the days become shorter, and remain in a slump until spring, when things begin to light up again. This condition is called SAD, or seasonal affective disorder, and is brought about by the decrease in sunlight.

Psychiatrist Thomas Wehr, chief of psychobiology at the National Institute of Mental Health, has found that the opposite happens as well. Some people get depressed in the hot, muggy summer months, and endure spells of anxiety, including panic attacks. The culprit? Again the hypothalamus, the part of the brain that helps your body adjust to outside conditions, including both light and temperature.

Psychological

Though some contend it's possible to have what appears a panic attack for a purely biomedical reason, others claim there is no such thing—that mind and body are too intimately connected. Whatever the primary cause, anxiety often colors our coping abilities, our relationships and our state of mind. And it's often precipitated by a stress event or trauma.

Stress!!

Jerry, a twenty-three-year old recent law graduate, felt terrific pressure to pass the bar exam. His father was a lawyer, as was his grandfather before him. But now his father was in a nursing home, incapacitated by the later stages of multiple sclerosis. Jerry, who had witnessed his father's deterioration for many years, was terrified he too would get the dreaded disease.

While studying late in the night, Jerry went to jot some notes on a piece of paper. Suddenly, his hand just seemed to stop in mid-air. He felt as if he couldn't move it. Terrified, he started to shake and tried to get up from the chair but felt as if he couldn't move his legs.

Close to hysteria, he called a friend who drove him to the nearest emergency room. He arrived frozen in the doorway, convinced he had the first signs of multiple sclerosis. Upon examination, the ER physician assured him he did not have any preliminary signs of the disease, characterized by tingling in the arms and legs, visual disturbances, and temporary weakness, and sent him home with some tranquilizers.

If illness can mimic panic, Jerry demonstrates the opposite: how stress can create acute anxiety that in turn can manifest in apparent illness. His case also points to how difficult it may be to tease out the soma from the psyche—the body from the mind. Stress wears down our system, inviting all sorts of upheaval: ulcers in some, panic attacks in others as anxiety skyrockets. The stress of experiencing loss can especially trigger the first attack, including loss of:

➤ A significant other through death, divorce or separation

➤ Employment

➤ Health through illness

➤ Lifestyle as a result of a major financial reversal

In some vulnerable people, the stress of simple lifestyle changes can create enough anxiety to cause a panic attack. Changes such as:

➤ Marriage

➤ Divorce

➤ Having a baby

➤ Moving

➤ Job change

➤ Going into the military

➤ Illness

Trauma

Specific phobias often result from trauma. It often takes only one good fall from a horse to fear horses, one near drowning to fear water, one car accident to fear driving, or one rape to fear sex. Trauma and its aftermath will be discussed in detail in Chapters 18 and 21.

The Least You Need to Know

➤ Medical illness can produce the same symptoms as a panic attack.

➤ Many prescription and some non-prescription drugs create panic like symptoms.

➤ Nutritional imbalances, inner-ear dysfunction, and environmental stimuli can in some cases mimic panic or at least exacerbate or enhance it.

➤ While some contend that a purely biomedical panic attack is possible, others insist that the interconnectedness between mind and body make this impossible.

Chapter 4

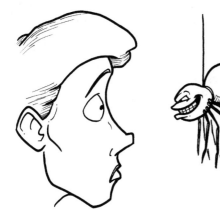

Face to Face with Your Demons

In This Chapter

➤ Identifying your fears

➤ Who is most vulnerable to fears

➤ How fears need to be attacked

➤ Getting started

What are you afraid of? Some fears, like that of snakes, may be obvious to you. But others might be neatly tucked away in your unconscious—perhaps a fear of making mistakes, of being alone, or of dying. In this chapter, you will find a Fear List that will help you pinpoint your fears and how intensely you feel them.

Armed with this information, you will also learn why some people come, see and conquer, while others come and run—how genes, individual biochemistry, and life experiences interact to form our unique behavior patterns. You will learn as well something of the origins of fears and, lastly, how to take your first steps in conquering them.

Name Your Poison

What stimulus set off your fears? To find out, you might want to take a minute and fill in the following Fear List. How much something distresses you will range from some fear to "terror" or a full blown panic attack. Some things that you fear may not be on the list. You can write them in by "Other."

Fear List

	Some Fear	Much Fear	Very Much Fear	Terror
Angry people	___	___	___	___
Bats	___	___	___	___
Being alone	___	___	___	___
Being criticized	___	___	___	___
Being hurt	___	___	___	___
Being in an elevator	___	___	___	___
Being in strange places	___	___	___	___
Being robbed	___	___	___	___
Birds	___	___	___	___
Blood (animal)	___	___	___	___
Blood (human)	___	___	___	___
Blushing	___	___	___	___
Cats	___	___	___	___
Closed places	___	___	___	___
Crowds	___	___	___	___
Crossing a bridge	___	___	___	___
Darkness	___	___	___	___
Dead bodies	___	___	___	___
Deep water	___	___	___	___
Dentists	___	___	___	___
Doctors	___	___	___	___
Dogs	___	___	___	___
Driving	___	___	___	___
Dying	___	___	___	___
Failure	___	___	___	___
Falling	___	___	___	___
Fighting	___	___	___	___
Fire	___	___	___	___
Flying	___	___	___	___
Germs	___	___	___	___
Ghosts	___	___	___	___
Illness	___	___	___	___
Imaginary creatures	___	___	___	___
Insects	___	___	___	___
High places	___	___	___	___

	Some Fear	Much Fear	Very Much Fear	Terror
Hypodermic needles	____	____	____	____
Large open spaces	____	____	____	____
Losing control	____	____	____	____
Loud noises	____	____	____	____
Loud sirens	____	____	____	____
Loud voices	____	____	____	____
Opposite sex	____	____	____	____
Pain	____	____	____	____
Physical assault	____	____	____	____
Riding a Ferris wheel	____	____	____	____
Riding a roller coaster	____	____	____	____
Riding down an escalator	____	____	____	____
Riding in a car	____	____	____	____
Snakes	____	____	____	____
Speaking in front of a group	____	____	____	____
Strangers	____	____	____	____
Suffocating	____	____	____	____
Surgical operations	____	____	____	____
Swinging on a swing	____	____	____	____
Thunder	____	____	____	____
Weapons	____	____	____	____
Worms	____	____	____	____
Other	____	____	____	____

Different Strokes

Now that you've named your fears and how intensely you experience them, imagine your significant other filling in your Fear List. How close might he/she come to estimating your fears?

My friend Candice would probably say that her husband John would miss most of them. She is one of these tough-talking people—independent, self-reliant, in control. Or so it seems. On the inside, all sorts of things are simmering—fear of being alone, of the dark, of getting breast cancer, of her husband leaving her, of dying. Some of these fears are threatening to brew over. But she'll never let on. Instead, she has colitis and a constant skin rash.

Renetta, on the other hand, is quiet, blushes easily and rarely parties. When asked to go deep sea diving with the wild bunch at work, they never expected her to say yes. But she did. And though when they got there, she readily admitted some fear of the water, with a little reassurance from her buddies, she donned a tank suit, took a deep breath, and plunged into the cold ocean.

People react differently to fear. Some panic, others react mildly. Some get cramps, some pace back and forth, some shake all over, some do all three. Some people readily express their fears, as did Renetta. Others appear cool as a cucumber while inwardly boiling, like Candice. Of course, when faced with a charging bull, even Arnold Schwartzennegger would shake in his boots and flee in fright.

What kind of person are you? Fear-prone or fear-resilient? Can you openly admit to your fears or do you need to hide them? And how did you get that way? The answer lies in a combination of heredity, childhood environment and cumulative stress.

Born Wired

Jonathan cries easily. He's not supposed to. He's a 35-year-old married advertising executive, with three children. But he does because he's a nervous person, full of terror and trembling, and always has been. As a child, he feared the dark, monsters, thunderstorms, his parents leaving him, his sister hitting him, and that was only the start. He peed in his bed until he was nine, stuttered through high school, and shook when asking a girl for a date. All his life he's heard, "toughen up," "don't let things get to you," "get over it." And he's tried. But things just seem to, well, bother him.

You may have been born touchy, your fear alarm preset to go off sooner than others. If so, you are among those prone to excessive fears and anxieties. Quickly keyed up and agitated, you possess a sharp antenna that easily picks up the vibes from the environment, good and bad, to which you react with great excitement *and* great trepidation. People accuse you of "getting carried away with your emotions," "overreacting." "Yes," you tell them, "I feel things more intensely than other people."

When a situation seems potentially threatening—taking an elevator which could malfunction—your autonomic nervous system may go into high gear and a thumping heart and sweaty palms cause your fears to quickly escalate.

If you are shy, you are especially vulnerable to becoming fearful and easily agitated by new people and events. Children and adolescents that are shy develop more phobias and panic attacks than do their more outgoing counterparts.

If you are fear-prone, think back on whether anyone in your immediate family suffers or has suffered from panic attacks, phobias, or chronic anxiety. If so, it's not surprising.

Research shows that a tendency to fearfulness is often inherited. If you've grown up with an agoraphobic parent, for instance, there's a fifteen to twenty percent chance of becoming agoraphobic yourself.

Further evidence of fear's genetic component can be found from studying twins. From as early as three months of age, identical twins, who have the same genetic make-up, respond more similarly to fears than do fraternal twins. And identical twins often develop similar phobias even when raised separately.

Angst Bulletin

Could you have inherited your fears from your parents? Puppies can. Two groups of pointer dogs were bred with each other: one group was fearful, one stable. By the second breeding, 90 percent of the puppies of the fearful group would cower, freeze, or flee when approached by strangers. Eighty percent of the stable dogs, on the other hand, showed little fear.

A propensity toward fearfulness may also result from maternal anxiety during pregnancy or, as some people believe, birth trauma.

Nurture/Nature

Genetic make-up may leave you prone to fearfulness, but it takes more than worry genes to become phobic. Environment plays its role through childhood experiences, how you were conditioned to react to fear and the amount of current and past stress in your life. This mixture of nature and nurture scripts the kind and intensity of the fears that get played out in your life.

Faulty Attachments

Regardless of where your anxieties stem, at heart they hold the same meaning for you: Fear for your own survival—physical or emotional. The more we feel protected from danger, the more secure we feel. Fear-resilient genes help, as does good health. So do warm, loving parents.

Our mother is our first relationship. The quality of our attachment to her—secure or insecure—relates to how inwardly secure we feel and serves as a blueprint for later relationships.

Secure Attachment

Some people are born with a silver spoon in their mouths—rich in spoon-fed love and adoration. Born to sensitive, warm and loving parents, the payoff is lifetime security, nurtured in the belief that someone will always be there to shield you from life's demons. Could you ask for a better buffer from all the witches and wolves out there?

As a child, you comfortably explored your world, confident that should harm befall you, waiting arms would scoop you up and protect you. Your needs quickly met and your feelings acknowledged and respected, you easily expressed your fear and turned to others for protection and consolation.

If you were born fear-prone and were easily overexcited and agitated, your mother took the extra time needed to calm you—holding you tight, stroking your brow and gently rocking you into a quiet sleep. Later, the good enough mother inside you enabled you to talk yourself into a calm state, equipping you to disarm your own fears. Security and self-love; these are the gifts your mother's loving touch bestowed upon you. And their benefits last a life-time. Some people, after the death of a loving parent, imagine their mother or father looking down upon them from the heavens, watching over them.

Insecure Anxious–Ambivalent Attachment

You too were spoon-fed love, but unpredictably: sometimes your mother was there for you, sometimes not, depending on her mood. Unsure she would protect you in times of need, you continually sought her attention. Maybe you were naughty and hit your sister. Or hit your mother. Or maybe you behaved like a helpless baby, or flashed those pearly whites to charm her. Whatever your strategy, it served its purpose: her eyes and ears were upon you.

But if they weren't, and especially if she left or threatened to do so, you became quickly anxious and clung to her. If she pushed you away, you screamed and lay on the floor, kicking your legs and flailing your arms.

The greater your separation anxiety, the greater the likelihood that your childhood temper tantrums would, given enough stress, later become panic attacks. And this is where the fear-prone personality comes in: highly fearful to begin with and unable to easily pull yourself together, you respond with terror to separation from your source of protection. You did as a child, and you probably do now to a greater extent than other people do. Insecure, dependent on others, and often anxious, you dread being alone and your worst fear is abandonment. And so you seek the constant companionship of others—at times whomever is available.

Angst Bulletin

If your parents are fearful and anxious, there is a greater likelihood that you will be as well.

Insecure Anxious-Avoidant Attachment

Along with your food, you had to swallow uncomfortable feelings from the person feeding you: indifference, intrusiveness, annoyance, anger (overt or subtle) or anxiety. It's a lot to put on an infant's plate, and it left you starved for love.

It started with your cry, which elicited your mother's own unmet needs for nurturing and made her anxious. And so she delayed picking you up. Or she came soon enough but felt a bit tense, annoyed or even angry. Picking up on her discomfort, you started to squirm and fuss. She became more annoyed. You cried more. Well, it didn't take long for you to learn your lesson. If you're upset, don't count on people for solace.

Soon you discovered how you could control her irritation. Don't show her you're upset but inhibit your emotions—the best defense you could devise against such overwhelming excitation and the uncomfortable feeling that the person in charge of nurturing you often didn't much like you. If you were fear-resilient, and therefore less easily overwrought and more able to calm yourself, you found that you could control your distress by tuning her out and twirling your hair or playing with your toys. But if you were fear-prone, you experienced a double whammy: easy irritability and a mother who, rather than buffer your distress, intensified it. Achieving any sort of emotional balance has been a life-long challenge.

Since you lacked confidence that anyone would come to your aide in time of need, you took on an "I-can-do-it-myself!" attitude and became (falsely) independent, "It's not that you won't answer my cry, I just don't need you." But inside lay a pool of unshed tears and anxiety seeped out in other ways:

➤ Eating problems

➤ Sleep problems

➤ Excessive thumb-sucking

➤ Excessive rocking

➤ Excessive masturbation

Later, more got added to the list:

- ➤ Nail biting
- ➤ Stomach aches
- ➤ Eye blinking
- ➤ Stuttering

- ➤ Nightmares
- ➤ Bed-wetting
- ➤ Headaches
- ➤ Illnesses

Watch It!

In a recent study that followed subjects for 35 years, severe anxiety was the best marker for later illness; the anxious group developed cardiovascular disease, hypertension, ulcers, migraines, and other illnesses. At the same time, the anxious group reported a less warm and loving relationship with their parents.

Take Anna. She was born emotional and touchy and to a mother who was high-strung, on edge, insensitive, and who showed Anna little tenderness. Her memories of her mother were all the same: her mother snapping at her. If Anna openly showed distress, her mother became more nervous and screamed, "Don't get hysterical!" Her mother's own hysteria intensified Anna's anxiety and her perception of the world as dangerous and added a new burden for her to carry: in addition to consoling herself, she had to console her mother as well. Her father, angry and hostile, mostly ignored her or behaved seductively toward her. For instance, as an adolescent he would frequently slap her fanny playfully.

Her childhood was fraught with monsters and heaviness. She was sick often with colds, viruses, stomachaches and the like and for awhile found herself unable to stop blinking her eyes. She sought to please parents who never seemed pleased—meeting her at every turn with criticism, disapproval, lack of support, rejection or indifference. Life felt full of continual threats; she became constantly vigilant and anxious.

She did her best to keep her anxiety from exploding and succeeded all the way through high school. But at nineteen, the dam of welled-up fright broke loose and constant uncomfortable overexcitement and dread turned to panic attacks. They served the purpose of eliciting concern from her parents, and sometimes even a warm touch, without her having to openly express her need for their nurturance.

Anxiety-filled days, mixed with profound depression, turned to anxiety-filled years. As she aged, her body too began to rebel as well and physical symptoms emerged— irritable bowel syndrome, TMJ, mitral valve prolapse, arthritis and then chronic fatigue syndrome.

Experiencing people as rejecting, indifferent, hurtful or disappointing in the least, she found it hard to find a "safe person" to help her cope with her fears and found herself mostly alone.

Dangerous Attachments

In spite of everything, Anna was lucky. She did not experience trauma or tragedy in her life, which further predispose people to react fearfully. The following are strong risk factors for later psychiatric disorders:

➤ Neglect

➤ Abandonment through divorce or death

➤ Physical abuse

➤ Sexual abuse

➤ Alcoholism in one or both parents

The more these combine with a highly reactive temperament and insecure parenting, the greater the likelihood of crippling anxiety overwhelming your ability to cope.

Early Stress

How was your childhood? Happy? Sad? A little of both? Or is your childhood something you've put in the back of your mind, like Anna, filed under "forget?"

If you are anxious and fearful, and especially if you experienced insecure attachments to your parents, chances are you've been anxious for a longtime—and especially if you experienced early trauma.

The kinds of things parents do, day in and day out, map the blueprint of the child's developing brain. One mother softly soothes her crying infant; another one jiggles the buggy. One father gently rocks his baby to sleep; another one awkwardly shakes the baby. Those parents who calm their infants may be reinforcing electrical and chemical signals in the brain that connect our rational brain to our emotional brain, a process that appears to take place between 10 and 18 months. When in pain, the child learns how to self-calm. But insensitive parenting confuses these connections and they fail to strengthen. Later, it's much harder to self-nurture.

Early stress and threats rewire the emotion circuits in the brain as well, specifically in the amygdala, an almond-shaped mass of gray matter deep in the limbic system of your brain, as the research of Bruce Perry of Baylor College of Medicine shows. The job of the amygdala is to monitor incoming sights and sounds for emotional content and it does this quickly—before the information gets to our neocortex, our thinking brain. If a sight, sound, touch, smell reminds you of something painful in the past—Dad's growl turned to a slap—then the first "Shut up!" floods the amygdala with stress chemistry before the brain knows what's happening, explains Perry. If this happens over and over again, the slightest stress and cortisol (your stress hormone) surges through your brain. The impact is profound: anxiety, hyperactivity and impulsive behavior, and an ongoing hyper-vigilant "I-better-be-prepared-next-time" stance that keeps the child defensively cued to anything that might signal danger, like a frown, an edge in the voice, eyes that turn away or glare. Prepped to perceive the world as dangerous, stress starts building literally from infancy on.

Angst Bulletin

Trauma elevates stress hormones, such as cortisol, that destroy brain cells. The regions in the brain responsible for emotions, including attachment, are 20 to 30 percent smaller in abused children than in children who were not abused, found Dr. Bruce Perry of the Baylor College of Medicine. In adults who were abused as children, the memory-making hippocampus is smaller as well.

Carried or Cached as an Infant

Do you know how you were carried as an infant? In your mother's arms? Or mostly in a baby carriage or stroller? If you answer the latter, and you experience panic attacks and phobias, there may be some connection.

Remember last chapter when I talked about the functions controlled by our inner-ear or cerebellar-vestibular system (CVS), such as our sense of balance and orientation in space? Well, carrying, rocking and swaying babies stimulates their vestibular apparatus. Yet babies today spend the majority of their day separated from their mothers in a container, where they often move little. What might this mean? Increased vulnerability to later vertigo for one, as well as a feeling of physical insecurity in space in general. Consider:

➤ Whereas carried babies receive vestibular stimulation throughout the day, our babies, lying still much of the day, receive little vestibular stimulation.

➤ When lying on their backs in a buggy or crib, babies' limbs are generally uncontained and this increases random movements that startle and frighten infants, especially the very young.

➤ Young babies carried in plastic seats are frequently jostled, such as when the seat is picked up and put down, and this often causes them to startle.

➤ Frequently out of human arms, our infants are picked up and put down frequently throughout the day for feeding, diapering, playing, and consoling. Every time they go from vertical to horizontal and vice versa, there's an alarming moment when one kind of support is removed before the other is established. This places babies, in the first six months of life, at risk for the Moro startle response (babies reflexively extend both arms and legs, cry persistently and move about in an agitated manner).

Secret Weapons

The Navajo Indians, carried throughout infancy on a cradleboard on their mother's back, felt the safe containement of the mother's womb. Later, they felt so secure in space that they were frequently employed to work on constructing high-rise buildings where they worked *in bare feet without harnesses.*

The more pronounced their feeling of instability in space, as well as the co-occurrence with other risk factors—ear infections, unstable parenting, fear-prone personality, emotional liability, traumas—the greater the vulnerability to later anxiety, panic attacks and phobias, especially phobias related to space, such as:

➤ Fear of open spaces (agoraphobia)

➤ Fear of heights (acrophobia)

➤ Fear of flying (aerophobia)—sometimes experienced as a dread of losing ground and flying out in open space

Babies carried extensively during infancy feel safe in space and appear to not suffer vertigo as adults. Held safely against the parent's body, their limbs safely contained, they feel the security of the womb. This greater security in space lessens later vulnerability to certain space-related phobias like agoraphobia, acrophobia, and aviophobia.

Now the Good News

Now that you've had all the bad news of what woes fearful genes and the sins of our fathers can bestow on our ability to later cope with our fears, we come to the bottom line: Like it or not, it's your life and only you can change it. If you were born fear-prone, if you've had an unhappy childhood, if you've endured horrific trauma in your life, there's still much you can do to change your life. But to do so, you must use every means possible to make yourself feel safer in the world. And this starts with increasing control: The more you can rely on your mind and body, the more power you have to scare away your fears.

Take the legend of Harry Houdini. Famous for his ability to escape from tight spaces, he fearlessly crawled into steamer trunks that would be dunked in water, or safes, which would be dangled high above the ground. But twice in his life, when he was not in control of the confinement, he panicked—once when accidentally trapped in a phone booth and again in a bathroom stall. After that, he never left home without his special lock picks that could free him from inside. He could do powerful magic when he felt in charge, mind-boggling stunts that assured him immortality. But when not in control, terror struck. Let it be a lesson for all.

Fear Forum

"In the midst of winter, I finally learned that there was in me an invincible summer."
—Albert Camus

First Steps

You are now ready to take the first steps in conquering your fears. You might want to start with a Fear Journal. You can begin by taking the fears that you checked off in the "Very Much Fear" and "Terror" column of the earlier Fear List and answering the following questions for each:

I am most afraid of _____

When I encounter this fear, I feel _____

My response is to _____

This fear first began _____

This fear stops me from doing _____

I want to understand why I feel afraid of_____

I want to overcome the fear of _____

You may also find it helpful to categorize your fears under categories such as:

- ➤ Fear of heights
- ➤ Fear of being trapped
- ➤ Fear of social ridicule
- ➤ Fear of physical deformity
- ➤ Fear of animals
- ➤ Fear of separation
- ➤ Fear of going crazy

The Least You Need to Know

➤ Some people are more fear-prone than others.

➤ People express their fears differently.

➤ A secure start in life helps to buffer our fears.

➤ Child-rearing impacts how we later respond to anxieties.

Chapter 5

Chasing Away Your Child's Monsters

In This Chapter

➤ Different ages, different fears

➤ When to worry

➤ Parent's bag of magic scare tricks

➤ What *not* to do and say

Three-year-olds Shakita, Nicky and Chris are running on the playground laughing. All of a sudden, Chris grits his teeth, clenches his fingers into claws, growls and starts chasing Shakita and Nicky. They run in "fright" yelling, "the monster!"

This "Monster Chase" is spontaneously played out in childcare centers everywhere. In fact, if you observe preschool children in free play, you won't have to wait long for it to begin. It is the child's attempt to master the dangerous monsters that inhabit his mind: thunderstorms that roar; lions that roar; parents that roar.

It's scary being a child, with all the giants out there. Lacking strong muscles, quick legs, guns, and charge accounts with which to defend yourself, there's much to fear. You might want to console your child by telling her that she won't be so scared when she gets bigger. But don't count on it. As children mature and learn to distinguish reality from fantasy, their intense fear of monsters, the dark, strangers and the like do abate. But as her world broadens, so does recognition of the real dangers out there.

Don't be afraid of your child's fears—scare them away as early as you can with your support, reassurance and protective presence. Left to incubate, childhood fears grow and may later become phobias. Most of our adult fears are unresolved childhood fright.

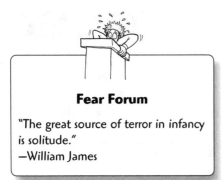

This chapter will answer some of your pressing questions regarding childhood fears: Where do they come from? How do they evolve? When should you worry that your child's fears are excessive? How can you help?

Fear Forum

"The great source of terror in infancy is solitude."
—William James

The Building Blocks of Fear

At two, Billie is afraid of the vacuum cleaner. At four, Sari is terrified of the dog next door. At seven, Bambi is afraid of ghosts. And 11-year-old Sam is horrified of taking tests.

As your child's mind grows and develops, what she perceives as dangerous or safe changes. Infants fear the uncontrollable and the unfamiliar. By preschool, fears of the imaginary begin. In the school years, fear shifts more to concrete, realistic concerns. And by the teens, fears reflect the adolescent issues of self-image.

Childhood Fears

0-6 months	7-12 months	1 year
Loss of support	Strangers	Separation from parent
Loud noises	Heights and falling	Toilet
	Sudden, unexpected, and looming objects	Injury
		Strangers

2 years	3-4 years	5-6 years
Loud noises (vacuum cleaners, sirens and alarms, trucks and thunder)	Imaginary dangers (monsters, ghosts, bad dreams, Frankenstein)	Imaginary dangers
Animals (large dogs)	Animals	Animals
Dark rooms	Dark	Dark rooms and closets
Separation from parent	Separation from parent	Separation from parent
Doctors—both the pain and the intrusiveness	Noises (including noises at night)	Sleeping or staying alone
	Masks	"Bad" people
		Bodily harm
		Thunder and lightning

7-8 years	9-12 years	Teens
Supernatural beings (ghosts, spooky things, aliens)	Tests and examinations in school	Fear of failure
Dark	School performances	Social fears
Bodily injury	Bodily injury	Sexuality
Staying alone	Physical appearance	Physical appearance
More realistic fears (natural disasters, media reports of violence, war, death, and so on)	Thunder and lightning	
	Death	
	Dark	

In Arms

At six-months, Serita cooed happily in her Grandmother's arms and there was nothing to indicate she would later be frightened of falling down the stairs. But at eight months, when Serita crawled to the edge of the stairs, she looked down and started to cry. When Grandma, whom she hadn't seen for a few weeks, picked her up, she burst into tears. She didn't stop crying until her mother walked in the room, said "poor baby" and took Serita into her arms.

Though young infants will be startled and become distressed at loud noises or loss of support, your baby won't show actual fear until the second half of the first year. Fear of heights begins when she becomes good at crawling. Fear of strangers starts at around eight months of age when your baby now recognizes you as "mother" or "father": she is now officially attached to you, and no one else will quite do. When Grandma tried to soothe Serita, she didn't match her "working model" of her mother—her touch, her smell, her voice, her face. This discrepancy between the familiar and unfamiliar, explains Harvard developmental psychologist Jerome Kagan, is at the heart of stranger anxiety. If Grandma sat down to play with a content Serita, Serita may have found the newness of Grandma interesting. But because Serita felt threatened, the discrepancy between the familiar and unfamiliar was too great for her to handle and mother's comfort was not replaceable.

Secret Weapons

If your child shows strong stranger anxiety, don't allow the stranger to come in and pick up your crying, fearful baby; discourage strangers from making eye contact; and respect your child's fear and try to soothe her.

Some children react mildly to strangers with a wary look, while others scream in terror if left with a stranger. The intensity of your child's response depends on:

➤ Temperament: Emotionally reactive and shy children react with greater stranger anxiety

➤ Parental availability: The further from the parent, the more the child feels in harm's way

➤ Quality of parent/baby attachment: Securely attached infants, who trust people as reliable and available, react less fearfully than insecurely attached infants

➤ How strange is the stranger: The more novel the stranger, the more intense the child's fear

➤ Environment: The more unfamiliar the environment, the more stress intensifies and stranger anxiety increases

In addition to stranger anxiety, by one year of age, babies show separation anxiety, especially at night, when it's dark. If your child wakes up and doesn't sense your warm touch or soothing odor, out of sight is out of mind and your baby feels you have disappeared. Actually, she feels she has disappeared as well. And so she cries, which is her separation distress call.

On the Lap

Two-year-old Billie's dad, who wanted to surprise him for Halloween, donned a gorilla mask. He thought Billie would laugh but Billie surprised him and burst into tears. Incapable of understanding how things can be different from what they are—a chair is a chair; Daddy is Daddy—small children become frightened when the familiar becomes too strange.

Also frightening are things that can eat or swoop him up, like noisy vacuum cleaners and bathtubs, where the water goes down the drain, so maybe he can too. Bathtubs are also slippery, too hot or too cold, and the place where he gets soap in his eyes. As for toilets, not only does the flush startle him, but if his feces—a part of his body—can get flushed away, perhaps he can too.

Here are some ways to squash the "me-too-disappear" fears:

1. Let your child control the switch on the vacuum cleaner
2. Have your child flush the toilet himself
3. Bathe your child on a bath table
4. Take your child gradually into the tub with you
5. Use a wading or swimming pool to help your child get over the fear
6. Get each part of her body a little wet, a little more wet and so on.

7. Initially, take your child out of the tub and let her be the one to pull the plug

8. Let her give a bath to her toys and control the water

Secret Weapons

To help ease separation anxiety, provide trust and caring while encouraging independence and individuality. Offer your child a "brave companion," like a fierce stuffed animal.

At two, Billie is less frightened of strangers. But he still shows separation anxiety when Mommy or Daddy want to leave him, especially at night, where he sleeps alone in his own room. To ease him into sleep and make the night seem less dark, his parents have put a clown night-light next to his bed.

By Your Side

In school, four year-old Matthew saw the movie *Hansel and Gretel*. That night, when his mother left him with a babysitter, Matthew screamed, afraid his mother too would abandon him to witches and dark forests.

By preschool, your child is good at imagining what he's actually never seen, but bad at distinguishing reality from fantasy. Fear of imaginary creatures, "bad" people like robbers, bodily injury, abandonment and loss of love, death, and being alone are now added to his fear list—big time! Some fears will drop out, some abate, some re-emerge in a different form—fear of the dark becomes fear of robbers, for example.

During the day, your child may be able to handle his fears well enough. But at night, the dark now really spooks him, as his imagination spins out of control of all the evil out there. It's not the darkness, with all its eerie noises and shadows, that frightens him, as it did when he was two. It's all the things, like burglars and monsters, that can be lurking out of sight. That little night-light next to his bed helps but doesn't seem to stop a bear from sneaking under his bed and into his dreams now and then. Occasional nightmares, which peak in children between the ages of four and six, are common.

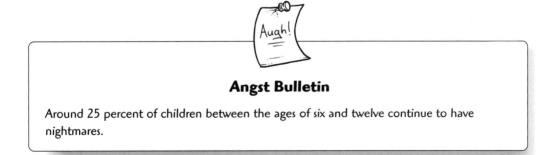

Angst Bulletin

Around 25 percent of children between the ages of six and twelve continue to have nightmares.

Out the Door

Eight-year-old Danny doesn't fear monsters so much anymore. He's more afraid that Hurricane Hugo, whirling away in the Bahamas, will hit Miami where he lives and blow his house away. He's also afraid that the bully, Jeff, will carry through his threat about beating him up on the playground and that Mr. Sanford will blame him for the fight and send him to the office. Though he's big enough to run from a burglar, or call 911, he doesn't feel powerful enough to combat night terrors and still has occasional nightmares.

The "age of reason" begins by the age of seven or so, and your child no longer blurs fact and fantasy. Concrete, tangible fears, related to situations where the child knows enough to recognize danger, but is not old enough to feel control in protecting herself, now upstage imaginary fears. But they don't quite end then. At this age, your child's imagination can still run away with her: imaginary creatures, along with real ones like robbers, or the possibility of accidents and events associated with the dark, increase throughout the school years.

Fortunately, your child, armed with her new weapon—being able to distinguish real from fantasy—has the capacity to talk herself out of the fear. "There is no Frankenstein in my closet because there is no Frankenstein," Cindy tells herself as she goes to bed.

Hi and Goodbye

Twelve-year old Maisie is afraid that her father will punish her for getting a "C" in geometry. Fifteen-year-old Cynthia fears that heartthrob Randy won't call her again because she's convinced she has bad breath. Sixteen-year-old Richard is terrified that he will forget his lines and make a fool of himself when he recites the *Declaration of Independence* in front of his class next week.

Between nine and eighteen years of age, fears of personal safety decline. In their place are fears pertaining to school—worries about grades, fears of teachers, and performance fright—as well as fears about sexuality, parental criticism and peer rejection.

Child's Responses

Children react differently to fear according to age, temperament, and life circumstances.

The Changing Face of Fear

When it started to thunder, two-year-old Alicia opened her eyes wide in fear, started to cry and ran for her mother. While her brother DeShawn, who's three, hid under the table and sucked his thumb.

Seven-year-old Nadia stood frozen and silent as her eight-year-old sister Mandy, at the top of the monkey bars, asked her to climb up. When Nadia shook her head no, her father laughed and called her "scaredy-cat." That night she peed in her bed and dreamt that she had fallen down a steep staircase.

When the lights in the house suddenly went out, nine-year-old Frankie ran around laughing and punching his younger sister and brothers, while his twelve-year-old sister Barbara didn't let on that she was afraid, but had diarrhea all night.

Watch It!

Aggressive behavior in children is often a cover-up of intense fears—an impulse to fight in response to a perceived danger.

While infants will cry loudly when frightened, there are many variations on the fear theme as children age. Some children easily show their fears, while others hide them or mask them in aggressive acting out, as did Frankie. Young children often seek out the protective parent but may, like DeShawn, run for cover. Regression to thumb sucking, or bed-wetting, or crying is common, as is covering up fears with psychosomatic symptoms like stomachaches and headaches. In this way, children get the needed attention and care-giving without showing what they are feeling.

Born That Way

Why did Mandy easily climb the monkey bars while her sister Nadia stood frozen in fear? Inborn temperament likely has much to do with the difference in their responses. Even when they were babies, Nadia was more fearful. Upon hearing a dog bark, she would start to cry, whereas Mandy would screech and crawl over to pet the dog.

Angst Bulletin

If you observe a group of monkeys, you can see the same temperamental differences as in humans. J. D. Higley of the National Institute on Alcohol Abuse, who studies the behavior and physiology of rhesus monkeys, says that within minutes of watching them, you can point out the meek, who peek at you from around the corner, from the bold, who leave the group and approach you in hopes of a treat.

Nadia was born more cautious, more attuned and sensitive to any changes around her. She was the first to notice a new toy in her bedroom, or that mother was trying to sneak spinach into her mashed potatoes. She reacted more strongly to noises, lights, touch, new things—to anything in her environment—than did her sister. And things haven't changed much. If we measured the sister's heart rates and respiration when Smokey, the neighbor's dog, came charging into their backyard, we would find that Nadia's elevated higher and more quickly than Mandy's, and that cortisol, the stress hormone, was greater in Nadia's bloodstream.

Sensitive and inhibited, Nadia will be more fear-prone than her sister all her life, so her parents will have to work harder to reassure her that the world is safe.

It's a Zoo Out There

Four-year-old Larry lives alone with his mother in a housing project and goes to sleep to the sound of gunshots. Though he was not born cautious and fearful, he has learned to become vigilant and, because of the dangerous world that he inhabits, experiences more fears than his average middle-class counterpart. Often, he sneaks into his ten-year-old brother Jimmy's bed at night—if Jimmy doesn't sneak into his first.

The more real fears in the child's life, both at home, on television, and in the surrounding neighborhood, the more the child's imagination will conjure up potential monsters to hurt her, make her bleed, go to the doctor, even kill her.

Even small bodily damage frightens the child. It's not just the pain. As your child develops and becomes more aware of himself as "I," he views his body as the encasement of his person. This is why young children often approach scratches, cuts and bruises as mortal wounds.

Angst Bulletin

"The two-year-old feels 'whole' again when his scratch is covered by the Band-Aid," wrote child psychoanalyst Selma Fraiberg in *The Magic Years*. "It's as if a leak in the container, the body, is sealed up and his completeness as a personality is re-established by this magic act."

By school age, as your child's self-image has matured, she is less worried about cuts and scratches. But by the time children become teenagers, and their bodies erupt into manhood and womanhood, new fears about the body emerge: being too fat; too short; too flat-chested; too pimply; and on and on. I'll talk more about this in Chapter 22.

Helplessness

The younger you are, the more powerless and dependent you are on others to protect you from the bear under the bed, which has a meaning beyond imagined dangers. It is also the lion/father who roars and sometimes hits you, as well as your own monstrous bad behavior that so vexes Mommy and Daddy and makes you fear that maybe they'll give you to someone else.

How well children cope with their powerlessness and dependency relates to the nature of the parent-child relationship. When the attachment to the parent is secure, your child feels she can trust you to be there to scare away the monsters and so her fears are more manageable. When children do not feel this sense of trust in their parent's availability to protect them, they fear abandonment and life becomes an on-going threat. Safe places and safe people are harder to find, increasing the child's sense of helplessness and powerlessness, and the likelihood for later anxieties and phobias.

When You Need to Worry

Six-year-old Debbie has nightmares several times a week and has for the past year. Seven-year-old Miguel has regressed to bed-wetting and sucking his thumb. Nine-year-old Diana refuses to spend the night away from home. Ten-year-old David won't sleep without a night-light.

Though children experience a number of fears, some extreme, all of which are normal, parents need to know when fears go beyond the norm. The following signs of trouble will guide you:

➤ Regardless of reassurance, the fear lingers or even worsens

➤ Fear disrupts child's friendships, schoolwork, eating, and sleeping

➤ The child fears going to new places or even familiar ones

➤ Fears are not age-appropriate—a teenager refusing to sleep alone

➤ Extreme reactions: trembling, weight loss, insomnia, diarrhea and vomiting, hysteria, panic

➤ Denial of all fears

➤ Psychosomatic complaints like a constant stomachache or headache

➤ Development of obsessions and compulsions

➤ Avoidance of places, people or objects, such as school, water, elevators, dogs, and so on

If you suspect your child's fears are extreme, don't assume he will outgrow them. Many of our adult fears are extensions of childhood fears that we *never* overcame.

Roots of Fears

Where do fears come from? Some, as you recall, are innate, like fear of falling, of loud noises, of the dark and of strangers. Other fears we learn.

Classical Conditioning

When eight-month-old Molly sees her doctor, she starts to cry. She has become conditioned to associate the sight of her doctor with the pain of getting an injection. In fact, she starts to cry when she sees any man in a white shirt or beard, like her doctor. Children learn a lot of fears through classical conditioning of a neutral stimulus—the doctor—with an unconditioned response—pain. Often, they generalize these fears to similar persons or situations, as did Molly.

In the 1920s, the behaviorist John Watson conducted one of the earliest demonstrations of classical conditioning that showed that emotions such as fear can be conditioned. As an 11-month-old baby known as "Little Albert," who loved furry animals, was about to grasp a white rat, a loud noise frightened him, and he began to cry. After repeated pairings of the rat with the loud noise, the child whimpered with fear when he saw the rat. The fear also generalized to rabbits, dogs, a Santa Claus mask, and other furry white objects.

Watch It!

Your children can pick up your fears. The last message you want to give your child is that you are too frightened to protect them.

Operant Conditioning

When Molly starts to cry, her mother holds her tight and soothes her. This reduces Molly's fear. In a sense, it also rewards Molly for feeling fearful since it gets her mother's attention and nurturance. With her mother's tender love and care, Molly will likely outgrow this fear. Nevertheless, parents can unwittingly encourage fears by positively reinforcing them with attention. For instance, when eight-year-old Yaacov said he didn't feel like going to school, his mother kept him home where he watched television all day and ate chocolate cookies. The next day he announced to his mother that he'd like to stay home all week!

Imitation

Your own reactions also lay the groundwork for unwittingly creating fears in your children. If you cower at the sight of thunder, your child picks up that there's a reason to be afraid and may imitate your reaction. In fact, parents and children often have similar fears.

TV

Horror movies and television violence scare children, especially the young ones who confuse fantasy and reality, and may stimulate nightmares. I will talk more about this in Chapter 19.

Combat the Fears

Children, with limited power, are full of fears. Fortunately, they have their omnipotent parents, endowed with endless magical powers, to help them cope. What can you do?

1. Being there: Your presence and helpful reassurance is your child's best line of defense. Sensitively allow him to talk about and explore his fears. Don't say, "There's nothing to be afraid of." Remember that we are frightened not just of what *can* harm us but of what we *think* can harm us. And that varies with age, understanding of the world, life experiences and our ability to protect ourselves. Teasing your child—"you know there isn't a bear under your bed"—will make him lose trust that he can turn to you for understanding and protection and ultimately increase his fears. Children will not express their fears if they fear the parent's disinterest, misunderstanding or rejection.

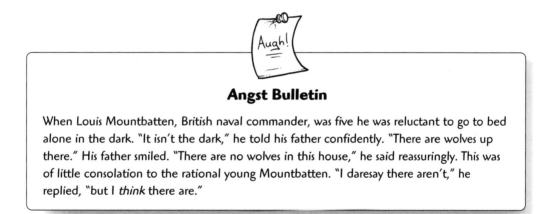

Angst Bulletin

When Louis Mountbatten, British naval commander, was five he was reluctant to go to bed alone in the dark. "It isn't the dark," he told his father confidently. "There are wolves up there." His father smiled. "There are no wolves in this house," he said reassuringly. This was of little consolation to the rational young Mountbatten. "I daresay there aren't," he replied, "but I *think* there are."

2. Facing fears: Encourage your child to gradually confront her fears but don't use the "sink or swim" approach and push her all at once. Forcing a child to take risks before she is mentally ready may ultimately frighten her more.

3. Don't make your child afraid of you: Avoid criticizing your child or getting angry with her. Your "roar" will ultimately elicit more fear and helpless anger, responses that are maladaptive. Use discipline rather than severe punishment: ghosts, lions, witches, which the child usually associates with being seriously hurt

or killed, may be symbolic substitutes of feared parental punishment. Try not to impose standards of behavior that are too high for your child to meet, or to be overly negative about their behavior or accomplishments—"Only a B. I expected an A."

4. Stay calm: Overreacting exacerbates your child's perception of the world as dangerous.

5. Create a protective environment: Control exposure to fear-producing stimuli like scary TV programs and movies that can cause your child to become over-stimulated, which encourages their behavior to get out of control.

Chapters 19 through 22 explain additional ways in which you can help your children cope with their fears.

The Least You Need to Know

➤ Childhood fears are normal and expected.

➤ Different fears predominate at different ages.

➤ Childhood fears that go beyond the norm warrant attention.

➤ Parents can do much to help their children cope.

Part 2
Making It All Better

"To be thus is nothing; But to be safely thus."—William Shakespeare, Macbeth

The first step in treating anxiety disorders is a proper diagnosis. Although psychological problems underlie most out-of-control fears and anxiety, medical conditions can, in some cases, mimic anxiety and panic, or at least exacerbate the symptoms.

If medical conditions for your anxiety are ruled out, your next step should be to attack your fears on as many fronts as possible: physiological, behavioral, and psychological. Part 2 covers all these areas: relaxation techniques, nutritional supplements, exercise, body work, psychoactive drugs (if you wish) and the spiritual route, as well as the various psychological therapies that help change avoidance behavior and perpetual worry and apprehension.

Huff
Huff

Chapter 6

Chill Out Time

In This Chapter

➤ Tensing your muscles to relax them

➤ How to breathe like a baby

➤ Finding out if you're a hyperventilator

➤ Finding inner stillness

"Whenever I feel afraid, I hold my head erect and whistle a happy tune, so no one will suspect I'm afraid." So goes the song from Rodgers and Hammerstein's *The King and I*. Unfortunately, if you're an anxious type, and especially if you have panic attacks, it's hard to think of anything but fleeing when you're afraid.

A brain flooded with adrenaline is an unreasonable brain, obedient to chemical messengers commanding it to run from the charging bull. To take control of your body and master your anxiety, you need to first slow it down—to release your natural powers of relaxation that are being drowned out by an out-of-control flight/fight response. Once you are able to quiet your body at will, then you can begin to take command of it in any situation. That includes profiting from therapies such as systematic desensitization and visualization, that require a relaxed state as a starting point. These are described in the next chapter.

There are different routes to inner tranquility. In this chapter I will concentrate on three major ones: deep diaphragmatic breathing, progressive relaxation, and meditation, and in Chapter 9, I will discuss body work and exercise. If you make them your own, you will find that they work amazingly well in helping you to calm yourself.

Deep Relaxation

Most people think of relaxing as unwinding in front of the TV set at the end of the day, reading a juicy novel, or soaking in a lavender scented hot bath. That's all right, but it won't help you achieve calmness as a mode of being, nor reduce the frequency or intensity of panic attacks. For that, you need to learn the *relaxation response,* a state of *deep relaxation* that is a distinct physiological state the exact opposite of the way your body reacts under stress or during a panic attack.

Angst Bulletin

The **relaxation response**, so named by Dr. Herbert Benson, author of *The Relaxation Response* and *Beyond the Relaxation Response*, refers to the inborn capacity for the body to enter a special state of deep relaxation characterized by lower heart rate, breathing rate and blood pressure, along with slower brain waves (alpha wave activity like the state just preceding lapsing into sleep), and reduced metabolic rate and oxygen consumption.

Daily deep relaxation gives your body a chance to recuperate from the day's stresses and to prevent stress from piling up. Over time, you will start to feel calmer, sleep deeper and more soundly, and feel more energized and more productive. You will experience less "age of stress" illnesses, like hypertension, migraines, headaches, asthma, and ulcers. And you will feel more in touch with your feelings, since you are less focused on stress, bodily symptoms and how to cope.

Here's how to prepare for your unwind time and to achieve maximum benefit from the exercises:

1. Find or create a quiet, relaxing place where noise, lights, bothersome odors and other distractions are minimal.

2. Find a comfortable position. You can sit up, lie back in a reclining chair, or lie down flat, but don't let this position seduce you into a snooze, which is counter-productive.

3. Wear comfortable, loose clothing and take off anything that puts pressure against your skin—shoes, watches, glasses, etc.

4. Practice at regular times to discipline yourself. Generally, the best times are just after waking, before going to bed or before meals. A full stomach tends to disrupt deep relaxation, since your system is working to digest your food.

5. Practice at least 20 to 30 minutes per day and preferably twice a day.

If your body does not easily chill out at first, don't try to force it. It will take practice to retrain your body out of your usual hyper-alert, tense state, and at first, it will seem hard and effortful. Once you learn deep relaxation, you return to the world with a different consciousness and sense of yourself that makes it addicting. Without it, the day seems incomplete.

Secret Weapons

Try to do your relaxation routine daily for at least 21 days, the amount of time it takes to make something into a habit.

A Sigh of Relief: Proper Breathing

Notice how you are breathing. Do you breathe slowly or quickly? Is your breathing deep or shallow? Do you breathe from your abdomen or from your chest? If you are chronically anxious or experiencing panic attacks or phobias, odds are your breathing is quick, shallow, and from your chest.

The first indicator that you are anxious is your breathing. You gasp, suck in your abdomen, and breathe high into your chest with short, shallow spurts to ready your body for quick flight. Once the cause of your stress has passed, your parasympathetic nervous system (PSN) kicks in and your body calms, returning you to a baseline of relaxed, regular breathing from your abdomen.

But if anxiety is your constant companion, your sympathetic nervous system (SNS) remains aroused, creating agitation, and prevents you from returning to a baseline of normal, diaphragmatic "belly" breathing. Instead, you breathe routinely in a restricted chest-breathing pattern: upper chest projected forward, surface muscles tightened, and length of exhalation reduced. This prevents the *diaphragm,* the muscle that separates the lung cavity from the abdominal cavity, from descending completely in order to inhale. Unable to get the air you need, you may fight even harder on the next breath to suck the air in and set up a vicious cycle: The harder you try, the less air you get.

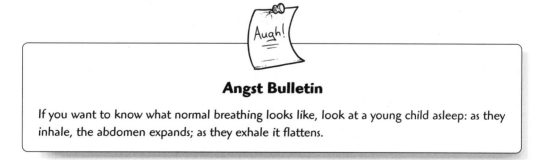

Angst Bulletin

If you want to know what normal breathing looks like, look at a young child asleep: as they inhale, the abdomen expands; as they exhale it flattens.

The more stressed you feel, the quicker and more shallow your breathing becomes. This breathing pattern in turn increases your stress level in a continuous negative feedback cycle. This is why you often feel hyper-alert—your breathing keeps you in a state of perpetual overarousal that you experience as tension or agitation.

Once chest-breathing becomes a habit, it affects your whole body. As Donna Fahri explains in her helpful book, *The Breathing Book,* when you breathe only from your chest, you learn to rely almost entirely on your upper body muscles to breathe, which are weaker than the primary muscles that make up your diaphragm. This results in:

➤ Chronic tension in the neck, shoulders and upper back

➤ Chronically tightened abdominal muscles from not expanding your abdomen, which in turn, prevents the organs in your lower body from getting sufficient circulation, which affects your digestion, assimilation and elimination

➤ Reduced blood flow to the heart, since during chest breathing the diaphragm is prevented from descending completely

Unfortunately, these aren't the only consequences of chest breathing. Unable to breathe in fully, we can't breathe out fully. To compensate, we start breathing more quickly: we hyperventilate.

Shallow Breathing and Hyperventilation

When you hyperventilate, you breathe out too much carbon dioxide relative to the amount of oxygen in your bloodstream. Carbon dioxide is crucial in helping the body maintain the right combination of acid and alkaline that is essential for cell metabolism. When this acid-alkaline balance is off even slightly, there are marked changes in the rates of chemical reactions in the cells, slowing down some, speeding up others. This imbalance can set up a whole chain of unfortunate events:

Secret Weapons

If you are a chest breather, eliminate from your wardrobe tight-fitting clothes, restrictive belts, and clothes too small for you.

➤ Less oxygen is released to the tissues, causing dizziness and a feeling of breathlessness

➤ Diminished blood flow to the brain and other parts of the body causes headaches and lack of concentration

➤ An increase in alkalinity creates excess calcium in muscles and nerves, making them hyperactive and causing muscle tension

➤ Reduced blood flow to the extremities of the body causes cold hands and feet

➤ An overexcited nervous system causes irritability, overreacting, rushed reactions and inappropriate responses

Conditions Related to Hyperventilation

Fatigue	Insomnia and nightmares
Exhaustion	Loss of concentration and memory
Heart Palpitations	A feeling of a lump in the throat
Chest pain	Stomach irritation
Rapid pulse	Feelings of unreality and depersonalization
Dizziness	Increased sensitivity to light and sound
Faintness	Pain in neck and shoulders
Distorted vision	Difficulty in swallowing
Shortness of breath	Free-floating anxiety
Yawning	Burping (sometimes bringing up fluid with it)
Aching muscles	Numbness and tingling in the limbs
Cramps and stiffness	Ringing in ears (tinnitus)
Irritability	Increased effect to alcohol
Depression	Decrease in pain sensation
Allergies	Feeling of "losing one's mind"

Angst Bulletin

There is a direct correlation between chest breathing, and heart disease and hypertension.

If you experience panic attacks, many of the above conditions probably sound all too familiar. Hyperventilation and panic are frequent travelling companions, though it's not always clear who invited whom. Some people over-breathe, which elicits the fear that they are having a panic attack and actually sets one off. In this case, hyperventilation mimics panic, causing a state of anxious agitation that, colored by catastrophic thoughts like "I'm losing control," or "Something terrible is happening to me," sets off genuine panic. Others begin to over-breathe in response to the panic, breathing too fast or too deeply and taking in too little oxygen, thereby aggravating perturbing physical symptoms.

A host of other things can trigger hyperventilation: tension, depression, chest troubles, a stuffy nose, allergies, disease, wearing tight clothes or a spinal brace, folding your arms across your chest, holding in emotional pain, overreacting to stress, drug effects and withdrawal from drugs, or even just faulty breathing.

Signs of Hyperventilation

How do you know if you're hyperventilating? There are two kinds of hyperventilation—acute and chronic. Acute hyperventilation is easier to recognize than chronic. Here are the signs:

➤ Your breaths are erratic, noisy, and rapid

➤ Your chest is heaving and your abdomen is barely moving

➤ You may feel the need to take an occasional deep breath

➤ You may find it difficult to breathe out and may sigh at intervals to relieve this

➤ You may feel dizzy

Secret Weapons

To "catch" how you routinely breathe, try putting red or bright pink dots at conspicuous places throughout your house—the refrigerator, bathroom mirror, computer monitor, a reading lamp. When you see the dot, notice your breathing pattern. Is it too fast? Are you chest breathing? Mouth breathing? If so, stop a moment and breathe slowly and deeply into your abdomen and through your nose.

Chronic hyperventilation, which can be subtle, can go unrecognized. You may be a chronic hyperventilator if the following describe your breathing pattern:

➤ Upper chest breathing

➤ Breathing through the mouth rather than the nose

➤ Breathing 18 or more breaths per minute (normal breathing is 12-14 BPM for men and 14-15 BPM for women)

➤ Frequent sighing, gasps, yawning, coughing or clearing the throat

➤ Moistening of the lips

➤ Apparent "heavy" breathing

If you feel you are a chronic over-breather, you must break this bad breathing cycle, especially if you experience panic attacks. If not, you will never achieve a comfort zone—the place where calmness and alertness are felt as a steady state. But don't despair. You were once an infant in your mother's arms, breathing deeply and peacefully. The memory is there and can be restored.

Diaphragmatic Breathing Practice

You weren't born an over-breather; you learned it. You can also unlearn it and train yourself to breathe normally. The following deep breathing exercise will help teach you to slow down your breathing and to breathe from your abdomen, or diaphragm. This will increase the amount of oxygen getting to your brain and muscles and stimulate your parasympathetic nervous system (PSN) to override your sympathetic nervous system (SNS), thereby inviting the relaxation response to take over. If you take yoga class, you will probably recognize this exercise as "ujjayi" breathing.

Here's how to do it:

1. Lie down, close your eyes and note the tension you're feeling and your breathing pattern. (If you're chronically stressed, you've become accustomed to feeling overanxious and take it for granted. It's important to become aware of how your breathing pattern reflects your level of tension.)

2. Place one hand on your abdomen, beneath your rib cage, and the other on your chest.

Angst Bulletin

Sixty percent of all panic attacks are accompanied by acute hyperventilation.

3. Place the tip of your tongue against the back of your top front teeth. Inhale slowly and deeply through your nose to the count of four or five (one thousand, two thousand...), creating a yawning sensation in the back of your nose and throat and expanding your abdomen like a balloon. Your hand should rise as you feel your navel rise to the ceiling. You should hear your breath filling your lungs and rising up to where your throat and the back of your nose meet and you should feel your throat vibrating. Your chest should move only slightly while your abdomen expands. If you only feel your belly expand without the sensation of air rising up to where your throat and the back of your nose meet, you are breathing incorrectly.

Watch It!

If you are anxious, it is not a good idea to do breathing exercises in which you hold your breath briefly on the inhale. Holding your breath extends SNS arousal, which you don't want to do, while pausing following exhalation extends PNS arousal, which will help prolong a feeling of calm.

4. Place the tip of your tongue behind your bottom front teeth. With slightly pursed lips, breathe out through your mouth, slowly pushing the stale air out of your lungs to the count of five (if you breathed in on four), or six or seven (if you breathed in on five). Don't force it. Feel your navel collapse towards the floor, minimizing your upper chest motion. The hand on your chest should stay as still as possible. Be sure to squeeze all the air out of your lungs and allow your whole body to just let go. You can also breathe out though your mouth, emphasizing the exhalation by making a "hah" sound with your mouth open and relaxed.

5. Pause briefly at the end of the exhalation and let your next inhalation begin on its own.

6. Do at least ten full abdominal breaths slowly and smoothly, prolonging your exhale. Slowly increase the amount to forty cycles a session. Take a few regular breaths between ten breath cycles.

If you spend three to ten minutes a day (10 to 40 breathing cycles), twice a day doing this exercise, you should begin to feel less jittery, and experience fewer early symptoms of panic. If you are having severe symptoms, panic, or agoraphobia, you may need to do it for longer periods and more often. Regular practice of deep breathing will increase your lung capacity and help you breathe more deeply—when my yoga teacher, who has been doing "Ujjayi" breathing for years, demonstrates it, you can hear her lungs fill, like a surge of wind, from the back of a large room. As your lung capacity increases, you will be able to train yourself to breathe between 8 and 12 times per minute. This in turn will greatly increase your energy level.

If you find yourself unable to slow down your breathing, don't be discouraged. If you hyperventilate, breath control does not come easy. And it's hard to breathe properly when you're overanxious. Try taking a yoga class, which incorporates breathing exercises. At home, try relaxing your muscles through progressive relaxation before you get out of bed in the morning. This will automatically slow down your breathing and allow you to begin your deep breathing exercise.

If during the deep breathing exercise you find the need to catch your breath, this will subside. You want to breathe in quickly because your brain is telling you that you are suffocating. And, since it takes a few minutes for the symptoms associated with hyperventilating to subside, the pause after the exhalation again triggers a perception that you are suffocating. Try to breathe slowly and deeply, but gently. The more vigorous or forced your breathing, the more you may become light-headed—an indication of a rapid lowering of carbon dioxide levels. If this happens, stop briefly and then start again.

If light-headedness continues, it's probably because the muscles involved in breathing, namely the chest, diaphragm and, for some people, the throat muscles, remain tense. The following exercises will help relax your chest, diaphragm and throat muscles:

Chest muscles

1. Square your shoulders and bend your elbows so your forearms are straight out in a 90-degree angle, like a puppy begging for food.

2. Try to touch your shoulder blades together and hold the tension felt in your chest muscles for three seconds (one thousand, two...).

3. Release the tension and relax your chest.

4. Repeat three to five more times until you feel your chest area relaxed.

Diaphragm muscles

1. Suck your stomach in and up under your rib cage.

2. Hold the tension for five seconds.

3. Release the tension and relax your stomach.

4. Repeat until your light-headedness dissipates.

Throat muscles

1. Point your chin toward the ceiling, stretching the throat muscles as much as you can.

2. Place your tongue in the roof of your mouth and push with your tongue as hard as you can.

3. Hold the tension for five seconds.

4. Release the tension and relax your throat.

5. Repeat three to five times, or until you feel the tension in your throat muscles dissipate.

Watch It!

Research has found that the moment your fingers rest on a computer keyboard, most people brace with their upper bodies. While typing, they chest breathe and breathe quickly.

Secret Weapons

To get a thorough review of proper breathing techniques and exercises, I suggest reading *The Art of Breathing* by Nancy Zi and *The Breathing Book* by Donna Fahri.

Shifting the center of your breathing from your chest to your abdomen, so you can breathe diaphragmatically easily and spontaneously on an on-going basis, will take time and effort. Don't forget, you haven't used these muscles in a long time. They need to be developed again. So, have patience. But once learned, you should be able to re-train your nervous system to an overall more relaxed state. And you will begin to be able to monitor your level of stress and self-calm before you get locked into anxiety's grip.

Tense to Calm: Progressive Relaxation

Do you feel "uptight" or "tense?" Are your muscles taut and knotted, especially in your shoulders and neck? Progressive relaxation, a short exercise that involves tensing and then releasing or relaxing each muscle group, calms within minutes.

Like the pendulum's swing, the more you pull your muscles into one direction, tension, the farther they will swing to the other direction, relaxation—an oxymoron of tensing to relax. So as you do progressive relaxation, don't be afraid to really tense up. As you get proficient, your body awareness of both the sensation of tension and the sensation of relaxation will increase.

To get some idea of your level of tension, do a quick body scan. The following symptoms will reveal your level of tension.

➤ Holding head on one side

➤ Head and chin jutted forward

➤ Tight jaw

➤ Raised shoulders

➤ Shoulders curved toward front of body

➤ Fists clenched

➤ Hands fiercely gripping pen, telephone, steering wheel, cup handle, computer mouse

➤ Stomach tightened

➤ Chest tightened

Are you tense? If so, get ready to *really* tense so you can *really* relax.

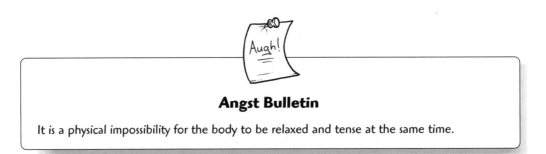

Angst Bulletin

It is a physical impossibility for the body to be relaxed and tense at the same time.

Ready to Tense!

The progressive relaxation sequence begins from head to toe, but you can vary the order. Some people like to begin with their hands or feet and end with their head. Though you will pick up the sequence after a few sessions, you may want to make your own recording of the sequence or pick up one that is commercially made.

Before getting started, check out these general guidelines:

Watch It!

If your muscles are very tense, or if you're withdrawing from tranquilizers or alcohol, tensing your muscles may create spasms. If so, try tensing only those muscle groups that do not spasm or avoid the protocol until bodily tension reduces.

➤ Lie down if you can

➤ For each muscle group in the sequence described below, hold the tension for 7-10 seconds

➤ Release abruptly, feeling the muscle group go limp. Relax for 15-20 seconds, breathing deeply

➤ Concentrate on the heaviness and greater awareness of the muscle groups that were tensed and relaxed

➤ Some especially tight muscle groups, like the shoulders or neck, might need to be repeated twice

➤ If you feel pain in any muscle group, omit it until the pain or extreme tension subsides

Here's how you do it:

1. Start by closing your eyes, lying still and taking in a few deep abdominal breaths.

2. Forehead: Wrinkle up your forehead. Hold...hold...hold...let go. Relax and feel your forehead relaxing and smoothing out. Breathe deeply making certain you are not chest breathing.

3. Eyes: Squint your eyes tightly shut. Hold...hold...hold...let go. Relax, take a deep breath and imagine relaxation spreading all around your eyes. Breathe deeply.

4. Mouth: Open your mouth as wide as you can, stretching the muscles around the hinges of your jaw. Hold...hold...hold...let go. Relax and gently close your mouth. Breathe deeply.

5. Tongue: Close your mouth and push your tongue against the roof of your mouth. Feel the tension. Hold...hold...hold...let go. Relax and feel your tongue smooth out comfortably in your mouth and your lips fall slightly apart. Breathe deeply.

6. Jaw: Clench your jaw tightly. Hold...hold...hold...let go. Relax and let your lips part and allow your jaw to hang loose. Breathe deeply.

Secret Weapons

If you suffer from Temporomandibu-lar Joint Problem (TMJ), try this exercise. Extend your lower jaw as far forward as possible and hold for five seconds. Release and relax. Repeat three to five times.

7. Neck: Pull your head way back, as if you were going to touch your head to your back but do it gently to avoid injury. Focus only on tensing the muscles in your neck. Hold…hold…hold…let go and feel the tension leave your neck. Breathe deeply.

8. Head: Push your head into the surface of wherever you are lying and feel its weight. Hold…hold…hold… Let go and let your head gently rock from side to side or front to back, feeling the tension slip away. Breathe deeply.

9. Shoulders: Shrug your shoulders and raise them up toward your ears. Hold…hold…hold…let go. Relax and let any tension melt away.Breathe deeply.

10. Shoulder blades: Tighten the muscles around your shoulder blades as if trying to touch them together. Hold…hold…hold… Let go and relax.

11. Hands: Clench your fists. Hold…hold…hold… Let go and relax. Breathe deeply.

12. Biceps: Build up the tension in your upper arms by drawing your forearms up toward your shoulders and making a muscle with both arms. Try to keep the muscles in other parts of your body relaxed. Focus on the sensations of tension. Hold…hold…hold… Let go and relax. Breathe deeply.

13. Triceps: Tighten the muscles on the underside of your upper arms by extending your arms out straight and locking your muscles. Hold…hold…hold… Now let go and relax your arms. Breathe deeply.

14. Chest: Take in a deep breath and hold it for ten seconds as you feel your chest expanded, and the muscles stretched around your chest. Now slowly let the air escape and resume normal breathing. Let the airflow in and out, smoothly and easily. Be aware of the difference as your muscles relax. Breathe deeply.

15. Back: Arch your back up. Hold…hold…hold… Let go and relax. Breathe deeply.

16. Stomach: Tighten the muscles in your stomach by pulling it towards your spine, as if to touch your backbone. Hold…hold…hold…let go. Relax and take a deep breath, and as you exhale, feel the tension seeping out of your stomach and a wave of relaxation coming over you. Breathe deeply.

17. Buttocks: Tighten your buttocks by pulling them together. Hold…hold…hold… Let go and relax, letting your hips spread out. Breathe deeply.

18. Thighs: Tighten your thigh muscles all the way down to your knees. Hold…hold…hold… Let go and relax as you feel your thigh muscles smoothing out. Breathe deeply.

19. Calves: Squeeze your calf muscles as tightly as you can. Hold...hold...hold... Let go and relax. Breathe deeply.

20. Feet: Clench your feet, pulling your toes in as if grasping something with your foot. Hold...hold...hold... Let go and relax your feet as you feel your toes gently open out. Breathe deeply.

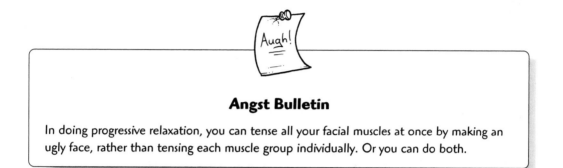

Angst Bulletin

In doing progressive relaxation, you can tense all your facial muscles at once by making an ugly face, rather than tensing each muscle group individually. Or you can do both.

Lie still and comfortable for a few minutes, focusing on your breathing, which is now regular and smooth. Free your mind of any thoughts. Feel your body become heavy, sinking into the ground. Imagine a white, warm light traveling up your body, from your toes to the top of your head. Stay in this state of calm for at least five minutes. When you're ready, open your eyes slowly. Your heart rate and blood pressure have probably dropped so you will want to avoid sitting up abruptly.

From Tense to Relaxed

If you have been in a chronic state of stress, you probably still feel some anxiety following progressive relaxation. Or you may feel initially relaxed but find yourself soon tense again. This is because your baseline state is dominated by sympathetic nervous system activity, or overarousal, thus you continually feel keyed up or agitated. As you repeat the protocol and make it a daily ritual, and as you learn to breathe diaphragmatically, you will feel greater and longer lasting relief from immediate tension.

Over time, you should experience a reduction of panic attacks and decreased anxiety, including the anticipatory anxiety related to phobias. You will be less bothered by tension headaches, backaches, tightness in the jaw, tightness around the eyes, muscle spasms, and insomnia. Since a relaxed body makes for a relaxed mind, your thoughts won't race as much and your concentration should improve.

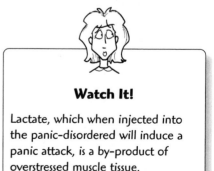

Watch It!

Lactate, which when injected into the panic-disordered will induce a panic attack, is a by-product of overstressed muscle tissue.

During the day, if you feel tension building, slow down your breathing for a few minutes and focus on each muscle group in turn, reminding yourself how it feels when these muscles are relaxed. To quickly get into an alpha state, try to concentrate on the sensation of heaviness, warmth, or a floating feeling. Or you can scan your body, starting at your toes, telling each body part to relax.

The Inner Glass Booth: Meditation

Now that your muscles are relaxed and you've done your breathing exercises, you are ready to enter another state of consciousness: the state achieved through meditation. Meditation brings you to a place of deep peace and quiet, where you can "just be," free of thoughts and worries—a land where you are resting deeply, as in sleep, but are wide awake inside. This is the ultimate in deep relaxation, and the more you master it, the more able you will be to control both mind and body. This will empower you, making you feel less victimized by helplessness and fear.

The secret to achieving this deep inner stillness is twofold: proper breathing and the ability to let go of the thoughts racing through your mind. Some reach this land of tranquility by repeating a mantra, visualizing a peaceful image, or focusing on their breathing. Others chant or stare at a physical object like a candle. For me, slowly rocking from side to side, my body locked into its own internal rhythm, is what does it. And it happens for me regardless of position—lying down, sitting cross-legged or in a chair. But it's not important how you get there. Only that you get there. Because "there" is Nirvana.

Nirvana. The Yogis define it as a state that transcends pain, suffering, and individual consciousness. The Western scientific definition is a bit more technical. It is a state in which, Herbert Benson discovered, we experience:

➤ Lower heart rate

➤ Lower blood pressure

➤ A reduced need for oxygen consumption

➤ Lower metabolic rate

➤ Lower concentration of lactic acid in your blood

➤ Increased circulation

➤ Increased alpha brain wave activity

That all sounds good to me.

Fear Forum

"An anxious mind cannot exist in a relaxed body."
—Dr. Edmund Jacobson, the founder of Progressive Relaxation

If you meditate consistently, you will feel generally more relaxed. If you do it over the long haul, in time you will discover yourself more alert, energetic and productive, more patient and open to experiences, and less self-critical. You will feel a greater sense of identity and self-worth, and decreased dependence on alcohol or recreational drugs. And you will be less vulnerable to illness because meditation enhances immune function.

That Still Place

For meditation to work, you must discipline yourself to do it regularly for at least 15 to 20 minutes or more. Here's how to do it:

1. Sit comfortably in a straight-backed chair, with your feet on the floor and legs uncrossed, hands on your thighs. Or sit yogi style—cross-legged on the floor, leaning slightly forward, with a pillow supporting your buttocks. Try not to lie down, because doing so invites sleep.

2. Play a tape of soft, instrumental sounds, or sounds from nature like the sound of ocean waves. Or play a guided meditation tape, which often includes visualizations.

3. Close your eyes. When thoughts or daydreams come to your mind, allow them to come and go. (The experience is similar to sitting in front of your aquarium and watching the fish swim.)

4. Do it daily if you can, even if only for five minutes.

Choose Your Mind Potion

One of the most popular means for going deep down under is Transcendental Meditation (TM). An instructor selects a Sanskrit mantra (a word or sound) for you, such as "Om." While sitting in a quiet place, you repeat the sound mentally, concentrating completely on the mantra and letting distractions just pass through your mind. Or you may select your own word or phrase—something personally meaningful. Or, as Dr. Herbert Benson suggests, you may repeat "one" on each exhalation.

Another way of getting into a meditative state is through visualizing a scene in your mind. To give you some idea of how strongly your imagination can impact your behavior, close your eyes and imagine yourself biting into a lemon. Notice how you immediately begin to salivate. Such is the power of visualization. Here are some interesting scenes to let your imagination ride with:

➤ A quiet beach

➤ A stream in the mountains

➤ Lying back in a canoe on a calm lake, looking up at the stars or the sun setting

➤ A cozy fireside on a cold winter night

➤ Floating on a cloud

➤ Flying on a magic carpet

The more detail you visualize, the more the image will absorb your attention and free you from anxious thoughts, thereby deepening your state of relaxation.

If you find that neither repeating a word or sound, nor visualizing an image works for you, try concentrating on the inflow and outflow of your breath, counting as you inhale and exhale.

Give Peace a Chance

Initially, you may want to start out with short periods of 5-10 minutes meditation and then gradually lengthen your time to 20-45 minutes.

If you are very tense, you may be unable to relax enough to go into a meditative state. It's all right. Most people, especially beginners, find that it takes a persistent and disciplined effort over a period of several months to become proficient at "getting inside your head." With enough persistence, it will eventually come. How do you know when you're there? You lose awareness of your breathing and your body, and find yourself floating in such serenity that it's hard to leave and return to the mundane everyday world. When you do, however, you feel more at peace.

The Least You Need to Know

➤ If you're anxious, you are probably over-breathing.

➤ Over-breathing perpetuates your tension and prevents you from achieving a generally relaxed state.

➤ Progressive relaxation is an easy to learn method for defusing tension in a short period of time.

➤ Meditation provides the deepest form of relaxation, though mastering it is not easy and can take time.

➤ If chronically tense, you may find it will take much effort to learn to retrain your system into a relaxed state—stick with it!

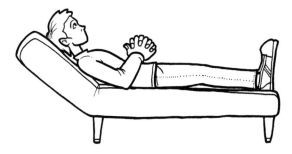

On the Couch

Ever want someone to just listen to you? Really listen and not say, "Oh, if you think you're a nervous wreck, let me tell you about how stressed out I am." Or "C'mon, just pull yourself up by your bootstraps and get over these silly fears."

When you go into psychotherapy, a treatment for mental and emotional disorders, you pay someone to listen to just you—your worries, fears, nightmares, crazy and silly thoughts. And you don't have to listen to theirs! (If you do, change therapists.) And this interchange is done in confidence—your wife will never find out that during sex you fantasize about your young secretary.

If the idea of seeking help makes you uneasy, rest assured—it does for many people. Self-reliance! Independence! These are the battle cries with which we're brought up, so seeking help comes to equal dependency and weakness. This is false. People are inter-dependent and reliant on each other. Seeking help is not a weakness but a form of self-nurturing—of taking care of your needs so that increased personal power and control make you less of a slave to uncomfortable fear and anxiety.

Moreover, since our patterns of behavior are set early in life through childhood experiences and seasoned by life events, they can be stubborn to change without profes-sional help. An empathic listener, trained in ways to help you overcome your fears, might change your life significantly and you might emerge with a new best friend: yourself.

In this chapter, you will learn about the different kinds of therapies, what each has to offer for conquering fears and anxiety, and which appear to work best for specific anxiety disorders.

Psychotherapy: It's Come a Long Way

The quintessential picture of a person in *psychotherapy* is someone lying on a couch with a rather stern, older, bearded white man, often smoking a pipe, sitting behind them. The patient is talking their heart out while the analyst nods occasionally and says little.

Actually, this scenario is a parody on only a small percentage of people in psycho-therapy—those in *psychoanalysis*, a long-term intense psychological treatment of generally three to four days a week for three or more years.

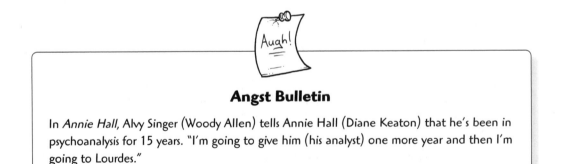

Angst Bulletin

In *Annie Hall*, Alvy Singer (Woody Allen) tells Annie Hall (Diane Keaton) that he's been in psychoanalysis for 15 years. "I'm going to give him (his analyst) one more year and then I'm going to Lourdes."

Today, most people are in some form of short-term therapy, ranging from weeks to months rather than years. The length varies depending on when you and your thera-pist agree that you've reached your goals. Rather than passively sitting back listening, the therapist will generally give frequent feedback and helpful suggestions for change and may do as much talking as you do. The choice is wide—there are over 250 types of psychotherapy that derive from psychology's major personality theories, psychoana-lytic, humanistic, behavioral, and cognitive. Treatment can be conducted on a one-to-one basis, in groups, with couples, or with entire families.

The most effective treatments for anxiety disorders are behaviorism and cognitive-behavioral therapy. Typically not as effective initially is *psychodynamic therapy*—a shorter and less intense form of psychoanalysis that is based on the same underlying principles.

Though the techniques may be different, most forms of psychotherapy have similar goals, that is, to help those in therapy to overcome their fears and anxiety.

Here is how psychotherapy can help to effect change:

Terror Talk

Psychodynamic therapy is a type of psychological treatment that utilizes psychoanalytic principles of treatment to help people gain insight into their problems. Current problems are understood by exploring their roots in childhood experiences. Therapist and client generally sit face-to-face and meet once a week for a few months to a few years.

1. Behavior: reduce avoidance and increase assertiveness

2. Feelings: identify, manage and express feelings appropriately

3. Thoughts: change negative self-talk

4. Relationships: increase capacity for establishing and maintaining healthy, supportive relationships

5. Sense of Self: increase self-esteem, self-knowledge, personal control, and self-identity

However, the style of therapy that works for one person may not work for you so you may have to shop around. If you feel depressed as well as anxious, and the two often go hand in hand, you should seek a professional, competent in treating both anxiety disorders and depression.

Freud Is Alive and Well

Consciously, you sincerely desire to overcome your fears. Yet, often people find it difficult to maintain their motivation for change. Fearing people, you tell yourself to get out there and overcome your shyness. Yet, when your friend suggests going to a party where you might have to strike up a conversation with strangers, you find yourself with a sudden headache. Fearing flying, you promise your brother you'll overcome it and be on that plane for his wedding. But the night before the flight, you feel suddenly too ill to travel. Fearing failure, you're determined to get over it, or you'll never get ahead. Yet you manage to arrive too late to take your final exam in your marketing class and end up not graduating.

Why do we behave contrary to our own best interest? To Sigmund Freud, the answer lay deep within our unconscious: therein lie strong forces that often conflict with and overpower our conscious desires, a thought or feeling that we believe is sinful or wrong. Perhaps you feel intense rage and/or the desire to harm someone close to you—a parent, a spouse, a child. Or you may wish to be taken care of like a child. Conscious awareness of these anxiety-provoking feelings might be catastrophic to your sense of well being: you might feel overwhelmed with guilt or shame or go insane altogether.

You protect yourself from bringing these feelings into conscious awareness by erecting defenses—repression, denial, avoidance and withdrawal, or displacement, for instance. As these defense mechanisms tighten their grip, your anxiety increases and eventually may spill over into symptoms like phobias, or obsessions and compulsions. Phobias, for instance, *displace* your anxiety away from the repressed desire or stressful loss and onto an external object: a spider, an airplane, a bridge. Since you perceive these external objects as less threatening than your feelings and you can avoid them, you feel less fearful.

To loosen the grip of your unconscious mind over your conscious motivation, you have to uncover what truly motivates your symptoms. For instance, underlying a fear of public speaking may be a fear of disapproval, reminding you of the times when your father failed to acknowledge your efforts; regardless of your accomplishments, you feel you will only disappoint people. Underlying a fear of dating may be the feeling that you are unlovable. The person will soon find out and leave you anyway.

Angst Bulletin

Freud treated a woman with an intense fear of rubber. When she was a child, her father brought her younger sister, whom she resented, and her each a balloon. When she burst her younger sister's balloon, she was severely punished and forced to give her balloon to her sister. Freud interpreted the burst balloon as symbolic of her wish to see her younger sister dead, which created guilt that she buried into her unconscious. Later, rubber objects stirred these feelings; hence the phobia.

When you avoid the fear-provoking person or situation, you experience "secondary" gains that perpetuate them—conscious or unconscious rewards for holding onto your symptoms, like attention, sympathy, or nurturance. Take Beth. She is too frightened to drive across bridges unless accompanied by her husband, who holds her hand during the ordeal, as she safely leans up against him. Deep within her is a basic fear of abandonment and of being swallowed up by strong dependency needs, as the water would swallow her up should the bridge collapse. To lessen the chance of her husband leaving her, she denies her own needs and lives her life to please him. Her phobia serves two purposes: it maintains her dependency on her husband which, in her mind, assures that he won't leave her and it affords her moments of physical closeness that they don't often share.

To help unlock the demons lurking in the caverns of your unconscious, the psychoanalyst's picklocks consist of free association (saying whatever comes into your mind), hypnosis, dream and transference interpretations (the feelings for the analyst linked with other relationships, such as love or hatred for a parent). For instance, common falling dreams may symbolize a host of current concerns:

1. Falling from grace
2. Falling through the cracks
3. Falling flat on your face
4. Falling in/out of love
5. Falling ill
6. Falling apart
7. Falling short
8. Falling behind

The primal terror you experience during the dream is the most basic fear of all: falling kerplunk like Humpty-Dumpty.

The following might represent a transference interpretation. A patient says, "I forgot my wife's birthday and she isn't speaking to me." The analyst responds, "Sounds like she's pretty angry at you." The patient yells, "You siding with her? You, who knows that she hasn't slept with me for a month and constantly burns my food?" The analyst might then interpret the patient's outburst as relating not to cues coming from the analyst "siding" with the wife, but rather a faulty perception elicited by early feelings of not having felt defended as a child—how when his mother yelled at him for no apparent reason other than her own foul mood, his father would not stick up for him.

As feelings and memories surface in a safe, non-critical and non-punitive environment, you experience *catharsis* (cleansing of pent-up emotions) and *abreaction* (resolution of neurotic behavior by reviving forgotten or repressed memories) and these terrors presumably lose their power over you. With the help of your therapist, you work through these conflicts and the phobia, no longer needed, disappears.

Triggering a Repressed Memory

Sometimes, something triggers long-term repression of these feelings. Kara, a dancer, was surprised to discover that when her father, whom she had adored, died, she felt not grief but hate for him.

A few months following his death, Kara was hired to dance in her first Broadway show, her dream. Rather than experiencing joy, she felt increasingly edgy and anxious. What if she couldn't dance up to their standards? What if they fired her? Suddenly, a memory

91

hit her. When she was eight, she was given the star role of the princess in her dance school performance. Her father received the news with indifference. In fact, he undermined her confidence, saying, "Are you sure you dance well enough to be the star?" Being offered a role in a Broadway chorus jiggled her memories of all the times her father failed to support her talents and desires, how he had greeted her accomplishments with apathy and doubt of her abilities.

Filled with rage, she collapsed in sobs on the floor, ripping to shreds a photo of her father and shouting how he never appreciated her. Afterwards, she felt drained but relieved and her anxiety abated.

Angst Bulletin

Freud himself saw the limitations of traditional psychotherapy when treating agoraphobia and other phobias, stating that "one can hardly master a phobia if one waits till the patient lets the analyst influence him to give it up."

Freudian Doubts

In spite of the relief of gaining insight into your behavior, thereby forgiving yourself all your imaginable crimes, psychodynamic treatment has shortcomings in treating anxiety disorders:

➤ Gaining insight into your behavior does not alone guarantee freedom from phobias or anxiety.

➤ Psychoanalysis and psychodynamic therapy is a long, complex mode of treatment.

➤ Emphasizing thoughts or feelings prior to a panic attack, psychodynamic therapists often ignore the physical causes of panic attacks and phobias. This not only perpetuates the mind-body split, but limits the efficacy of treatment.

➤ Psychodynamic therapy has a poor success rate for eliminating panic attacks and phobias.

Nevertheless, once anxiety is brought under control with employing other forms of therapy, such as cognitive-behavioral therapy, research has found psychodynamic therapy useful for those who want a greater understanding of what fuels anxiety and allows it to thrive. A small percentage, generally those highly verbal, introspective, educated, and with financial means to do so, will seek out long-term psychoanalysis. The intense relationship developed with the analyst allows for much re-parenting, that is, the person comes to feel more nurtured, valued, understood, and accepted. Many report profound behavioral transformations and deepened self-identity and self-worth.

Today, many psychodynamic therapists are eclectic and use a variety of interventions, some beginning with cognitive-behavioral treatments and then switching over to in-depth psychodynamic therapy when the patient's symptoms abate.

Humanistic Therapy

Like the Freudians, the *humanistic* therapists assume that anxiety arises from intrapsychic conflicts. Unlike the Freudians, however, the battle is not between the conscious and the unconscious mind, but between our ideal self, who we would like to be, and our actual self, who we view ourselves as being. Their emphasis is on the here and now, rather than past causes, and they encourage the client to take responsibility for their behavior.

Treatment consists of empathetically listening to and accepting the person uncondi-tionally, without judgment. This is based on the premise that feeling validated and accepted for who they are helps the person narrow the gap between their actual and ideal self.

Terror Talk

Humanistic therapy is a type of psychological treatment that emphasizes people's inherent potential for self-fulfillment and helps them grow in self-awareness and self-acceptance. It utilizes the technique, developed largely by Carl Rogers, of active listening within a genuine, accepting, empathic environment that facilitates the client's growth.

Angst Bulletin

Modern day psychoanalysis, as pioneered by the theories of people such as Heinz Kohut, combines much of humanistic therapy—it emphasizes empathic responding and a focus on development of the self more than on intrapsychic conflict.

As with psychoanalytic treatment, humanistic therapy also ignores physiological symptoms, which are a major component of panic attacks and require intervention beyond just talking about them—relaxation exercises, for instance, as well as constructive self-talk for keeping the panic attacks in perspective. Thus, though warmly embraced by many people seeking psychic healing, who often feel better understood than in other therapies, it has been largely ineffective in controlling panic attacks.

Face It, Kid: Systematic Desensitization

Insight and self-awareness may be nice, say the *behaviorists*, but the real problem is your behavior: if you don't change that, the self you know may remain anxious. For instance, you can understand why you're trembling as you ask someone for a date, but understanding will not necessarily relieve the anxiety you feel.

Terror Talk

Behavioral therapy eliminates fear by applying counter-conditioning, based on classical conditioning, in which you pair an unpleasant stimulus with a pleasant response to eliminate avoidance behavior. Classical conditioning was originally conceived at the turn of the century by the Russian physiologist Ivan Pavlov.

Behavioral therapy is a short-termed psychological treatment that focuses on fear as a learned behavior. Let's say that on the way to see your accountant, you suddenly feel terror while riding the elevator (not to be confused with the ordinary "panic" many feel when visiting their accountant). By the time you get off at the eighteenth floor, you are shaking and are drenched in sweat. Through simple classical conditioning, you now pair elevators with fear and start to avoid them. This puts a real damper on your life: you work fourteen floors up, your girlfriend lives eight floors up, to say nothing of the clients you must visit high in the sky. In other words, this fear has the potential to change your entire lifestyle, greatly limiting your choices in life. You must do something—and quick.

Fortunately, behavioral therapy can come to the rescue. It changes phobic behavior within a relatively short period of time by applying learning principles. Through *counter-conditioning,* you will learn to pair the trigger stimulus—taking an elevator—with a new response that is incompatible with fear—relaxation.

Typically, counter-conditioning takes place through *systematic desensitization*—the most successful non-pharmacological therapy for phobias and panic attacks. During systematic desensitization, you associate a pleasant, relaxed state with gradually increasing anxiety-triggering stimuli. This is a standard scenario:

1. A behavior therapist asks you to construct all the steps leading up to getting into the elevator, starting with leaving your house.

2. The therapist teaches you how to relax, for instance through progressive relaxation.

3. Once in a drowsy and comfortable state, you close your eyes and imagine a mildly anxiety-inducing situation, like standing before an elevator.

4. If this image creates anxiety, you signal so to the therapist by raising your finger.

5. The therapist instructs you to turn off the mental image and return to a state of deep relaxation.

This sequence is repeated until you can mentally play out the scene without anxiety. The therapist progresses up your anxiety hierarchy, using the relaxed state to desensitize you to each imagined situation. For elevators, your anxiety hierarchy may look like this:

1. Stand in front of an elevator and watch it come and go

2. Step into the elevator with your support person

3. Ride up one floor with your support person

4. Stand in an elevator alone

5. Ride up one floor alone, with your support person waiting for you on the floor on which you get out

6. Ride up one floor without a support person

7. Ride up two to three floors with your support person

8. Ride up two to three floors alone, with your support person waiting for you on the floor on which you get out

9. Lengthen the number of floors you can travel with a support person and then alone with that person waiting for you

10. Ride an elevator alone without a support person

After several therapy sessions, you practice the imagined behaviors in actual situations. You begin with relatively easy tasks and gradually move up your anxiety hierarchy until your fears are gone. In contextual therapy, originated by psychiatrist Manual Zane, founder of one of the first phobia clinics at the White Plains Medical Hospital Center in White Plains, New York, therapists accompany phobics as they expose themselves to the feared situations and help them recognize the difference between imagined and real dangers. Today, patients can also play out their fear in virtual reality.

Other, more aggressive forms of counter-conditioning include:

➤ Rapid exposure, which is also call flooding, and implosion therapy: You imagine (implosion) and then experience (flooding) the worst possible scenario. For instance, if you fear heights, you picture yourself falling from the top of a tall high-rise. Your therapist immediately takes you to the top of such a building. Though working for some people, this "laugh-in-the-face-of-fear" approach is too intense for many who need more gradual exposure.

➤ Paradoxical intention: In this technique, phobics create the frightening physical symptoms of fear, as in causing yourself to hyperventilate. You are then asked to control these symptoms using the slow breathing technique. This reassures you that your worst fears of becoming totally overwhelmed by your symptoms will not happen.

As people begin to conquer their fears, they gain self-confidence and feel greater control of their lives. However, if your catastrophic beliefs continue, you will remain vulnerable to panic. Cognitive therapy, often combined with behavioral therapy, may help you change negative thought patterns.

Terror Talk

Cognitive therapy is a short-term psychological treatment to help overcome restrictions to everyday life by breaking the vicious cycle of negative thoughts. Fear-provoking thoughts are changed by repeatedly replacing them with positive encouragement.

Banish Those Bad Thoughts

While the Freudians focus on feelings, and the behaviorists on behavior, *cognitive therapy*, originated by Dr. Aaron Beck, focuses on thoughts.

Like a tango, our thoughts and feeling dance in synchrony: often, it's hard to discern who's leading whom. If your thinking is upbeat, your feelings move in that direction; if you think the blues, your feelings drag along—and vice versa. Cognitive therapy works on the premise that changing maladaptive thought processes ultimately alters feelings and self-perceptions.

If your thinking is distorted, as happens when you view the world through the negative lenses of a wounded psyche, your feelings are based on thoughts that aren't true. Fear producing self-talk and frightening feelings lead to a faulty self-image that breeds and maintains your fears. For instance, you might think that you "can't" call a girl and ask her out on a date because you might stammer and sound foolish and she would only reject you. Fear of failure prevents you from taking the first step.

To banish your fears and improve your self-image, you work on changing faulty self-perceptions. This goal, set by your therapist, happens in three steps:

1. Identify your thoughts: You are unworthy if she doesn't accept the date.

2. Check how accurately this reflects the reality of the situation: If she doesn't accept the date, does this truly make you less worthy? Perhaps the problem lies in her character and a kinder, more sensitive woman might be more worthwhile.

3. Restructure your thoughts in a positive way: Substitute constructive and affirming self-statements, like "I am a person of worth" or "many people like me," for destructive thoughts. Next time you want to ask a girl out on a date, you would repeat these affirmations to yourself.

One shortcoming of cognitive-behavioral therapy is that anxiety often interferes with learning. Working hard to control your thought processes while your mind is racing and your stomach is churning can sabotage the process. This is why behaviorists and cognitive therapists often first try to get you into a relaxed state to give you the energy and focus you need to make changes. Generally, this succeeds. If not, there are new non-conventional approaches showing much promise.

Mind Games

As scientists are studying and learning more about the brain, they are finding newer techniques for overcoming fears by accessing our nervous system in unique ways. Though seemingly unconventional, some show good results.

Your Eyes: Windows to Your Mind

One day in 1987, Dr. Francine Shapiro was walking through a park. Anxious thoughts began to flash through her mind. She moved her eyes from side to side and noticed that her disturbing thoughts immediately disappeared. Since then, she and other clinicians have applied EMDR (eye movement desensitization and reprocessing), which she describes in her book *EMDR* (Basic Books, 1997), to more than one million victims of post-traumatic stress disorder (PTSD), panic disorder, and agoraphobia. Though she reports dramatic results, many remain skeptical. For every therapist that finds it effective, there is another who finds no changes. If it works, some feel it does so primarily in victims of PTSD.

Getting in Touch with Both Sides of Your Brain

In the film *All of Me*, Steve Martin and Lily Tomlin play madly opposite personalities who reside side-by-side—in Martin's brain. According to Harvard psychiatrist Dr. Fredric Schiffer, author of the book *Of Two Minds* (Free Press, 1998), that's exactly what happens to people with psychological problems: each side of your brain possesses its own persona—one rational, stable, and mature, the other emotional, impulsive, and child-like.

In most people, the two halves of the brain co-exist in peace. But stress or childhood trauma can cause one side to become more troubled and result in a mental war. Proof is found in a simple pair of plastic goggles that Schiffer created. They block all vision except to the far left or far right and thus activate only one half of the brain at a time. When seventy therapy patients donned them, 30 percent described two different experiences: anxiety, anger or sadness when looking in one direction, calmness and rationality when looking in the other.

Secret Weapons

To try visual lateralization on yourself, cover your left eye with your left hand and the middle of your right eye with your right hand, which triggers the left side of your brain. Remain still for a minute and then rate your level of anxiety from one to five (none, mild, moderate, quite a bit, or extreme). Now switch to the other side, which will trigger the right side of your brain, and do the same.

Wearing the goggles (or using your hands to cover your eyes) is not a panacea, says Schiffer, but a means of helping people explore both sides of their brain and to demonstrate how each has its own set of memories, motivations and behaviors. You can, however, use this technique to evoke your more mature brain when anxious. Generally the right side of your brain, where negative emotions originate, evokes anxiety, but in some the left side is the troubled partner.

Neurolinguistic Programming (NLP)

Neurolinguistic programming theorizes that distancing yourself from your phobia frees you from it. To accomplish this, the therapist starts by helping you relax and visualize a time when you felt completely calm and at ease. As this "movie" plays in your mind, and you enjoy the evoked feelings and memories, the therapist "anchors" this experience in your subconscious by touching you on your arm or leg.

Next, you play the movie of the earliest memory you have of feeling afraid of the situation you fear. The therapist touches your arm to release the good feelings that were anchored in, and the physical symptoms of fear that you normally experience when thinking of your phobic situation disappear.

NLP, pioneered by psychologist Richard Bandler, M.A., and John Grinder, Ph.D. in linguistics, appears to work well for some people. You can undergo therapy by a professional trained in NLP or attend courses that will help you practice this therapy on your own.

The Five-Minute Phobia Cure

In *The Five-Minute Phobia Cure* (Enterprise Publishing, 1985), Dr. Roger Callahan describes how applied kinesiology can quickly dispel fears. The method, used mostly by chiropractors, is based on the theory that there are meridians at different locations on the surface of the body, identical or similar to Chinese acupuncture points. If certain points on these meridians are tapped, Callahan claims an 85 percent rate in permanently curing phobias. At this time, his claims are mostly anecdotal and lack the backing of research.

Safety in Numbers—Group Therapy

Individual therapy can get expensive. Group therapy, more economical and comprised of other fearful people with similar experiences as yours, can have a powerful effect. Often, the group becomes like a big family, where you laugh and cry together, fight and make up together and where, under the guidance of a trained therapist, you feel safe in trying out new behaviors.

The Least You Need to Know

➤ Psychotherapy can significantly change your life, alleviating anxiety symptoms, increasing self-esteem, changing maladaptive thought patterns and teaching better coping strategies.

➤ The most common psychotherapies for treating anxiety include behavioral and cognitive and, less successful initially, psychodynamic.

➤ Systematic desensitization is the most effective non-pharmacological therapy for treating phobias.

➤ Reducing anxiety symptoms alone will not eliminate future panic without also changing maladaptive thought patterns.

➤ Some new, non-conventional therapy treatments claim success in alleviating anxiety.

Chapter 8

The Doctor Is In

In This Chapter

➤ How psychoactive drugs help alleviate anxiety

➤ The pros and cons of taking psychoactive drugs

➤ What are the anti-anxiety and anti-depressant drugs

➤ How nature has her own anxiety busters

Anxiety disorders were not built in a day, but pile up after years of stress, maladaptive thinking and poor coping skills. As such, it may take some time to reprogram your brain out of the jittery mode. Drugs, both prescription and natural, change your brain's biochemistry, providing quick relief from overwhelming angst and helping you cope better with your nervousness.

Thirty years ago, anxiety sufferers relied primarily on Valium, which left them zonked and, as it turned out, dependent. Today, you can get quick help from intolerable panic from a variety of magic bullets, called "psychoactive drugs," including anti-depressants as well as anti-anxiety drugs. But that option is open, should you and your physician or psychotherapist decide that this is your best route. In this chapter I discuss the pros and cons of drug use to help you decide if you would like to take that route.

If you are leery about using prescription drugs, consider zapping your anxiety via the natural drug route. Some people find herbs such as Kava, a natural tranquilizer, as effective in treating anxiety.

Take a Pill?

Barbara, a 43-year-old nurse who worked the night shift, started to feel terrifying panic attacks when driving her car to the hospital. Suddenly, she would feel as if she'd forgotten how to use the steering wheel and constantly worried about swerving into another car. She switched to taking the bus, though the route went through dingy, run-down neighborhoods and took her twice as long. When she got home, she was too jumpy to fall asleep. She also found herself increasingly short with her patients and family. Then, she experienced panic attacks when taking the elevator in the hospital. Since she worked on the sixth floor, she feared she might have to give up her job altogether.

At her wit's end, her physician prescribed Xanax, an anti-anxiety drug, along with Prozac, an antidepressant. Though generally opposed to taking prescription medication, she felt that her suffering was intolerable. Within two weeks time, the panic attacks ceased. She was able to drive to work, take the elevator without trepidation, and to sleep better.

"O.K., you take one little blue one for malheurs,
and two little yellow ones for angst."

If you suffer from anxiety, one of your toughest decisions is to swallow the pill or to go drug free. Why suffer needlessly, some say? Drugs will quickly alleviate your symptoms, as they did for Barbara. There is no such thing as a free lunch, say the naturalists, because with drugs can come unpleasant and sometimes serious side effects, possible dependency, head fogginess and the feeling that the drug, not you, is in control of your behavior. What to do?

If you look to the experts, don't expect easy answers. In the tug of war between the mind and the body, psychologists, psychiatrists and physicians often lock horns as to the role of each in causing anxiety disorders. Some say that anxiety disorders are chiefly biological, making drug therapy the logical primary treatment. Others say that anxiety disorders are primarily psychological and maintain that effective psychotherapy render drugs unnecessary. While still others caution that the causes of anxiety disorders are too intertwined to be teased out, suggesting that a combination of drugs and psychotherapy would work best.

In making your decision, be suspicious of extremists at either end. Where there's body there's mind and vice-versa: behavior is biological and psychological (try laughing or crying without using your body!). Changes in how one functions produces changes in the other. A sense of balance, of being in that "just right zone," happens when you feel physically at ease and mentally alert. When your biochemistry is out of whack, so are you: depressed when understimulated; anxious when overstimulated.

Drugs work by altering biochemistry, coaxing our brain out of feeling fearful or sad, and they do it quicker than other therapeutic interventions. There's good reason for that. In the anxiety prone, and especially with panic disorder and obsessive-compulsive disorder, a biological imbalance—too little of this chemical, too much of that chemical—appears to be what sets off our symptoms. Colluding with this imbalance are maladaptive thoughts, feelings, and behavior that feed our biological vulnerability to overreact and perpetuate our symptoms. But our unique biochemical make-up appears to determine how our symptoms manifest themselves, whether it be in the form of panic, compulsive hand-washing, drug addiction, violence, or whatever.

Secret Weapons

People don't will themselves bold or cautious, but are born that way. The National Cancer Institute has uncovered two distinct temperamental genes: one for novelty seeking, for people who plunge right into the water; and one for harm avoidance, for people who toe the water first and then gingerly step in.

My Biology Made Me Do It

Not everyone buys into the notion of a largely biological origin for anxiety disorders. But the evidence is weighty. Consider genetic factors:

➤ Fear-proneness is evident in early infancy. In response to new situations, cautious or shy infants are more fearful than more outgoing infants, and, starting in adolescence, shy children show a higher incidence of panic attacks than their more fearless peers. (For more information on this, see Chapters 12 and 20.)

Secret Weapons

Numerous studies show that combining therapy and drug intervention for anxiety disorders work more effectively than either used alone.

➤ Anxiety disorders often run in families.

➤ A greater number of both identical twins than both fraternal twins experience panic attacks.

➤ There's a higher incidence of mitral valve prolapse in people who have panic attacks.

➤ Under similar high stress, such as combat, one person will have a panic attack, while another downs a fifth of gin and another has a heart attack, suggesting different biological vulnerabilities.

There is more evidence for a biological basis for anxiety disorders. In people who experience panic attacks, an injection of sodium lactate, which is a by-product of exercise, can spontaneously trigger a panic attack. Yet, the same dosage will rarely do so in those suffering from non-panic anxiety. This suggests a biological vulnerability to panic attacks.

Angst Bulletin

Bulimics, who often experience panic attacks, show a high rate of panic attacks when injected with sodium lactate. Interestingly, almost 50 percent of bulimics who don't experience panic attacks will experience one after lactate infusion.

Finally, the strongest evidence for a biological origin for anxiety disorders are the working of the drugs themselves.

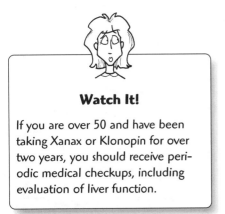

Watch It!

If you are over 50 and have been taking Xanax or Klonopin for over two years, you should receive periodic medical checkups, including evaluation of liver function.

Brain Chemistry

Psychoactive drugs balance your biochemistry and affect your mood by elevating the number of *neurotransmitters* in your brain, the chemical messengers through which neurons (nerve cells) communicate. When you have too little of the neurotransmitter *serotonin* leap-frogging across the synapses (the gap between neurons) in your brain, you feel anxious and down and may even become aggressive and violent. Your sleep, appetite, mood, and sexual interest are all affected.

The *noradrenergic* system in our brain is especially sensitive to the neurotransmitter *norepinephrine*, which is similar to a hormone called epinephrine (adrenaline), and is released from our adrenal glands during times of stress. Within this system is the locus cerulus, a little group of nerves deep in our brain that regulates the fear response. If you inherit an over-sensitivity in this center, it takes less of a threat to push your fear button and release norepinephrine into your bloodstream. In other words, you are born more vulnerable to biochemical imbalance.

Medications and the Treatment of Anxiety Disorders

See the following table for a list of the medications used in the treatment of anxiety disorders.

Medications Used in the Treatment of Anxiety Disorders

Generic Name	Common Brand Name(s)
Serotonin Specific Reuptake Inhibitors (SSRIs)	
fluoxetine	Prozac
sertraline	Zoloft
paroxetine	Paxil
fluvoxamine	Luvox
Tricyclic Antidepressants	
imipramine	Tofranil
desipramine	Norpramin, Pertofrane
nortriptyline	Aventyl, Pamelor
amitriptyline	Elavil
clomipramine	Anafranil
doxepin	Sinequan
Monoamine Oxidase Inhibitors (MAOIs)	
phenelzine	Nardil
tranylcypromine	Parnate
isocarboxazid	Marplan
New Antidepressants	
venlafaxine	Effexor
Benzodiazepines	
alprazolam	Xanax
clonazepam	Klonopin
diazepam	Valium

continues

continued

Medications Used in the Treatment of Anxiety Disorders

Generic Name	Common Brand Name(s)
New Anti-Anxiety Drugs	
buspirone	BuSpar
Beta Blockers	
propranolol	Inderal
atenolol	Tenormin

Let's begin by looking at the anti-depressants, the most commonly prescribed drugs for anxiety disorders.

Watch It!

Though the SSRI antidepressants are less likely to have side effects like dry mouth and weight gain, occasionally people do report a problem with these drugs.

Antidepressants

Many of the antidepressants enhance or alter neurotransmitter levels in our brain, making them useful to treat anxiety disorders. Different people react differently to them. You may have to try several before finding the right one. They do not lead to physical dependence.

SSRIs (Selective Serotonin Reuptake Inhibitors)

The SSRIs are the newest antidepressants, which include the wonder drugs Prozac and Zoloft. They work by interfering with the re-absorption of mainly serotonin, thereby ensuring a sufficient supply streaming through your brain, and thus help in treating panic disorder, agoraphobia, social phobia, and OCD. People prefer them to the older antidepressants since the dose regimen is easier to follow and they generally do not have some of the bothersome side effects, like dry mouth, weight gain, and oversedation. There are, however, other side effects, including:

➤ Headaches
➤ Sleep problems
➤ Agitation and restlessness
➤ Constipation or diarrhea
➤ Nausea and vomiting
➤ Skin rashes
➤ Impaired sexual function

Angst Bulletin

Twenty-five to thirty percent of people stop taking anti-depressants because of initial side effects.

Tricyclics

These are the older antidepressants that work by boosting the brain's supply of norepinephrine and serotonin. Though used to treat panic attacks, (especially Tofranil) and to relieve the depression that frequently accompanies panic disorder and agoraphobia, they are now generally used only if the newer ones don't work or have too many side effects. Clomipramine is commonly used to treat obsessive-compulsive disorder.

The tricyclics take four to eight weeks before an effect takes place. Side effects can occur, though starting off with low dosages and gradually increasing the dosage minimizes these.

Potential side effects include:

➤ Increased heart rate

➤ Dry mouth from limited saliva production (which can lead to dental problems)

➤ Dry skin

➤ Blurred vision

➤ Constipation

➤ Confusion

➤ Drowsiness

➤ Agitation and anxiety

➤ Lowered blood pressure

Monoamine Oxidase Inhibitors (MAOIs)

MAOIs keep the neurotransmitters serotonin, dopamine and norepinephrine elevated by destroying enzymes that burn them up. They are prescribed primarily to treat panic disorder and social phobia. They are especially effective in people who do not respond to other antidepressants.

This sounds good, but beware—there are serious problems with their use. When combined with foods that contain a substance called *tyramine*, they can spike up your blood pressure to levels high enough to cause a stroke and even death. Though rare, it does happen, so if you decide to use them be sure and follow the dietary restrictions. Also, MAOIs should never be combined with other classes of antidepressants. If you experience headaches or nausea while taking MAOIs, see your physician immediately.

New Antidepressants

Some new antidepressants, prescribed when others don't work, are Wellbutrin (bupropion) and Effexor (venlafaxine). Wellbutrin, which may work well as an antidepressant, is the only antidepressant believed ineffective in panic disorder. Effexor combines a cyclic antidepressant with an SSRI in one pill. At this point, its usefulness in controlling anxiety disorders has not been established.

Benzodiazepines

Benzodiazepines, or anti-anxiety drugs, decrease anxiety by depressing the activity of the central nervous system. In higher doses they act as sedatives, inducing sleep. Traditionally, panic attacks were treated with the tranquilizer Valium. Today, Xanax and Klonopin appear more effective. Xanax is often prescribed on a short-term basis for acute anxiety and, in lower doses, on a long-term basis to prevent panic attacks and agoraphobia. For best effect, they should be taken reguarly, not as needed. There are advantages and disadvantages to its use:

On the plus side:

➤ Less of a sedative effect than other tranquilizers

➤ It's fast-acting: Taken sublingually (under the tongue), it blocks panic in five to ten minutes

➤ Diminishes panic symptoms in low doses and suppresses them in higher doses

On the downside:

➤ Physical dependence: After taking Xanax or Klonopin for a few months, you will likely experience withdrawal symptoms if you discontinue using it. Following long-term use, withdrawal can be as difficult as that from alcohol or heroin. Moreover, anxiety and panic attacks can reoccur while tapering off use.

➤ Once fully withdrawn from the drug, you may re-experience your original anxiety and panic attacks, making it only a temporary solution.

➤ Anti-anxiety drugs dull emotions in general. Since identifying, acknowledging, and expressing your feelings is a major goal in recovery from anxiety disorders, the use of tranquilizers, especially in higher doses, can be counter-productive.

Buspirone

Buspirone (BuSpar) is a new anti-anxiety drug FDA approved for the treatment of generalized anxiety disorder (GAD) and among the safest drugs known. Though slow-acting compared to the benzodiazepines, it has numerous advantages. It is non-sedating and non-habit forming, without the usual side effects.

Watch It!

If currently taking Xanax on Klonopin, and you wish to discontinue taking them, to avoid withdrawal effects, you must wean yourself gradually, which can take several months. Abrupt withdrawal may get you right back to square one: panic attacks, severe anxiety, confusion, muscle tension, irritability, insomnia and even seizures.

Beta Blockers

Beta blockers are sometimes prescribed for anxiety disorders. Inderal and Tenormin, commonly used to treat high blood pressure, may help in blocking the pounding heart, tremors and sweating associated with stage fright or performance anxiety. They need to be taken about one hour before your anticipated speech or performance.

The Big Decision

Now that you've gotten an overview of today's wonder drugs, what are the advantages and disadvantages of taking them? It's a tough decision because, although medication can be helpful, there are always risk factors. You and your doctor need to weigh the risks and the benefits of any drug, and whether it makes sense given your particular symptoms. Here are advantages and disadvantages of drug use.

On the plus side:

➤ Much of the time they work.

➤ Why suffer needlessly?

➤ Rather than diminish control, the drug helps some patients gain control.

➤ If started at a low dose, the risk of side effects is minimal.

➤ Since panic attacks have a biological origin, a biological intervention seems reasonable and appropriate.

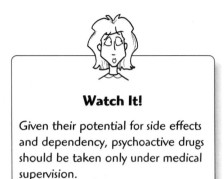

On the downside:

➤ There are side effects during the first week or two of usage, though starting off with low dosages and gradually increasing the dosage minimizes these.

➤ They typically take four to six weeks to take effect, except for Benzodiazepines.

➤ You may have to experiment before you find a drug and dosage that works for you.

➤ Fifty percent of people experience a relapse of panic attacks after discontinuing use of anti-depressants.

➤ Though not physically addicting, they can create psychological dependency.

➤ Many people overcome panic attacks and phobias *without* their use.

In deciding whether or not to self-medicate, try not to be swayed by another's claim to have overcome anxiety without drug use. True, people are capable of balancing mind and body without drug intervention. Some yogis and monks can even control physiological factors like body temperature. And recently psychological intervention alone was shown to eventually produce changes in brain chemistry in OCD (see Chapter 17).

But individuals differ. Needing chemical support is not a sign of weakness. In fact, it may indicate strength, since you are willing to take steps toward easing your suffering, which is not your fault. Each person's situation is a compilation of individual biochemistry, inborn temperament, and childhood and life experiences, the sum total of which differs from anyone else's. As such, each of us copes differently with life's stresses. What's important is to find the regimen that works best for you. Drugs are especially recommended if you find yourself so overwhelmed with anxiety that you are unable to function.

If you do decide to use drugs, most professionals in the field recommend that you do so as part of a total therapeutic program. Though drugs will block symptoms, they will not address the underlying issues and problems that produced your anxiety to begin with. Moreover, without therapeutic intervention designed to teach better coping skills, symptoms often return after discontinuation. This can be demoralizing and leave you nothing within yourself to fall back upon.

Nature's "Tranquilizer"

If you are leery of using drugs and of introducing chemicals into your system, there's good news. Mother Nature has her own medicine cabinet for relief from anxiety. On the shelf next to the herb St. John's Wort, which is nature's "Prozac" for mild to moderate depression, sits the herb kava, nature's "Valium." Although it doesn't work for all, some report relief similar to anti-anxiety drugs. Dina, a 52-year old social worker, is one.

Dina was chronically stressed and had been for years. A knot in her stomach, tensed muscles, and constricted breathing, as if something pressing against her chest, were constant companions. Then she started taking a daily dosage of two dropperfuls of kava. She was amazed. Within an hour, she would find the knot had disappeared and that her breathing was relaxed and full, feelings that she had almost forgotten. All this from an herb.

Angst Bulletin

In the last ten years, five kava studies were conducted in Germany, all with positive results. In one in 1995, 100 people suffering from anxiety and stress were given 210 mg (milligrams) of kava's active compounds (kavapyrones) a day. After eight weeks, the people taking the kava were clearly improved compared with those receiving a placebo.

You know all the warnings on the labels of prescription tranquilizers: side effects; potentially addictive—can cause drowsiness? Well, kava calms *without* these potential hazards. It is safe, non-addictive, with minimal to no side effects, relatively inexpensive and available without prescription.

Relaxing both muscles and emotions, kava calms without sedating and causing you to lose mental sharpness, as prescription tranquilizers often do. In fact, writes Dr. Hyla Cass in her book *Kava*, kava appears to enhance perception, awareness, and clear thinking.

Only recently introduced into the United States, kava has been used for hundreds of years by Pacific Islanders in religious and social rituals. They grate the underground stem of the kava plant, mix it with water, strain it and then drink it down and mellow out.

In Europe, particularly in Germany, kava is commonly prescribed for anxiety. The German Commission E, the equivalent of the FDA (and also recognized as the world's leading authority on herbs), gave kava its stamp of approval in 1990. They deemed it beneficial for relieving nervous anxiety, stress, and restlessness.

How Kava Works

Some fifteen different chemical compounds known as *pyrones* account for kava's anxiety-easing and muscle-relaxing effects. These appear to reduce activity at the spinal part of the nervous system. Kava also acts upon the limbic system, our emotional

Secret Weapons

Kava has minimal side effects. In over 4,000 patients who consumed 105 mg of kavapyrones daily for seven weeks, there were 61 cases (1.5 percent) of mostly minor undesired effects, like stomach upsets or allergic skin reactions. Of 3,000 patients taking a higher dose (240 mg daily) in a four-week study, 2.3 percent showed similar side effects.

Watch It!

The German Commission E recommends not taking kava continuously (vs. "as needed") for longer than three months without medical advice. Long term use above the recommended level without medical advice could potentially result in: yellow discoloration of the skin, nails, and hair; allergic skin reactions; visual disturbances; difficulty in maintaining balance. However, a recent six-month project of daily usage found no ill effects.

brain, and specifically on the amygdala, where it dampens fear and anger, thereby perking up pleasant feelings. These effects are felt within a half-hour to two hours. When you're restless, kava in somewhat larger doses will help ease you into sleep.

Taking Kava

Kava comes in tinctures (alcohol based), tablets, soft-gel encased paste, encapsulated powdered extract, sprays and powdered extract. For fast absorption, use the liquid forms—sprays, tinctures and reconstituted extract. Use whole extracts rather than "active ingredients."

In her book *Kava*, Hyla Cass recommends the following dosages:

For general anxiety or stress relief:

➤ Seventy to 210 mg daily, in divided doses. Do not exceed 300 mg per day, or four doses of 70 mg each.

➤ With most tinctures, the dose is 40 drops, three to four times a day.

For sleep:

➤ Seventy to 210 mg, or up to three doses at once, one hour before bedtime.

➤ One to two droppers full, adjusted as needed. Liquid, which works more quickly, can be taken closer to bedtime.

As with any medication, need varies. So you may have to play around a bit to find the amount and frequency that works best for you.

If taking psychoactive drugs, consult your physician before taking kava. In higher doses, it may adversely affect motor reflexes and judgment for driving and/or operating heavy machinery. Do not take kava if you are pregnant, nursing or depressed.

Angst Bulletin

In two placebo-controlled, double-blind studies of 80 women with menopause related symptoms, the kava group reported reductions in anxiety symptoms, hot flashes, and other menopausal symptoms, along with improvements in sleep, mood, and a subjective sense of well-being.

Kava Combining

To enhance kava's effectiveness, try combining it with other herbs, depending on your malady. The following are some recommendations:

➤ Insomnia: Kava with valerian root (50 to 100 mg valerian taken two to three times daily, and 150 to 300 mg taken 45 minutes before bedtime, using a standardized dose of 0.8 percent valeric acid.) You can also add passionflower to the mixture.

➤ Mixed anxiety and mild depression: kava and St. John's Wort, nature's prozac for mild to moderate depression (300 mg of standardized extract, 0.3 percent hypericin, two to three times daily, in tablets, capsules, or tincture).

➤ Memory and concentration loss: kava and Ginkgo biloba (120 to 160 mg daily in two or three divided doses).

➤ Fatigue, mental dullness and test anxiety: kava, Siberian ginseng (200 mg, two to three times daily).

In Chapter 9, you will find more natural substances to relieve both anxiety and depression.

The Least You Need to Know

➤ There are a host of psychoactive "magic bullets" to help ease your anxiety and depression.

➤ Antidepressants and benzodiazepines, which can cause side effects and, in the case of tranquilizers even addiction, should only be taken under medical supervision.

➤ To decide if you want to take the drug route, you need to weigh both risks and benefits.

➤ Kava, the natural valium, works well for some in relieving mild to moderate anxiety.

Chapter 9

And There's More...

The symphony of life consists of the rhythm of the body, the melody of the mind and the harmony of the soul.

In this chapter, I will explain the necessity of proper nutrition for balancing your nervous system. You will learn that if you don't exercise you may not have a means for releasing excess stress chemicals in your bloodstream. You will discover how bodywork can help release muscle tension and help you relax. And you will learn how finding meaning in your life will help you to achieve inner harmony and how, for many people, spirituality serves this purpose.

Food for Healthy Thoughts

Psychotropic drugs alter brain chemistry by causing the neurotransmitters in your brain to behave differently. Food is also a drug. What you eat directly and significantly impacts your body's internal physiology and biochemistry. Certain foods create additional stress and anxiety, while others foster a calming affect, and still others have an antidepressant effect.

Watch It!

If you wish to wean yourself off of caffeine, do so gradually over a period of several months—some people experience withdrawal symptoms when quitting cold turkey.

Secret Weapons

Food must be partially predigested in your mouth for adequate digestion later, so you should chew your food at least 15–20 times per mouthful. Also, limit drinking during meals to one cup of fluid because drinking too much with your meals can dilute stomach acid and digestive enzymes.

Foods that Aggravate the Jitters

If you are the nervous type, beware of foods that increase stress. To start, avoid or minimize substances that act as stimulants on your nervous system.

➤ Caffeine: There's nothing like a cup of coffee to get you going in the morning… and going… and going. Coffee, tea, colas, cocoa and chocolate, and some over-the-counter drugs all contain caffeine. Caffeine increases the level of norepinephrine in your brain, causing you to feel alert and awake. This is good. But it also increases sympathetic nervous system activity and releases adrenalin—the same physiological arousal response triggered by stress. Too much caffeine can keep you chronically tense and keyed-up, the last thing you want if you're vulnerable to anxiety and panic attacks. If anxiety-prone, and especially if you experience panic attacks, you should not consume more than 100 mg/day of caffeine: one cup of percolated coffee; two diet cola beverages.

➤ Nicotine: If you smoke, with every inhale, you are making yourself more nervous. Nicotine stimulates increased physiological agitation and makes your heart work harder. Make it a personal challenge to stop smoking. Doing so will not only lessen your anxiety, but will also increase personal empowerment and your capacity to take control of your life.

➤ Stimulant Drugs: Some prescription drugs, including Benzedrine, Dexedrine, Methedrine, and Ritalin, contain amphetamines. If you have a history of panic attacks, they are risky to take.

In addition to stimulants, other substances that stress the body include:

➤ Preservatives: Commercial food processing presently uses some 5,000 chemical additives. Common artificial preservatives include nitrites, nitrates, potassium bisulfite, monosodium glutamate (MSG), BHT, BHA, and artificial colorings and flavorings. Our bodies were not designed to handle these artificial substances, nor do we know, in many cases, their long-term effect. Eat fresh, natural foods as much as possible and try to buy organic foods.

Anxiety and Eating Habits

Are you eating on the go, wolfing down your food? Do you try to chomp away tension until you feel stuffed? Both of these bad habits put strain on your stomach and intestines. This interferes with proper digestion and assimilation of food and can create indigestion, bloating or cramps, as well as increasing your level of stress.

Another danger of improper eating habits is malabsorption of essential nutrients. Food not first properly digested in your mouth and stomach may pass undigested through your intestines. There it putrefies and ferments, resulting in bloating, cramps, and gas. Unknowingly, you miss out on much of the nutrition potentially available in your food. You can be undernourished even if you eat highly nutritious food.

Watch It!

During the flight/fight response, digestion and other bodily functions slow down to conserve energy. If you're under chronic stress, your SNS is continually activated, preventing adequate digestion of your food and causing malabsorption.

Hypoglycemia and Anxiety

Sugar! We crave it and eat too much of it, even though it makes us fat, rots our teeth, and robs us of proper nutrition. Still, our body needs sugar to survive. Glucose, or sugar in its naturally occurring form, is the very substance that provides the energy to sustain life. We obtain much of it from carbohydrate-rich foods, such as bread, cereal, potatoes, vegetables, fruit, pasta, and so on, whose starches gradually break down into glucose.

Simple sugars, on the other hand, like refined white sugar, brown sugar, and honey, break down rapidly into glucose and too quickly overload our system with sugar. This can result in excessively high levels of blood sugar, or diabetes, or, more commonly, in periodic drops of blood sugar below normal, a condition called hypoglycemia. This drop upsets your whole system, resulting in symptoms similar to a panic attack:

➤ Palpitations

➤ Anxiety

➤ Light-headedness

➤ Trembling

➤ Unsteadiness or weakness

➤ Agitation

➤ Blurred vision

➤ Panic feelings

➤ Chest pain

Angst Bulletin

For detailed information on diet and control of blood sugar level, see: *Sugar Blues* by William Duffy, *Hypoglycemia: A Better Approach* by Paavo Airola, *Low Blood Sugar and You* by Carlton Fredericks, and *The Zone* by Barry Sears.

Stress, a time when your body burns up sugar very rapidly, can also quickly deplete sugar. As a result, your brain does not get enough sugar and you feel trembly, confused, spacey and anxious. You feel more anxious and agitated as well because your adrenal glands release adrenaline and cortisol to prompt your liver to release stored sugar to stabilize your sugar level.

If you suspect you may be hypoglycemic, your doctor can give you a glucose tolerance test. The following are signs of hypoglycemia:

➤ Anxiety, light-headedness, weakness, or irritability several hours following a meal, or in the middle of the night, that disappears soon after eating.

➤ An elevated mood after eating sugar that rapidly drops to depression, irritability or spaciness 20–30 minutes later.

➤ Anxiety, restlessness, and sometimes a rapid heart beat early in the morning, when your blood sugar is lowest, since you've fasted all night.

If you experience anxiety or panic like symptoms three or four hours following a meal, but which go away when you eat, hypoglycemia may be the cause. In the majority of panic attack sufferers, however, low blood sugar does not necessarily correlate with panic reactions, though it can aggravate anxiety and panic reactions from other causes.

Fortunately, hypoglycemia can be easily overcome. To maintain a steadier blood sugar level, consume a snack between meals. Some recommend a complex carbohydrate or protein snack, like nuts, a whole grain bagel with cheese, or a glass of orange juice. Others, like Barry Sears, recommend that to balance your insulin level, every meal should consist of 30 percent protein, 30 percent fat and 40 percent carbohydrates, snacks included.

Your diet should avoid foods and substances that are quickly absorbed, resulting in rapid changes of glucose levels in the blood. These consist largely of:

➤ Simple sugars: candy, cookies, cakes, colas, ice cream, honey, corn syrup, molasses, high fructose

➤ Simple starches: pasta, refined cereals, potato chips, and white bread

Food Allergies Trigger Anxiety

When you think of food allergies, you imagine someone breaking out in hives from peanuts, or getting diarrhea from cheese. Yet, food allergies can also have a toxic effect on your mood and well-being; they can make you dizzy, irritable, confused, tired, depressed, anxious and even panicked.

If you suspect food allergies, you can have your physician conduct a formal allergy test, or you can consult a qualified nutritionist. You can also use your body as a laboratory and systematically monitor your own reaction to foods. Obviously, you should avoid any foods to which you are allergic, and especially if you suspect they relate to panic attacks.

Nutritional Anxiety Busters

When stressed, anxious or depressed, your adrenal glands work overtime and your body has an enormously increased need for particular vitamins and minerals. Especially important to refurbish the nervous system are the B vitamins and vitamin C, which are rapidly depleted under stress and should be replenished daily. Vitamin B1, B2, B6, and B12 deficiencies in particular can lead to anxiety, irritability, restlessness, fatigue and emotional instability.

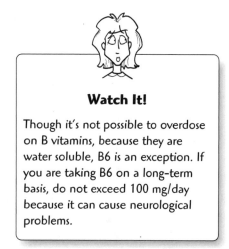

Watch It!

Though it's not possible to overdose on B vitamins, because they are water soluble, B6 is an exception. If you are taking B6 on a long-term basis, do not exceed 100 mg/day because it can cause neurological problems.

You also need sufficient amounts of the minerals calcium and magnesium. Calcium acts as a tranquilizer, which is why having a glass of milk before bedtime helps you sleep. You should take it in combination with magnesium, since these two minerals work synergistically. Chromium, critical in lowering insulin requirements, is another important mineral. Lower insulin levels aid healthy function of many body systems, including the serotonin system, which I'll discuss shortly.

The following are suggested daily dosages of these supplements:

Vitamins:

➤ B-complex: 50–100 mg of all 11 B vitamins once or twice a day. During high stress, take extra B5 (pantothenic acid), up to 1,000 mg in a time-release form.

➤ Vitamin C: 1,000 mg in a time-release form, twice to four times a day—preferably combined with bioflavonoids.

Minerals:

➤ Calcium and magnesium: 1,000 mg of calcium (chelates preferred over calcium carbonate), with magnesium.

➤ Chromium: 200 mg a day

Secret Weapons

Don't forget herbal mood boosters. St. John's Wort appears to raise serotonin and relieve mild to moderate depression. And the herb kava is a safe natural tranquilizer (see Chapter 8).

Taking a multivitamin daily, particularly one for "stress," will probably include most, if not all, of these vitamins and minerals, as well as vitamin E, selenium, zinc, copper, manganese and iron—also essential for the proper functioning of the nervous system. If not, you can supplement as needed.

Natural Serotonin Boosters

Levels of the neurotransmitter serotonin in our brain affect our mood. Low serotonin levels appear to cause depression, particularly in vulnerable individuals.

But how does serotonin level affect anxiety? It's a bit complex, writes Dr. Michael Norden in his book *Beyond Prozac*. Extreme stress, which creates anxiety, depletes serotonin levels; restoring those levels, as when taking Prozac, relieves anxiety. Apparently, though, high as well as low levels of serotonin can generate anxiety. It's unclear whether elevated serotonin during anxiety causes the anxious feeling or if it may be a helpful response to the stress.

To stabilize our state of being, the goal is to maintain healthy levels of serotonin in our brain. Food does this, which is why many call it literally a drug. We need vitamin C to make serotonin, along with sufficient quantities of vitamin E and the minerals magnesium, zinc, copper, manganese and iron. And we need the amino acid tryptophan—*the* building block of serotonin and which is contained in pineapple, bananas, turkey, chicken, tuna, eggs, yogurt and milk. Many people find it useful to treat depression and anxiety with L-tryptophan supplements. L-tryptophan, however, is not available in this country. Another form, 5-Hydroxy-Tryptophan (5-HTP), is sold over the counter in health food stores. Gamma amino butyric acid (GABA), an amino acid available in many health food stores, has a mildly tranquilizing effect. The amino acids DL-phenylalanine and tyrosine treat the depression often accompanying anxiety disorders. Though less potent than prescription antidepressants, they have fewer side effects.

Angst Bulletin

A 1974 Japanese study of 107 patients found 74 to improve with 5-HTP. A 1991 Swiss study compared 5-HTP with the antidepressant Luvox (fluvoxamine) and found them equally effective. However, both treatments produced side effects: 5-HTP most commonly caused nausea and other gastrointestinal distress.

Detoxify Your Life

If you are fear-prone, you are likely more aware of, and bothered by, aspects of your environment than other people. Becoming aware of what in your surroundings sets you off will help you take action to minimize exposure.

Sensory Defensiveness

Do you get overly stimulated easily by noise, bright lighting, odors, crowds, heights, and certain textures on your skin or light unexpected touch? If so, you may be sensory defensive, meaning that you perceive presumably harmless stimuli as dangerous, setting off your flight-fight response. The more sensory defensive, the more you overreact to fear provoking stimuli and the greater the likelihood, other factors considered, of anxiety turning into panic. Bright artificial lights exacerbate the agoraphobic's avoidance of public places such as malls.

To help modify your level of agitation, become aware of what sensations easily bother you and modify your environment accordingly. For more information on sensory defensiveness and how it can be treated, see Chapter 16 as well as Appendix B.

Chemical Sensitivities

Chemical sensitivities can precipitate allergic reactions and a host of psychological symptoms— including anxiety and panic (see Chapter 3). Offending substances include:

➤ Detergents

➤ Household cleaners

➤ Formaldehyde (in carpeting and furniture)

➤ Cleaning fluid in dry-cleaned clothes

➤ Synthetic fabrics

➤ Gasoline fumes

➤ Insect or exterminator spray

➤ Nail polish remover, kerosene, turpentine

➤ Fresh newspapers

➤ Perfumes

➤ Fresh tar

Watch It!

If exposure to certain chemical substances causes confusion, forgetfulness, irritability, fatigue, depression, panic, anxiety, hyperactivity, or hypoglycemic symptoms, you probably have a chemical allergy.

If you are mildly sensitive, self-help may be sufficient to reduce your reaction, starting with avoidance. If you suspect a chemical allergy, you should get a medical evaluation. For suggested nutritional supplements, see *No More Fears* by Dr. Douglas Hunt.

Get Moving!

Want an antidote to anxiety and depression that also improves your body image, makes your skin look younger and healthier, enhances your immune system, helps you live longer and better, and even makes you feel euphoric? Try exercise.

We think of exercise as something we "should" do—if only we had the time. This conception is anti-biological. Our cave-dwelling ancestors were constantly on the go, hunting and foraging for food and water. Later, both men and women worked in the fields, planting, tending and picking crops. It wasn't until machines took over at the turn of the century that we started to become sedentary.

Our bodies were designed to be used. Idleness comes at a price. In this country, we have greater obesity, higher blood pressure, more heart attacks and strokes, as well as increased anxiety, stress and depression. In the non-industrial world, where the demands of daily life gives bodies all the work they need, these problems appear not to be an issue. There's only one answer: to get moving.

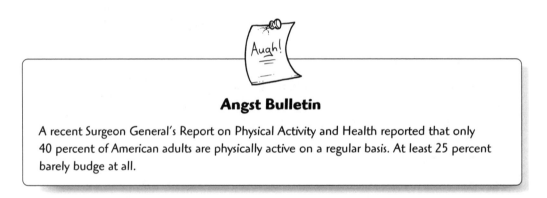

Angst Bulletin

A recent Surgeon General's Report on Physical Activity and Health reported that only 40 percent of American adults are physically active on a regular basis. At least 25 percent barely budge at all.

An active body is as important as an active mind for mental and physical health. It creates energy, stamina and relaxation, improves your self-image, and makes you stronger mentally and physically. Vigorous exercise can also be the acme of pleasure. If you exercise for more than 30 to 40 minutes, your body releases *endorphins*— natural opiates that relieve pain, regulate the body's response to stress and create the "runner's high."

Boogie the Jitters Away

For us fearful folks, regular, vigorous exercise is *sine qua non* to reduce generalized anxiety and overcome a predisposition to panic attacks. The false flight-fight response evoked when overly anxious, and big time when panicked, releases excessive adrenaline that has no outlet: there's nowhere to run, no one to punch. Exercise affords us this outlet.

In addition to releasing pent-up energy and frustration, exercise relaxes those tense muscles that contribute to our feeling "uptight." And it helps to distract us from our worries. Regular exercise also builds up serotonin in our brain that diminishes the anticipatory anxiety that leads to further panic attacks. This helps to speed up recovery from all kinds of phobias—from fear of public speaking to fear of being alone.

When you really whip yourself into shape, increased cardiorespiratory function and decreased body fat will enable you to be less stressed throughout the day. You will find that you can do the same amount of work with a lowered heart rate, blood pressure, and adrenaline production. Overall, you will feel more relaxed, more confident, more mentally sharp and less dependent on alcohol and drugs. You will also sleep better with less insomnia.

Choose Your Game Plan

The key to sticking to an exercise program is to find one that you enjoy and that fits into your lifestyle. Hopefully, this will include all three types of movement:

➤ Aerobics: Activities that increase heart and lung capacity, increasing stamina and reducing stress, such as running, swimming and biking.

➤ Strength: Activities that build your bones and muscles to increase muscle strength, like weight-lifting and isometric exercise.

➤ Stretching Exercises: Activities to increase joint and muscle flexibility, like yoga, Tai chi, ballet and American jazz dancing, gymnastics and calisthenics.

Secret Weapons

Exercise is one of our best health tonics: It enhances oxygenation of the blood and brain, increasing alertness and concentration; stimulates production of endorphins, which increases your sense of well-being; improves blood sugar regulation; lowers pH (increased acidity) of the blood, which increases your energy level; improves circulation, digestion, and elimination; decreases cholesterol levels and blood pressure; and helps in weight loss.

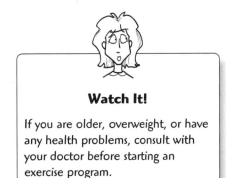

Watch It!

If you are older, overweight, or have any health problems, consult with your doctor before starting an exercise program.

Aerobic Exercise

If you are fear-prone, you should try to begin the day with some kind of aerobic exercise to slough off excess stress chemicals. Aerobic activities can be done conveniently in your own home. But if you have the luxury of time, getting out and making your exercise routine a social one greatly aids in toughing it out. Individual routines often become routine and increase the likelihood of you becoming an exercise dropout.

Aerobic Sports

Individual	Social Aerobics	Interactive Aerobics
running/jogging	aerobic dancing	tennis
vigorous cycling	cross-country skiing	racquetball
brisk walking	downhill skiing	handball
jumping rope	ice skating	table tennis
rowing	roller skating	basketball
stationary cycling	horseback riding	softball
swimming	volleyball	soccer

If you don't have time to fit in a daily workout, try incorporating physical activities into your daily routine. Take stairs rather than an elevator and, if you have stairs at home or work, run up and down a few flights at a time once or twice a day. Park farthest, rather than nearest, to the supermarket entrance. Fast walk while window shopping in the mall. Bend down in a gradual forward stretch while fetching something on the floor. Replace your electric can opener with a manual one. And a hard one—give up your TV remote!

Watch It!

Since exercise produces a sharp rise in lactic acid, some people warn that it may produce a panic attack in individuals with panic disorder. Other researchers deny this connection. If you are having panic attacks, you need to monitor yourself whether vigorous exercise seems to trigger panic.

Walking Off Steam

If you're not into sweat and huffing and puffing, don't worry. You don't have to bop until you drop to get a sufficient workout. Walking briskly 30 to 45 minutes (this should cover about three miles) for at least five days a week will give you all the aerobic activity you need.

Human beings, upright and bipedal, are meant to walk. Walking exercises our minds as well as our bodies. The cross-patterned movement of our limbs—right arm and left leg, then left arm and right leg—generates electrical activity in the brain, boosting serotonin and harmonizing the nervous system. Free, non-injurious, convenient, and requiring nothing more than a good pair of shoes, walking is a habit well worth incorporating into your lifestyle.

Lubricate Your System with Yoga

When most people think of yoga, they don't think of a work out—but just imagine someone sitting in a lotus position or standing on their head. Actually, yoga, which combines exercises, breathing, and meditation, offers much to improve overall fitness. Yoga oils your joints, stimulates your internal organs, and both calms and energizes. Some exercises are easy and you barely feel a bead of sweat; others are designed to build strength and endurance and you drip with sweat from start to finish.

For us anxious types, yoga is almost a necessity. In addition to everything else, yoga postures (asanas) help correct poor posture that typifies those of us living our lives on the lookout. When you are anxious, you tense up your muscles, particularly in your shoulders and neck, and they contract and shorten. This creates a chain reaction of tension in the muscles in your head, neck, shoulders, down your spine, through your pelvis and even in your legs. Your breathing constricts as well. Not correcting this posture makes it hard to breathe correctly and you can't learn to relax.

> **Terror Talk**
>
> **Yoga** is a 2,000-year-old program that combines exercises, or hatha yoga, with breathing and meditation. "Ha" means sun and equals the left side of the body; "tha" means moon and equals the right side of the body; "Hatha" means to bring both sides of the body in harmony. The word "yoga" itself means "union of body and soul."

Body Work

Sometimes people have been so uptight for so long, that their bodies have forgotten how to relax. Massages offer quick relief by:

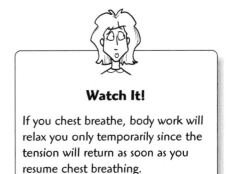

> **Watch It!**
>
> If you chest breathe, body work will relax you only temporarily since the tension will return as soon as you resume chest breathing.

➤ Stimulating circulation of the blood and lymph fluids

➤ Fueling the muscles with fresh oxygen and nutrients while flushing away metabolic waste products

➤ Releasing physical tension and soothing the nerves by lowering the stress hormones cortisol and norepinephrine and by releasing endorphins in the brain

Soul Food

Some people find themselves unable to overcome their fears because their lives lack purpose or direction: Not guided by an inner light, they stumble and fall in the dark. Balance for many people comes from feeling connected to something larger than ourselves which gives our lives meaning. For some it is God, for others Nature, for others the creation of something that we throw our whole being into—a poem, a song, a dance, a painting. Whatever it is that gets you to transcend self and merge with a larger entity, throw yourself into its pursuit. It is an important key to taming your psychological demons—a profound means of achieving inner security, strength, peace of mind, and a kinder view of the world.

Fear Mastery Progress Chart

Now that I've covered the many paths of self-help for conquering your fears and anxieties, you may find it helpful to chart your fear-busting efforts. The following daily checklist, which you can tailor to your individual regimen, will help you to monitor your daily progress.

Weekly Fear Master Progress Chart

(Activity)	Mon.	Tues.	Wed.	Thurs.	Fri.	Sat.	Sun.
Deep Breathing	___	___	___	___	___	___	___
Progressive Relaxation	___	___	___	___	___	___	___
Meditation	___	___	___	___	___	___	___
Visualization	___	___	___	___	___	___	___
Regular Aerobic Exercise	___	___	___	___	___	___	___
Yoga or T'ai Chi	___	___	___	___	___	___	___
Healthy Diet	___	___	___	___	___	___	___
Herbs & Vitamins	___	___	___	___	___	___	___
Body Work	___	___	___	___	___	___	___
Spirituality	___	___	___	___	___	___	___
Elimination of:							
Caffeine	___	___	___	___	___	___	___
Smoking	___	___	___	___	___	___	___
Recreational drugs	___	___	___	___	___	___	___
Environmental toxins	___	___	___	___	___	___	___

The Least You Need to Know

➤ Food is a powerful agent to help balance your nervous system.

➤ Food allergies have the potential to keep you tense and nervous.

➤ Environmental overstimulation feeds into stress and anxiety.

➤ Chemical sensitivities and especially chemical allergies play havoc with your nervous system, and in some cases, have been known to mimic panic symptoms.

➤ Exercise is one of your best allies against anxiety and depression.

➤ Massage offers quick relaxation.

➤ For many, spirituality helps in achieving comfort, peace and security.

Part 3
Overcoming Phobias

Imagine being too afraid to leave your house, to eat in a restaurant, or to use a public toilet. Picture what it would be like to step on a stage to perform and get struck with a panic attack that left you speechless and ready to faint. Envision a person giving up a free vacation to Hawaii for fear of flying. Think of what it might be like to so fear failure that you procrastinate and avoid until failure becomes inevitable.

The chapters in Part 3 talk about these common phobias—agoraphobia, social phobia, stage fright, fear of flying, and fear of failure...or success. You will learn what they are, where they come from and how to reduce or even eliminate their control over your life.

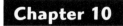

Chapter 10

Escape from Psychological House Arrest

> ## In This Chapter
>
> ➤ Agoraphobia: the fear of leaving the house
>
> ➤ Why someone becomes housebound
>
> ➤ Exploring the agoraphobic profile
>
> ➤ How to open the door and join the world again

Twenty-three-year-old Alicia was an aspiring interior designer. But the only interior that she saw for two months was that of her parent's house, where she had been living. For three weeks, she didn't leave the house at all. As soon as she stepped out the door, terror erupted in her body. Alicia is *agoraphobic*.

"There's nothing to fear but fear itself," said Franklin Delano Roosevelt. Franklin Roosevelt wasn't referring to agoraphobia, but he may as well have been.

Agoraphobia, the most common phobia, is the fear of an impending panic attack in a public place that makes a person retreat closer and closer to their safe home, venturing out only when accompanied by a safe person. It is the fear of fear.

In this chapter, I will talk about what makes someone psychologically housebound and how to unshackle the chains that keep them locked inside their psychological, as well as their real, house.

When You Don't Feel Safe Leaving Your Home

Two weeks after her boyfriend left her, Alicia experienced her first panic attack. It happened the day her boss called her into his office. Terrified of this harsh, cold man who reminded her of her foreboding father, Alicia crept toward his office with trepidation. He was on the phone and, with a sober look on his face, signaled for her to sit down. As she waited for him to get off the phone, she felt her stomach sinking as thoughts raced through her mind of what she could have done wrong.

Suddenly, the room began to seem strange, almost surreal. The bright overhead lighting appeared dull. Her vision seemed blurred and she couldn't focus on her boss's face. He seemed far away, as did her own body, as if not a part of her. Her head was spinning and she felt she might faint. She tried to catch her breath as waves of terror surged through her body. Shaking, sweaty and unsteady, she knew she had to get out of there, but didn't feel the power to command her arms and legs to move. She felt literally paralyzed with fear.

Unsteady, she managed to get up. She went to move her lips, but there were no sounds. She stared for a moment at her boss, frozen. Then she managed to blurt, "excuse me," and darted for the bathroom. There, she turned on the faucet and threw cold water on her face and leaned against the wall to steady herself. In a few moments, the terror passed, but she felt shaky, exhausted, confused, and embarrassed. Feigning the flu, she went home.

Angst Bulletin

Agoraphobic fears likely have an evolutionary basis. Fears of being alone, too far from home, or trapped in various situations would have served to protect vulnerable humans from predators and other physical dangers.

Over the next few days, Alicia obsessed over what had happened to her. Why had it happened? What triggered the attack? Would it happen again? She was all right for a week, but she then had a panic attack in line at the supermarket and another sitting on a bus. She began to feel petrified for no reason. Slipping steadily downhill, the attacks increased as the weeks went by and spread to any place where she felt that escape would be difficult. Everywhere she went, she sensed impending disaster. She was afraid to go back to work. What if she had another attack? She couldn't fake another case of the flu. She called, said she had hepatitis and needed a medical leave of absence. She then packed her bags and moved her things to her parent's house.

One night, she got high on marijuana with her friends, hoping it might relax her. Instead, she had the most frightening experience of all. She felt estranged from everyone around her, as if they were far away and she was a mere observer, cut off from her own body. This strange loss of self was more intense than in previous attacks and seemed to go on for hours. Terrified, she was convinced she was losing her self.

Afraid to leave the house, she lay most of the day in her mother's arms. When her mother wasn't home, she stayed in her bed under the covers and hugging her pillow—the phone within reach. With each breath she exhaled, she felt this horrifying, sinking feeling in her stomach that wouldn't go away, and that made her feel as if she were filled with inner demons.

She wanted to die. Not knowing what to do, she drank wine to drown herself into a stupor that would allow her to sleep. But she would awaken with nightmares: of having murdered someone; of lying on a table, broken in pieces; of falling down steep rows in a theatre and feeling her body crash as she hit each row. One night, she lay in bed watching *The Snake Pit*, an old movie about a woman in an insane asylum. She trembled with dread, convinced that she, too, was going crazy.

First Comes Panic

Agoraphobia generally begins with a panic attack. The panic, which commonly builds up for a ten-minute period or so, and then may last as long as another ten minutes or more, feels like a living nightmare. The experience itself, along with the loss of control it causes, looms like a true catastrophic event.

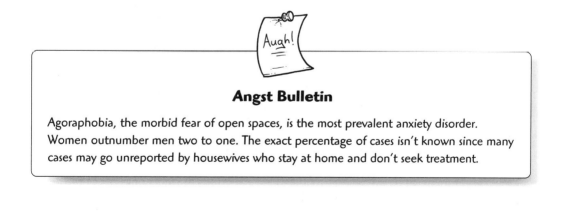

Angst Bulletin

Agoraphobia, the morbid fear of open spaces, is the most prevalent anxiety disorder. Women outnumber men two to one. The exact percentage of cases isn't known since many cases may go unreported by housewives who stay at home and don't seek treatment.

Avoidance: The Apparent Best Defense

After the first panic attack, you dread the thought of the awful anxiety of another. What if you find yourself in a situation in which you might panic and lose all control? You imagine the attack striking when you're carpooling your daughter and her friends to their dance class and you're unable to grip the wheel and command your foot to push the gas pedal. What would you say to them? What if you caused an accident? Or you think of what might happen if you have one on Sunday, while amidst the crowds at a baseball game with your family. You feel mortified as you see yourself running out of the stands looking ridiculous, as people all around gape at you.

Watch It!

Avoidance is a double-edged sword for the agoraphobic. Though avoiding panic-provoking situations helps them circumvent unbearable anxiety, this avoidance feeds their agoraphobia and further limits their freedom of movement.

These catastrophic thoughts paralyze you with fear and fill your days with intense anxiety. You feel the need to carefully watch your steps, lest the world swallow you up like quicksand. Minor bodily sensations seem a prelude to disaster: a fluttering heart signals an impending panic attack, as does a quickening breath, a moment of disorientation or dizziness. As this anticipatory anxiety builds up, sometimes it leads to a full-blown panic attack.

You begin to associate these attacks with situations where you might feel trapped, where escape would be difficult and embarrassing. This happens particularly in crowded or isolated places, or places from which you will be unable to get immediate help—an elevator, a crowded pew at church, standing in line at the supermarket, sitting in the middle row of a movie theatre, driving over a bridge or through a tunnel. To protect yourself from overwhelming panic, you begin to avoid these "unsafe" places and live your life according to how quickly you can reach safety. At this point, you've become agoraphobic. In some cases, it takes only a single panic attack to trigger agoraphobia.

Here are some common ways agoraphobics modify their lives:

➤ To facilitate quick escape in case of panic, agoraphobics sit in the aisle seat at the movies, theatre, or in church.

➤ They carry cellular phones for immediate access to a safe person.

➤ They live on the ground floor of apartment buildings to avoid the necessity of taking elevators.

➤ They prefer driving rather than take public transportation, whose stops they can't control.

➤ They drive down deserted streets and highways at odd hours to avoid traffic.

➤ They seek out all night supermarkets or convenience stores for their shopping to avoid standing in line.

➤ If they must be confined, as when taking public transportation, or when in a dentist's or hairdresser's chair, they try to have a protective companion accompany them.

➤ They devise legitimate excuses for escape should they have a panic attack—a headache, sick stomach, need to make a phone call, worry about a sick child.

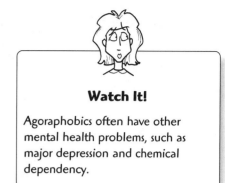

Watch It!

Agoraphobics often have other mental health problems, such as major depression and chemical dependency.

Though avoidance provides relief from panic, this relief comes at a cost: avoidance furthers avoidance behavior until it quickly dominates your life and intensifies your agoraphobia. The number of "safe zones," the places you can visit in relative comfort, narrow. Some, like Alicia, become increasingly imprisoned within their own homes (real and psychological).

The following is the common sequence of agoraphobia:

1. Panic attack occurs out of nowhere

2. Anticipatory anxiety of another attack

3. Overreaction to bodily cues that can intensify into a panic attack

4. Avoidance of panic provoking situations

5. Relief reinforces avoidance

6. Narrowing of the number of "safe places"

7. Sufferer becomes housebound

From Staying Close to Home to Staying Home

In some people, agoraphobia is so strong they haven't left their houses for ten, twenty, thirty years. In her book *Triumph Over Fear*, Jerilyn Ross reports of an agoraphobic woman that she successfully treated in 1978, who had not been out of the house since 1948! Some don't even open the door, lest terror fly in.

But not all agoraphobics become buried in their own digs. In fact, people can live relatively normal lives, with only mild avoidance, and with people unaware that they are agoraphobic. People go to work but may need to be accompanied to go shopping, to the movies, or to drive in a car on the highway. Often the illness fluctuates: During milder periods, you feel greater freedom of movement and especially when with a trusted companion.

Levels of Severity of Agoraphobia

Mild	Though uncomfortable in confined situations, you tolerate the discomfort and continue to work or shop on your own, but try to stay close to home.
Moderate	You start to avoid some situations, such as public transportation, elevators, driving far from home, or being in restaurants. Nevertheless, you can handle certain situations away from home or your safe person, even with discomfort.
Severe	You restrict all activities to the point of being housebound unless accompanied.

Angst Bulletin

Panic disorder in some women appears to relate to hormone fluctuation. Some women report the most panic attacks premenstrually, a time when excessive levels of the female hormone progesterone are present. Progesterone is known to stimulate some of the same nervous system sites that are sensitive to caffeine and sodium lactate, also implicated in producing panic attacks in some women. During pregnancy, panic disorder abates and resumes in full force after delivery—also suggesting a relationship between female hormone levels and panic attacks.

Agoraphobic's MO

Were you born doomed to become housebound or did you become that way? A bit of both. If you were a psychological sleuth and had to hunt down someone stowed away in his house, you would compile an MO that combined a biological predisposition to act fearfully, along with psychological factors that create a view of the world as more dangerous than your capacity to handle it. A typical profile might look like this:

Biological Factors

➤ Female: As a female, it's more socially acceptable for you to be housebound. What's more, you feel generally less control over your life than men do. You suffer from premenstrual syndrome (PMS), and feel heightened anxiety just before menstruating—the time at which you experience the most panic attacks.

➤ Childhood anxiety: As far back as you can remember, you've felt more fearful and anxious than others have. At least one of your parents may also be fear-prone.

➤ Sensory defensiveness: You get easily over-stimulated and irritated by certain sensory stimuli, such as bright lights, noise, unpleasant odors, certain textures on your skin and light or unexpected touch, as when someone comes up to you from behind and taps you on the shoulder. Crowds and heights make you anxious.

➤ Highly imaginative: You have a potent imagination that enables you to visualize your fears, increasing the likelihood that they will get out of control.

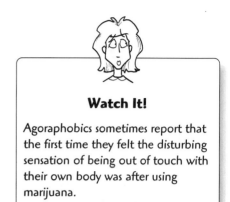

Watch It!

Agoraphobics sometimes report that the first time they felt the disturbing sensation of being out of touch with their own body was after using marijuana.

➤ Drug reactions: You react strongly to drugs. Caffeine and marijuana make you more nervous and prone to panic.

Psychological Factors

➤ Low self-esteem: You underrate your own value and abilities. Often, you set unreasonably high goals for yourself and then worry about failing, which would embarrass you intensely.

➤ Emotionally constricted: You tend to hide your emotions, especially fear, distress and anger.

➤ Strong fear of abandonment: You fear that people will leave you and find it hard to be alone. As a child, you were clingy and afraid to be separated from your mother. You may have refused to go to school at some point.

➤ Loss of a loved one: Preceding your first panic attack, you lost someone very close to you—through death, breakup of a relationship, or relocation.

➤ False independence: You see yourself as independent, but inside feel intense dependency, which you try to conceal. Were you to express this dependency, you worry no one would comfort you. Agoraphobic symptoms may serve the purpose of safely receiving needed care-giving without directly expressing the wish for intimacy. For instance, if you panic while at the supermarket, a sympathetic friend might hold your hand until you calm down. In this way, you get needed nurturing without revealing your longing for someone to love and take care of you.

➤ Stress: Stress has been an unwelcome companion for as long as you can remember. Preceding your first panic attack, you got whopped with a major stressor. If you are female, this was likely a change in your home or family life; if you are male, the stressful event likely involved work.

Angst Bulletin

Half of severe agoraphobics exhibited separation anxiety in childhood. This suggests that agoraphobia may be an extension of this childhood separation anxiety and represents the need to stay close to the protective mother. Only when you are with your safe person can you feel assured that you have not been abandoned and therefore safe enough to venture out into the world.

One Step at a Time

Agoraphobia is a serious and complicated disease that needs aggressive intervention in all of the four ways in which it manifests itself:

➤ Physical: Strange bodily sensations during panic and on-going agitation or anxiety

➤ Feelings: Uncomfortable fright, dread and free-floating anxiety

➤ Thoughts: Catastrophic worries of the worst case scenario

➤ Behavior: Avoidance of panic provoking situations

Watch It!

Agoraphobics tend to be especially bothered by the bright lighting in supermarkets and malls and often feel forced to flee. Some avoid bright areas altogether. During a panic attack, lights often seem intensely bright or dull.

As you read about the different interventions available, keep in mind that it takes time and effort to break loose from agoraphobia's chains and rarely can people do this on their own. You will be greatly aided by finding a therapist you can trust and using the material in this book to augment treatment, including the information in Chapter 15 on coping with panic attacks. Generally, agoraphobics show the best progress with cognitive-behavioral therapy.

Quieting Your Body

When you're constantly anxious, you feel continually tense and keyed up. Since it takes little to put you over the edge, it's hard to cope with day-to-day stresses, let alone panic attacks.

If you employ the self-help relaxation techniques outlined in Chapters 6, 8, and 9, you will help better balance your nervous system and increase the likelihood of achieving longer periods of calm and alert. Getting off the junk food track and fueling your body with proper nutrition, as well as avoiding the caffeine buzz, will also further this goal.

Relaxation Training

➤ Diaphragmatic or belly breathing: This will train you to slow down your physiological overarousal before it gains momentum and you become overly anxious. In this way, you can learn to bypass a panic attack or, should one occur, minimize its intensity. If you hyperventilate, "breathing lessons" are crucial to your recovery (see Chapter 6).

➤ Deep relaxation: With daily practice of progressive relaxation and, if possible, meditation, you can train your body to relax more easily. The affect is cumulative: Within a month or so, you begin to feel yourself more relaxed all the time (see Chapter 6).

Regular exercise

➤ Strenuous exercise helps metabolize excessive adrenaline, reduces muscle tension, and releases endorphins to increase your sense of well being. You can do whatever exercises you enjoy and will do consistently. The ideal is a half-hour of aerobic exercise four to five times per week. In addition, regular practice of yoga, which combines diaphragmatic breathing along with stretching exercise, promotes greater vitality, relaxation, suppleness and serenity (see Chapter 9).

Secret Weapons

Running, which releases pain killing endorphins that make it a powerful anti-depressant, is an excellent exercise for agoraphobics, who are generally depressed as well as anxious. If you wear running clothes while going somewhere panic-provoking, like the mall, you can quickly flee should you become anxious. Running will also help release the excess adrenaline streaming through your bloodstream.

Watch It!

Food allergies, warns Douglas Hunt in *No More Fears*, are common in agoraphobics and can trigger panic attacks. In one patient, oatmeal made her "spacey," wheat "panicky" and corn "tired and irritable." If you were to eat foods on a daily basis to which you were allergic and get these reactions, he warns that you might always feel on the edge of panic and suffer anticipatory anxiety.

Don't Fight Fear with Fear

One reason why not all people who have a panic attack become agoraphobic is the refusal to avoid situations that induce panic. This is the key to working your way out of agoraphobia: by facing your fears. In this way, you learn that nothing dangerous will happen to you during a panic attack.

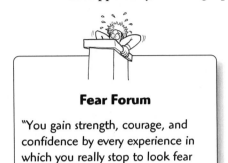

Fear Forum

"You gain strength, courage, and confidence by every experience in which you really stop to look fear in the face."
—Eleanor Roosevelt

The sink or swim approach for long-standing fears is not recommended, because this can easily overwhelm someone who is prone to feeling anxious. Instead, think of confronting your demons one manageable step at a time. Your goal is to stay in these frightening situations for longer and longer periods of time.

Here's how to get started:

➤ Make a list of clearly defined goals in order of difficulty, which will vary according to the severity of your agoraphobia:

1. Stepping outside my door
2. Walking to the corner
3. Walking three blocks to the grocery store
4. Sitting in the park by myself
5. Driving four blocks to the post office
6. Taking a bus
7. Shopping on the first floor of a department store
8. Taking an elevator to the second floor of a department store
9. Driving my car in heavy traffic

➤ Take the goals, one by one, and break them down into a series of specific steps that might look like this:

Going to the Park:

1. Walk (or run) to the park entrance, stand there for one minute and walk (run) back home.
2. Walk (or run) to the park, take a few steps into the park, stand there for one minute and walk (run) back home.
3. Walk (run) a block into the park, stand there for one minute and walk (run) back home.
4. Walk (run) a block into the park, stand there for five minutes and walk (run) back home.

5. Walk (run) into the park, sit on a bench for one minute, then walk (run) back home.

6. Walk (run) into the park, sit on a park bench for fifteen minutes doing an activity that will divert your attention away from bodily sensations—reading, sewing, drawing, a crossword puzzle—and walk (run) back home.

7. Walk (run) into the park, sit on a park bench for a half hour engaged in an absorbing activity and walk (run) back home.

➤ Before you actually take your first real step, run through each step you've outlined in your imagination. If you've been agoraphobic for a long time, even imagining taking an elevator may easily upset you. Have patience with yourself and go slowly, mastering the beginning goals first.

Secret Weapons

Some therapists do "home" visits and actually accompany their clients, step by step, to leave the house, and hold their hand if needed.

➤ When you can visualize the final step of your particular goal in detail without feeling overwhelmed by anxiety, you are ready for a real life walk (run) through.

➤ Practice daily to make progress. On days you don't, you might slip back. If you become panicky, know it will pass and try to "float" through it. Read Chapter 15 on coping with panic for strategies to control your anxiety before it spills over.

➤ If it's easier, begin to practice each step several times with the help of a safe person. This can be anyone with whom you feel support and protection: boyfriend or girlfriend, spouse, parent, or friend. If anxiety starts to build, stop and step back until the fear passes. In this way, you don't "overexpose" yourself and become too overwhelmed to continue.

A Penny for Your Thoughts

Agoraphobics are famous worriers, anticipating the worst before it happens with self-defeating "What if" statements like "What if I have another panic attack?" "What if I lose control of myself while driving?" To exorcise your inner demons, you must free yourself of these self-defeating negative thoughts, which feed into and perpetuate your panic attacks. Here are some suggestions to get you started:

➤ Write down your destructive thoughts in a notebook.

➤ Replace them with constructive ones.

➤ Go over the list several times.

➤ Keep your notebook with you. When you catch yourself thinking destructively, refer to it and try to replace the thought with a positive, constructive one.

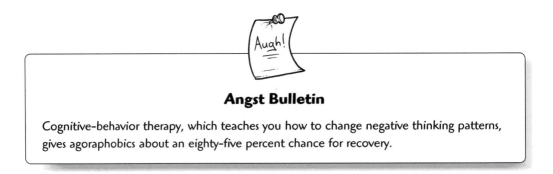

Angst Bulletin

Cognitive-behavior therapy, which teaches you how to change negative thinking patterns, gives agoraphobics about an eighty-five percent chance for recovery.

Here are some examples of changing destructive thoughts to positive, constructive ones:

Destructive and Constructive Thoughts

Destructive thought	Constructive thought
I'll never get rid of these feelings.	I can fight these feelings.
I've got to get out of here.	I can get through this.
I'll die if I have another attack.	I've survived them before and can again.
I'll never be able to go shopping alone again.	I will go shopping and buy myself something I've always wanted.
What if someone sees me looking so terrified?	People are too involved in their own lives to worry about me.
My heart's pounding so, I must be having a heart attack.	My heart has pounded like this when I've been in love too or run a mile.
Maybe I'll never get better.	I *will* get better.

If you can replace "scare talk" with constructive statements during a panic attack, you may be able to observe your bodily reactions, rather than react to them. In time, you may be able to avoid severe panic reactions altogether.

Free Your Imprisoned Feelings

Agoraphobics are often avoidant people who have a tendency to suppress negative feelings like anger, sadness, distress, and frustration. When these feelings surface, they feel anxious and seek to control their expression.

Secret Weapons

Buy a pillow that says, "this too will pass" and put it in a place where you can easily see it, like on your bed or a favorite chair.

During childhood, expressing negative feelings were not met with help in resolving them, but with increased parental annoyance, anger or rage, or withdrawal. Since angry or depressed parents didn't take care of you, you learned to deny these feelings and to behave to please your parents—to lay low and not make waves. Unable to turn to your parents for comfort when distressed, you became falsely independent and pretended to not need anyone.

These early experiences scarred your brain. Later, this pattern of behavior extends to other relationships: feelings were hidden; needs were denied; and behavior designed to please. Unable to say no to the demands of others and stand up for yourself, your sense of self was stunted.

But you can deny your feelings and your true sense of self only for so long; eventually, as Freud taught us, anxiety bursts through in psychological or psychosomatic symptoms. In some sense, a panic attack is an expression of intense feelings of frustration, anger, and grief in disguise, and agoraphobia a distress call that something is very wrong and you strongly need nurturing.

Freeing your imprisoned feelings may take aggressive therapeutic intervention (see Chapter 7). Remember, deeply embedded in your psyche is the notion that showing your feelings is dangerous: Not only will no one come to your aid, intensifying your distress, but if your rage and intense dependency needs spill out, they will surely scare the other person away.

Here are some ways you can help yourself:

➤ Try to identify your feeling states.

➤ Talk about your feelings with "safe" people.

➤ Write your feelings down in a daily journal.

➤ Explore your feelings through creative outlets, like painting, pottery, stained glass, playing a musical instrument, dance, drama, creative writing.

Fear Forum

"Move from worry to action, and the action will absorb the anxiety."
—Robert Ornstein and D. S. Sobel in 1994 in *Mental Medicine Update* III

➤ Watch movies, listen to music and read books that provoke intense feelings like sadness or joy, so you can learn to express the full range of your feeling.

➤ Practice expressing minor irritation.

➤ When you feel intensely angry, walk away from the situation or count to ten.

➤ Discharge your pent-up anger through exercise, hitting pillows or punching bags, screaming when you're alone in your car.

➤ When things cool off, practice in your mind telling someone how angry you were, including the worst case scenario of how this person might react, and then play it out in real time.

Love Thyself

Often, agoraphobics had cold, critical, angry, or withdrawn parents and grew up feeling unworthy and unlovable. This low self-esteem perpetuates the need to please others, which keeps you dependent and stunted in your growth as a person.

Secret Weapons

One of the best ways to become intimate with your feeling is to pause at the end of the day and write them down in a journal.

In addition to psychotherapy, you can take action on your own to develop a stronger sense of yourself and increase self-worth. Here are some ways:

➤ Taking care of your physical body and overall health

➤ Seeking pleasurable activities

➤ Assertiveness training

➤ Engaging in physical, mental, and creative activities that make you feel competent and successful

For details, see Chapter 14.

Find Your Guardian Angel

Finding a trusted companion with whom you feel safe is essential for anyone suffering from agoraphobia. Knowing you can trust this person to intervene should you panic will allow you to venture into feared situations that, if alone, would create unendurable anxiety.

In *Home Before Dark*, Susan Cheever's biography of her father John Cheever, she described how, at fourteen, her warm presence helped him through a panic attack that began as they crossed over the Tappan Zee Bridge. "I looked over at my father and saw that his foot was shaking against the accelerator. He was very pale. "Talk to me," he said. "About what?" I noticed that his hands were trembling, too. The car bucked along, edging toward the guardrail at the side of the bridge. "It doesn't matter, just talk." She described a novel she was reading and, by the time they reached the other side of the bridge, the shaking stopped and his face regained its normal color.

If you don't have such a "safe person," a favorite pet may be of help. Recovery depends tremendously on support.

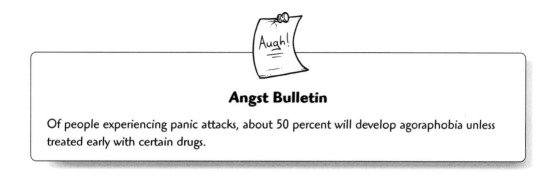

Angst Bulletin

Of people experiencing panic attacks, about 50 percent will develop agoraphobia unless treated early with certain drugs.

Prescription Relief

The most successful treatment for agoraphobia appears to be a combination of cognitive-behavioral therapy and drug therapy. Anti-anxiety drugs, such as Xanax or Klonopin, help reduce anxiety and enable the person to begin exposure treatment. The newer SSRI antidepressants, such as Paxil, Prozac, and Zoloft, help the agoraphobic follow through with exposure and in handling the depression that often accompanies agoraphobia.

The Least You Need to Know

➤ Some severe agoraphobics haven't left their homes for 20 or 30 years.

➤ Not all agoraphobics are housebound but function close to normal—working and going about, though these activities may be uncomfortable.

➤ Agoraphobia is a complex illness that needs aggressive treatment.

➤ Cognitive-behavioral therapy, along with drug intervention, appears to be the most successful treatment for agoraphobia.

Chapter 11

Glide Above Your Fear of Flying

In This Chapter

➤ How the media fuels a fear of flying

➤ The different flying fears

➤ Where fear of flying comes from

➤ From take off to landing without panic

My Aunt Sylvia lives in New York. When her son Jordie in San Diego decided to get married, she had a real dilemma: How to get there. Flying was out of the question. Please—did he want her to arrive alive? So she and my Uncle Herbie drove all the way to San Diego to attend their son's wedding.

But my Aunt Sylvia also wanted to visit Israel before she died and her husband didn't have the time to take a boat back and forth to the Holy Land. So, she decided that somehow she was going to overcome her fear of flying and get herself on an airplane. And eventually she did and flew the eleven hours to Tel Aviv. She wasn't wild about the flight, but she didn't panic.

It is estimated that as many as thirty-five million American adults refuse to fly. And this figure is probably low. Many, though, overcome their fear or at least learn to control it. In this chapter, you will learn why people fear flying and ways that you too can conquer that fear and take to the skies.

Fear Is in the Air

Why are so many people afraid to fly? Some, like Joe, have actually experienced danger on an airplane. Once, when flying from Seattle to Denver, Joe's plane ran into engine trouble and had to make an emergency landing. Several people were seriously injured. He was lucky and walked away with only some lacerations and shaky knees. Nowadays, he takes buses and trains from state to state.

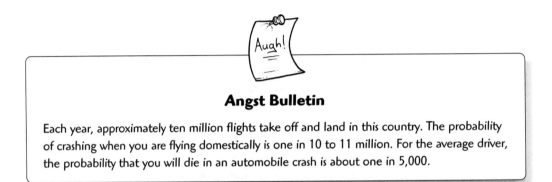

Angst Bulletin

Each year, approximately ten million flights take off and land in this country. The probability of crashing when you are flying domestically is one in 10 to 11 million. For the average driver, the probability that you will die in an automobile crash is about one in 5,000.

But most people who fear flying have not actually experienced danger in the air—they've simply learned to associate flying with danger. The media has much to do with this. Airplane crashes are big news and get much press. Pictures of a burned-out shell of an airplane, few or no survivors, and pieces of scattered body parts and personal belongings make the headlines—often for days.

Generally, the crash is not counterbalanced by the actual statistics of plane crashes and gives the false impression that taking an airplane is taking a chance. In actuality, a crash is extremely rare. You have a 99.99 percent chance of reaching your destination safely. This fact, however, makes little difference to those who have phobias about flying.

When There's No Way Out but Down

Jenny has never had a bad experience on an airplane. Nevertheless, each time she must fly, she is terrified that the plane will crash and cripple or kill her. She still flies, but for weeks before the flight, she worries and daily scours the papers for plane crashes. If she has a nightmare of a plane crash, she interprets the dream as an omen of a death foretold. She makes plans in case of her demise, like giving her daughter the key to her safety deposit box and updating her will. During the flight, she is hyper-alert to sounds, weather, other airplanes and any sign on the faces of flight attendants or in the voice of the pilot that something could be amiss with the flight. She spends much time with her eyes closed, praying. Jennifer is *aviophobic* (one who fears flying).

Raoul doesn't much like planes for the same reason he doesn't like elevators: he feels trapped in small, enclosed spaces. Raoul is *claustrophobic* (one who fears enclosed spaces) and will not fly.

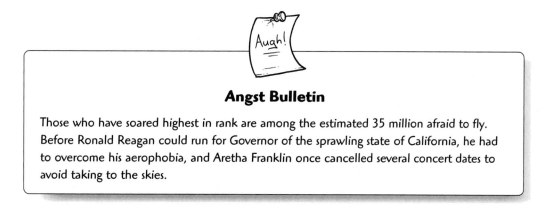

Angst Bulletin

Those who have soared highest in rank are among the estimated 35 million afraid to fly. Before Ronald Reagan could run for Governor of the sprawling state of California, he had to overcome his aerophobia, and Aretha Franklin once cancelled several concert dates to avoid taking to the skies.

Otis fears heights and hates to fly. He imagines the plane falling from the sky and crashing to the ground. If turbulence causes the plane to bounce or shake, he becomes petrified. Any moment, he expects a window to pop open and suck him out, sending him free-falling to the ground. Walking in the cabin, he even pictures that the floor will fall out from underneath him. Otis is *acrophobic* (one who fears heights).

Eddie has panic attacks. When he flies, all he can think about is what will happen if he has one during the flight. There would be no escape. Worse yet, what if his racing heart convinces him that he's really having a heart attack. He could die!

Jackie becomes anxious when not in control. She doesn't like trusting her fate to others, particularly people who don't know her—like pilots. She fears human error and, well, you never know if a hijacker is aboard a flight!

Terry, who has never flown on a plane, was about to take his first flight. With all the plane crashes that fill the news, he felt afraid. But after his first trip, his fear was dispelled. In fact, he found it exciting.

As you can see, fear of flying can encompass different underlying fears. Sometimes, these different fears are combined. Knowing more of why you fear flying will help you in devising ways to overcome it. Knowing the origin of your phobia may also help—although you can still overcome your fear without knowing how it got there.

Fear of Flying Profile

Though most everyone listens to the news and many read the newspapers, the majority of people who fly do so without terror. Sure, many close their eyes for two seconds and grip their armrest as the plane takes off. But when the flight attendant flashes a smile and hands them their bag of peanuts and maybe a Bloody Mary, they calm down and do their crossword puzzle or read their novel. What distinguishes these people from those who develop a full-blown flying phobia? The answer lies in some of the same roots that underlie other phobias.

Born Not to Fly?

Commonly, flying phobics have a genetic predisposition to react more fearfully. Other people in the same family may have other phobias, such as claustrophobia, acrophobia or agoraphobia.

Childhood Woes

Insecure attachment with one or more of your parents makes you unsure that people will protect you. This sets up a view of the world as generally unsafe and of people as untrustworthy. Convinced that only you can assure your own safety, you feel a stronger need to control aspects of your life to best govern the outcome. Thus, you are reluctant to trust others with your fate. Taking an airplane, which entails trust in the competence of many others, is a leap of faith that you may feel unsafe making. Some people solve this by learning how to pilot their own plane.

Some insecure parents, frightened themselves, are overprotective and "encourage" their children to believe that the world is a scary place and that people are "out to screw you." Prevented from taking risks, the children grow up feeling inadequate and anxious, and lack an inner locus of control. This makes them more worried about being thrown to fate, and they feel greater danger from external forces of disaster, like plane crashes.

Past Trauma

If you've experienced a horrific event, particularly one where harm has befallen you or a loved one, or a loved one has been killed, you might feel more fearful overall. You may feel as if disaster is waiting around the corner, and you become more cautious of situations that lend themselves to the potential for natural and man-made catastrophe. Boarding a plane triggers a feeling of danger.

Stress and Then Some

In the age of anxiety in which we live, stress piles up—day by day, moment by moment. If you're the nervous type, stress eventually wears you down and you can't cope as well. Mountains you may have scaled before now seem insurmountable and, after years of flying, you suddenly find yourself afraid and experiencing a heightened sense of your own mortality. This makes events that increase danger, like flying, risky. What might happen if you were to die, you wonder? What might you miss? What would happen to your children and spouse? Who would take your possessions and adopt your cat?

The Plane Will Crash!

Your husband tells you, "Plane crashes are rare." "Yeah," you say, "Well how come there's one on the news every other week?" We all pay attention to information that supports our belief system, and ignore or disconfirm information that is contrary to what we believe. If you are prone to think the worst, every plane mishap you hear or read about will strengthen the notion that planes are unsafe. You never think about the thousands of planes that fly everyday without mishap.

Angst Bulletin

People believe what they want to believe, as the saying goes, and will distort new information to fit into their belief system. Duane Brown and his wife Sandra co-designed and conduct seminars on fear of flying for American Airlines. In his book *Flying Without Fear*, he tells of one woman's comment as he was introduced to a group of fearful flyers. "I want you to know that I think American Airlines pays you to lie to us," said she.

Off Balance

For some who fear going "up, up and away," even being down on earth feels like shaky ground. These are people whose phobic-like symptoms appear to originate from impairment of the inner-ear system (see Chapter 8), which create symptoms similar to those associated with aviophobia, acrophobia and claustrophobia. These symptoms take three forms.

Sense of balance impairment symptoms:

➤ Anxiety

➤ Dizziness

➤ Light-headedness

➤ Spinning

➤ Falling

➤ Fainting

➤ A magnetic "tug" from the ground below

➤ Tipping or swaying

Orientation in space impairment symptoms:

➤ Anxiety

➤ Disorientation

➤ Confusion

➤ Spaciness

➤ Dizziness

Angst Bulletin

Speed, whether experienced in a plane, car, or train, unsettles some people. Many may have coordination problems as a result of inner ear or vestibular dysfunction. Difficulty stopping, starting and directing their bodies to a target gets displaced onto discomfort with speed of the vehicle in which they are traveling.

Sense of motion impairment symptoms:

➤ Anxiety

➤ Dizziness

➤ Nausea

➤ Vomiting

If you fear flying, and you experience any balance problems, or find that you easily experience vertigo, you may want to have a complete ear examination to see if inner ear dysfunction may be causing or contributing to your exaggerated fear response. Moreover, prolonged or turbulent air travel sickness can exacerbate inner-ear problems, and may in some people, contribute to aviophobia, acrophobia, and claustrophobia.

The Cost of Not Flying

LaToya, who fears flying, has won a free trip to Hawaii. If she doesn't get on that plane, her husband threatens to divorce her. Will she be motivated to conquer her fear? One clue is how much it would cost her, financially and emotionally, to lose her husband in contrast to the benefits of keeping him. Incredibly, many people would rather maintain their fear of flying, even at the cost of bypassing many of life's most precious benefits.

Fear of flying doesn't come cheap. People will sacrifice promotions, free trips to Paris (or wherever), miss weddings and funerals, and even damage and ruin relationships to avoid taking off into the wild blue yonder. They will spend extra time and money taking a train—simply to avoid flying.

The irony is that fear of flying, unlike other phobias (agoraphobia, for example) can generally be overcome quickly. And treatment has a high success rate. The American Airlines Air Born seminars last two days and have within that time about an 85 percent success rate.

Cruise Control

Assuming LaToya wishes to stay married to her husband, what can she do to get herself on that plane? Many things.

Secret Weapons

Dr. Roger Callahan, founder of the Five-Minute Phobia Cure, described in Chapter 7, claims his technique immediately eliminates fear of flying in many people. Sandy Shaw, co-author of *Life Extension*, had quit his job playing bass with the Righteous Brothers because he couldn't fly. After one treatment, he said he loves to fly. (See Appendix B for more information.)

First, suggests Duane Brown (*Flying Without Fear*, New Harbinger, 1996), she needs to pinpoint what she's actually afraid of: crashing, heights, enclosed spaces, loss of control or having a panic attack, or a combination thereof.

Overcoming the different phobias entail somewhat different strategies:

➤ Aviophobics, as well as neophyte flyers, are filled with misinformation. They need to hunt down reliable and trustworthy information to counter their misconceptions.

➤ Claustrophobics need foremost to understand what underlies their fear, and then develop strategies for dealing with it. Since enclosed spaces bring on a feeling of suffocation, they need to work on breath control. They will have an easier time flying on a large airplane and on a short enough trip so that they are unlikely to have to use the tiny lavatories.

➤ Acrophobics need information about the stability of airplanes (such as how they perform in turbulence), as well as strategies for dealing with their fear on the airplane.

➤ Panic attacks: People who suffer from panic attacks need primarily strategies for coping with panic attacks (see Chapter 15).

Angst Bulletin

Some people with acrophobia (fear of heights), including some pilots, do not feel afraid of heights while in an airplane. We are all born with a fear of heights that warns us so we don't fall off the side of a cliff. Since our ancestors did not have experience with airplanes, only heights like trees or mountains, they did not cultivate the fear of a cruising altitude of 35,000 feet.

Mental Flights

Once you know specifically what makes you afraid of flying, you need to identify the catastrophic thoughts flying inside your brain, such as "The plane will crash," "I'm going to die," that feed into your fear and paralyze you. You then need to change the direction of your mental flight to the positive, not the negative pole.

Here are some examples:

Aviophobic

➤ Destructive thought: This plane will crash, I know it!

➤ Constructive thought: Flying is far safer than automobiles and I drive one every day without fearing death.

Claustrophobic

➤ Destructive thought: I may panic and feel as if I can't breathe.

➤ Constructive thought: This is in my head. The air in a plane is changed frequently—at least every ten minutes. And there's even oxygen aboard should I need it!

Acrophobic

➤ Destructive thought: What if the window blows out and I get sucked out with it?

➤ Constructive thought: I'm more likely to get an allergic spider bite in the comfort of my own home and die from that. My fears are unrelated to reality.

Person with Panic Attacks

➤ Destructive thought: What if I have a panic attack during the whole one-hour flight?

➤ Constructive thought: If I have a panic attack, I know it will pass if I just ride with it. I will ask a flight attendant to act as a safe person and hold my hand.

Like Flying on a Cloud

If you spend weeks imagining the worst case scenario, your tension about flying escalates daily. By the time you get on the plane, you are so unnerved you may be ready for a straight jacket. With each flight, you effectively condition yourself into greater and greater anxiety. For this reason, flying does not improve aviophobia.

If you practice the relaxation techniques outlined in Chapter Six, you should be able to dampen pre-flight anxiety and use them in the event of jitters on the plane.

Watch It!

In an experiment conducted by Dr. Leslie Solyom of Allan Memorial Institute, McGill University, Montreal, a Fear Control Training program obtained poor results with participants who had done a lot of flying just prior to the FTC project. Each flight so reinforced their fear, it was hard to unlearn.

Here are more variations:

Before the Flight

➤ Armchair simulation: Sit in an armchair and imagine yourself on the plane. Go through the progressive relaxation exercise. You can do each muscle group, or only those muscles that are especially tense. Do this daily to progressively reduce your level of tension.

➤ Alternate Nostril Breathing (ANB): This breathing exercise helps you quickly achieve a calm and alert state. Sit comfortably in a chair or cross-legged on a cushion on the floor. Clear your nostrils by blowing each separately. Even better, sniff water through your nostrils and expel it from your mouth with the use of a Neti Pot (Ayurvedic Sinus Relief)—a great way to clear your sinuses. The ANB cycle is as follows:

1. Close the right nostril with your right thumb. Exhale completely through the left nostril.
2. Inhale slowly and evenly through the left nostril.
3. Hold the air for a few seconds, closing the left nostril with the left thumb.
4. Release the right nostril and exhale slowly through it.
5. Inhale through the right nostril.

This completes one cycle. Continue for up to 20 cycles and finish by exhaling through the left nostril.

Once you get the knack of it, your can try counting on each inhalation and exhalation with even counts. This will help keep your mind focused. You can start with a number that is comfortable for you, such as four, and gradually build it up as high as you can manage without force.

Up, Up and Away in Virtual Reality

Once you get yourself relaxed, you can, as with other phobias, desensitize your fears away by imagining anxiety provoking situations in a hierarchy of ascending terror. If you do this on your own, without a therapist, remember to completely relax and counter the fear before you begin to fantasize the next step.

Your fantasy hierarchy needs to be tailored to your own specific anxieties and should allow you to conjure up vivid fears. Here is an example of a useful fantasy hierarchy:

1. Driving to the airport
2. Going through the security gate
3. Checking in at the gate
4. Boarding the flight
5. Walking down the aisle to your seat
6. "Fasten Your Seat Belt" sign comes on
7. Demonstration of putting on an oxygen mask in case of depressurization, and explanation of the location of the emergency exits, and how to use your seat flotation devices should the plane make a landing in water
8. Announcing time for take-off
9. Plane begins to ascend the air
10. Announcement that you are cruising at 35,000 feet
11. Announcement that you will soon start to descend after an uneventful flight
12. "Fasten seat belts" sign goes on for no apparent reason
13. Plane shakes a bit
14. Plane gets wobblier and someone screams
15. Plane suddenly drops, things go flying through the air and the oxygen masks drop down
16. Pilot announces engine trouble and need to make an emergency landing

When you feel comfortable in imagining yourself in all these terrifying situations, your next step is reality desensitization.

Expose Yourself

Start with exposing yourself to everything regarding flying in an airplane but the actual flight. When you make it through this phase without undue anxiety, you graduate to your first test flight. Here is a sample of a fear hierarchy in real time.

1. Approach the airport with your spouse and drive around it.

2. Park at the airport with your spouse.

3. Enter the terminal with your spouse and walk around looking at the shopping and ticket areas.

4. Have your spouse leave you alone briefly.

5. Go to a departure gate or observation deck with your spouse and watch planes take off and land.

6. Observe the planes briefly on your own.

7. Go on a short shuttle flight (15-30 minutes) with your spouse.

8. Repeat the flight on your own.

9. Go on a longer flight with your spouse.

10. Go on a longer "solo" flight.

Secret Weapons

If you begin to feel anxious at any point in time during your fear exposure, repeat a previous step until you feel sufficiently calm to try again. For instance, if watching a plane take off gets you too anxious, go back into the airport and have a cup of warm herbal tea—remember that caffeine only exacerbates your tension—and take a few deep breaths.

If you are claustrophobic, construct your own fear hierarchy of the closed spaces that frighten you and begin to confront them. Do the same if you are afraid of heights with a graduated height hierarchy. Be aware that though systematic desensitization works well for most people, each person has his own timetable. Some people may have to repeat each step in increments of five, ten, twenty, thirty minutes, and so on until they begin to feel a modicum of comfort and the process can take months. Others successfully go through a run-through in real time in a weekend.

Getting Ready to Go to the Airport

➤ Call first to find out if your plane is leaving on time. You don't need extra time at the airport to talk yourself into a tizzy.

➤ Take with you whatever distraction ploys will work for you: crossword puzzles, needlepoint, a good novel, a gossipy magazine....

Watch It!

Many people prepare for a flight by knocking themselves out with drugs or alcohol. Be aware that many fearful flyers who down numerous cocktails or pop several Xanax report no lessening of fear.

➤ Bring along some relaxing essential oils, like lavender, bergamot, chamomile, neroli, or rose. You can rub some on your neck, your temples and the sides of your face and breathe in deeply.

➤ Bring along a relaxation tape that works well for you.

➤ Bring earplugs. When anxious, your hearing becomes more acute and the sounds of the plane, which are loud to begin with, intensify and annoy you that much more.

➤ Carry a "helping hands" wooden self-massager.

➤ Try taking some kava (see Chapter 8) just before the flight.

➤ Do strenuous exercise to work off stress chemicals.

At the Airport

➤ Buy yourself a treat at one of the airport shops as a later reward for your flight success.

➤ Board the plane as late as possible. In this way, you won't feel cramped between people in the jet bridge, which activates the fear of being trapped—you should do this especially if you're claustrophobic.

During the Flight

➤ Mentally scan your body, beginning with your toes, and telling each muscle group to relax or do progressive relaxation.

➤ Do your diaphragmatic breathing exercise.

➤ Sit wherever you feel most safe. Generally, phobics prefer the aisle seat, which affords the greatest freedom of movement. A middle of the row seat triggers the greatest feeling of being trapped. If you sit near the window and look out, fears of crashing and/or falling can intensify, especially if you fear heights. Although, some people find that looking out at land and clouds gives them a visual fix and they feel more grounded. And they can see what's going on.

➤ Tell the flight attendants about your fears. They're likely to reassure you and watch out for signs of panic.

Birds of a Feather Fly Together

Fear of flying groups are everywhere and are highly recommended. Many of the airlines offer them. Nothing bonds people like a common enemy—fear of flying—or a shared successful experience—conquering your fear.

The Least You Need to Know

➤ Flying, in spite of media attention, is very safe and far safer than driving a car.

➤ People who fear flying may fear crashing, entrapment, heights, loss of control or getting a panic attack.

➤ In some cases, inner ear malfunction may underlie or contribute to a fear of flying.

➤ Conquering fear of flying can be done quickly and has a high success rate.

Chapter 12

Antidote to People Allergy

In This Chapter

➤ Why life is often lonely for the people-shy

➤ What makes people afraid of people

➤ Situations that make you wish you could disappear

➤ Finding your comfort zone among people

If you fear elevators, you take the stairs. If you fear flying, you take the train. But what if you fear people? How do you live your life avoiding social contact? What alternative is available? This is the dilemma faced by the *social phobic*.

Millions of people are social phobics, though many don't know it. Unlike other phobias, for example, claustrophobia or aviophobia, social phobia can be camouflaged. You are aware of your loneliness, that you often alienate people, that you prefer solitude, and you find it hard to get close to others. But you attribute these problems to shyness, an unhappy childhood, too many rejections, or you believe that others are too shallow to understand and appreciate you.

Yet your avoidance of people is as irrational as walking up twenty flights of stairs to avoid taking an elevator, or passing up a vacation in Hawaii for fear of flying. And it strikes far more ferociously, imprisoning you emotionally and mentally, keeping you from that which makes life most worth living—human connections.

In this chapter, you will discover what makes people uncomfortable with other people. And you will learn ways to help you break free from your uneasiness and anxiety, to thus enable you to lead a fuller and more satisfying life.

Social Misfits

Do you think of yourself as shy? Many people do and experience mild social anxiety and worry about being rejected. But *social phobia* goes beyond shyness. Social phobics are *painfully* shy. Some feel so intensely awkward and anxious with others that they blush, tremble, perspire profusely, and continually run to the bathroom to urinate, and perhaps to hide.

Terror Talk

A **social phobia** is a persistent fear of one or more situations in which the person is exposed to possible scrutiny by others and worries about doing something or acting in a way that will be humiliating or embarrassing.

What is at the heart of such people fear? The concern that you will say or do something stupid that would invite criticism and contempt, and thus rejection. This is a fundamental fear of all humans since it results in abandonment by the group, which, certainly in earlier times, meant likely death. Because you are a person who strongly needs the understanding and approval of others, you feel the threat of banishment more intensely and find disapproval especially humiliating and shameful. To prevent such a catastrophe, you live with your head in the sand and prefer loneliness and melancholy to rebuff and disapproval.

Bryan, a handsome, 20-year-old computer science major at a prestigious college, is a garden-variety social phobic. He has always felt shy and never spoke up in class. At college, he tried to restrict his courses to large lectures, requiring neither classroom participation, nor oral presentations. He's afraid to ask a girl out for a date, worried that he won't know what to say and will mumble something ridiculous, or that he will become tongue-tied and say nothing. He belongs to no social groups. At parties, he feels like a fish out of water and sweats profusely, drinks too much, and almost never lets his back leave the wall.

Angst Bulletin

Only five percent of the population has social phobia, though as high as 40 percent of the population view themselves as shy.

He has one friend, but generally waits for him to call. Even then, he usually claims lack of time for getting together. Most of the time, he stays alone in his room where, studying and playing endless computer games, he doesn't have to worry about mumbling and blushing and feeling like he wants to disappear. His one on-going social contact is a sports club, where he does weight training and avoids making eye contact with others. If people initiate conversation, he answers politely but briefly and then averts his gaze.

Red All Over and Nowhere to Run

Social phobics like Bryan tend to be recluses. They avoid situations where public ridicule is possible. Here is a list of some of the most prevalent:

➤ Public speaking (see the next chapter)

➤ Entertaining an audience (see the next chapter)

➤ Taking tests (see Chapter 14) and writing

➤ Dating

➤ Writing or signing your name in front of others

➤ Eating and drinking in public

➤ Using public toilets

Watch It!

If you are a social phobic and experience some sexual dysfunction, such as impotence in men and frigidity in women, it may be related to your social phobia. After failing once in bed, you may be apprehensive about failing again, making you reluctant to enter into new relationships.

Let's look more closely at some of these situations:

➤ Taking tests and writing: Out of worry that whatever you produce won't be good enough or acceptable to other people, you freeze while taking an exam, or get blocked when trying to write something original. In Chapter 14, I will talk about taking tests and the fear of failure.

➤ Eating or drinking in front of other people: You worry about choking on, dropping or spilling food and consequently looking foolish.

➤ Writing in front of others: You worry that if people watch as you sign your name on a check or fill out a form, your hand might tense up and your handwriting will look like chicken scratching, which will make you look like a slob. Or you might misspell a word, appearing uneducated. Or your hand might shake, as if you were mentally unbalanced. Consequently, your hands may become stiff and start to tremble a bit.

➤ Using public toilets: You are self-conscious about relieving yourself in public but never dare told anyone. If you are female, and if someone else is present, you may worry that you must urinate in a hurry, lest that someone else need the stall. Consequently, though you were ready to pee in your pants, when you sit down on the toilet you suddenly have the "bashful bladder" syndrome, and can't pee a drop. You might also worry about taking too long and you imagine everyone

Fear Forum

"Twere blush, blush, blush with me every minute of the time, when she was speaking to me."
—Thomas Harding, *Far From the Madding Crowd*

wondering, "what's taking her so long?" You may be sensitive to the sounds you make and, if you pass gas, feel that no one else makes such loud noises and that people will wonder what's wrong with you. If you are a man with this phobia, you might have somewhat different concerns, since men's restrooms don't have private stalls for urinating. If other men are around when you use the urinal, you become anxious that you may be unable to urinate right away. When you don't, you worry that someone might think that you're masturbating, as if you're some kind of a pervert, or that you're gay or, if you are, that you will reveal yourself. These thoughts only make it more difficult for your bladder to relax and for you to urinate.

➤ Dating: The thought of asking someone for a date evokes two fears: rejection and acceptance. First, you worry that the person will refuse a date or, if they accept, they are doing so to be nice, or even out of pity. Should you go out with them, you fear behaving in such as way as to invite rejection or ridicule.

➤ Doing things alone: Lacking friends with whom to socialize, you sometimes try going alone to a restaurant, a movie, a sporting event, the theatre or even on a vacation. But the solo route only makes you feel defective and worry that people will look at you with pity and wonder why you're so unpopular. Thus, you generally opt for a rented video and fast food to sitting by yourself in a restaurant or movie theatre.

Some social phobics are apprehensive about many social situations, even all. Others fear only particular situations. Sally, insanely in love with Raffi, fantasized day and night about lying in his arms as they passionately kissed. But when she was with him, she felt so nervous that her hands shook uncontrollably. Horribly ashamed of what he might think of her, she avoided doing anything that involved her hands, like smoking or eating with him. Yet, she loved school and had no problem taking exams or speaking up in class. Jeff, on the other hand, was happily married to Sandra, an outgoing and understanding woman. But he dreaded any situation in which attention was focused on him—speaking in public, eating with friends in a restaurant, even using public telephones.

Is There a Hole I Can Crawl into?

What specifically do social phobics fear when under public scrutiny?

➤ Fear of being looked at: You become self-conscious when people focus their attention on you. For instance, when out to dinner with a group of friends, you begin to make a comment and become aware that people are looking at you. You feel uncomfortable and stop talking, or, out of nervousness, lose your train of thought and blurt out something to embarrass yourself. "Now everyone thinks I'm crazy and stupid," you think to yourself as you begin to feel yourself shrinking. To minimize the likelihood of future embarrassment, you rarely participate in conversation.

Watch It!

When bodily symptoms of anxiety come on rapidly and intensely in a social situation, causing you to feel a powerfully urgent need to flee, you may be in the throes of a panic attack or close to one. See Chapter 15 on how to handle a panic attack.

➤ Fear of people seeing your nervousness: You fear that people will notice your blushed face, sweaty palms, trembling hands, or a quivering voice and that they will view you with contempt or pity. You may begin to avoid situations where your anxiety will be "found out." If you are afraid of someone seeing your trembling hands, you avoid eating or smoking with people. If you fear sweaty palms, you avoid holding your date's hand and the social dancing that you so love. If you are afraid of someone hearing your quivering voice, you avoid public speaking.

➤ Fear of being revealed: You worry that if people really knew you, they would see that you are worthless, stupid, selfish, narcissistic and angry. Like the old Groucho Marx joke, you feel yourself so insignificant that you would not want to belong to a club that would have you as a member.

Angst Bulletin

In Woody Allen's movie *Annie Hall*, the character Annie Hall (Diane Keaton) is the quintessential social misfit—awkward, self-conscious, insecure and bumbling. The original title was Anne Hedonia from the psychological term "anhedonia," which means inability to experience pleasure which, if you're a social phobic, is often your reality.

➤ Fear of not being liked: Since you see yourself as innately flawed, you assume other people will perceive you as such and not like you. When rejected, you feel you are a social misfit—one who inevitably says or does the wrong thing and is better off a hermit. Yet, because you deeply need people—who doesn't?—you compensate for having so little to offer by feigning interest in the other and seeking to please; to avoid offending people, you let yourself be exploited. But since this behavior blocks expression of your real self, it only intensifies your discomfort and confirms your perception that social encounters are uncomfortable and to be avoided. If you do get rejected, you feel relentless shame that further advances avoidance behavior.

➤ Fear of looking foolish: Lacking appropriate social skills, or possessing them but becoming too anxious to use them, you worry that your awkwardness will show through in a social group and that inevitably you will do or say something to make yourself look stupid. The more you worry, the more nervous you get and, ultimately, the more you put your foot in your mouth. Do these situations sound familiar?

1. A lull in the conversation makes you worry about disinterest and rejection and you panic and mumble something inappropriate.

2. People conversing and not looking at you makes you feel uncomfortably ignored and you suddenly interrupt someone. All eyes turn to you. Self-conscious, your mouth fills with cotton and you forget what you were going to say. You turn bright red and blurt out a malapropism or erroneous information.

Symptoms of Social Phobia

Bodily

Blushing	Stomach aches	Nausea
Palpitations	Trembling	Dizziness
Sweating	Headaches	Muscle tenseness
Urinary urgency	Chills	Shortness of breath
Sinking feeling in stomach	Dry throat or mouth	

Thoughts

I look out of place.	I'm ugly.	People see how miserable I am.
People see how nervous I am.	I don't fit in.	I don't know what to say.
I'm talking too loud.	I can't keep up this fake smile.	If I start to speak, I'll stammer.

Feelings

Anxiety	Overwhelmed	Apprehension
Panic	Awkwardness	Pessimism
Confusion	Phoniness	Devastation
Regret	Embarrassment	Rejection
Fearfulness	Sadness	Foolish
Self-conscious	Gauche	Shame
Guilt	Shyness	Hateful
Sorry	Humiliation	Threatened
Ignored	Touchy	Inadequate
Trapped	Incompetent	Troubled
Inferior	Unappreciated	Inhibited
Unattractive	Insecure	Uncomfortable
Isolated	Uneasy	Lonely
Unfulfilled	Melancholy	Used
Miserable	Uptight	Misunderstood
Vulnerable	Muddled	Wishy-washy
Needy	Worried	

Behavior

Nervousness	Disengagement	Worry
Freezing	Self-preoccupation	Escape
Distraction	Avoidance	Substance abuse

Angst Bulletin

Social phobics often misinterpret behavior of others as displays of power or competence, and thus respond with behaviors that signal submission, writes John R. Marshall (*Social Phobia*). For example, they freeze, inhibit their own spontaneous interactions, cringe, crouch, smile appeasingly, anxiously attend, and try to please.

Roots of People Allergy

By now, you probably have discovered whether or not you think you have social phobia. If so, you may wonder what made you such a wallflower, approaching people as if they will bite you. The answer lies in a mixture of your genes, how you were treated, or mistreated, by your parents and life in general, and a maladaptive coping style that maintains your exaggerated fear of social scrutiny.

Born Shy

Shy adults are generally not made but born, as the work of Harvard developmental psychologist Jerome Kagan shows. Kagan has been studying "behaviorally inhibited" infants and children for many years. These babies are fidgety and fretful; they cry at the drop of a hat and get easily frightened. Behind this behavior is a distinct neuro-chemistry that makes the amygdala in the limbic system of their brain easily aroused. Confronted with noise, unpleasant odors, unfamiliar objects and people, their hearts race and blood pressure shoot up, and the stress hormone cortisol streams through their bloodstreams—a response that is not only intense but lasts a while. You can see this hyper-reactivity before birth. A fast heart beat in the womb foretells of an infant likely to be crabby and clingy. A low fetal heart rate foretells of an infant more likely to be smiley and cooey.

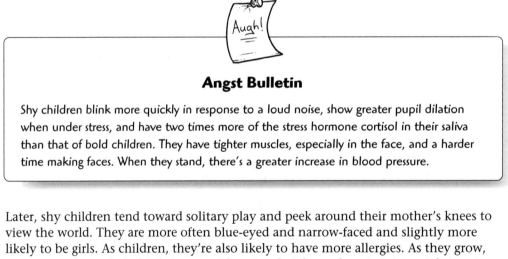

Angst Bulletin

Shy children blink more quickly in response to a loud noise, show greater pupil dilation when under stress, and have two times more of the stress hormone cortisol in their saliva than that of bold children. They have tighter muscles, especially in the face, and a harder time making faces. When they stand, there's a greater increase in blood pressure.

Later, shy children tend toward solitary play and peek around their mother's knees to view the world. They are more often blue-eyed and narrow-faced and slightly more likely to be girls. As children, they're also likely to have more allergies. As they grow, precursors of social phobia become evident in a heightened anxiety in social situations and a proneness to guilt and self-reproach. At the onset of puberty, ordinary alarms, like a first date or a big exam, can set off panic symptoms or even panic attacks.

A tendency for social phobia appears inherited. In a 1979 study by Dr. Svenn Torgerson, greater incidence of social fears, such as concerns about being watched by strangers while working or eating, were found to be more prevalent among identical twins than fraternal twins.

If shyness is part of our genetic endowment, a tendency to be alert to disapproval, which is at the heart of social phobia, is part of our evolutionary makeup. Since we must be aware of potential threats, we pay close attention to signs of disapproval from others—a frown, a grimace, a snarl. Shy infants, who are more sensitive to environmental cues, pick up signs of disapproval more easily and get more vexed by them—such as a mother's frowning face.

The social phobic's greater sensitivity to disapproval, along with an expectation of negative appraisal, helps explain why they avoid eye contact. Our eyes, the window to our soul, easily reveal our emotions. If disapproval is detected, looking away helps deflect some of the resulting humiliation and shame. Fright is also lessened, since looking away disarms the other person. Note how threatened animals avoid eye contact, which is perceived as aggression.

At the first sign of disapproval from others, very socially anxious people assume other submissive and appeasing behaviors as well: flattened voice tone; inability to speak up and project; curved, head-drooping body posture; and habitual apologies and self-denigrating statements.

Emotional Lessons and Shyness

If you were born shy, it's not necessarily a social death sentence. With the right emotional lessons, particularly those taught by your mother, many infants overcome their basic shyness and risk for social phobia. The key, found Kagan, is for the mother to gently prod her child to explore new people and situations. In this way, children learn how to cope with mild anxiety and frustration on their own and to gain some mastery over their fears.

How this emotional lesson is taught, however, is crucial. Imagine two different scenarios with shy children. Jillian's mother sits with her as she plays in the sand. After a bit, her mother smiles warmly and says, "I'll be right back, Jillian. Maybe you would like to show Jeremy your new shovel in the meantime." Confident that her mother will soon return, Jillian feels safe and is able to tolerate some discomfort and to play with Jeremy. Her mother approves of her and so, in spite of her greater anxiety, Jillian approves of herself.

Peter is not so lucky. His mother plops him down and says, "Peter, play in the sand with Jeremy" and then turns to her book. Peter looks warily around and just sits there. His mother looks up. "Oh, Peter,

Secret Weapons

Developmental psychologist Jerome Kagan found that if parents do not overprotect their shy children, many will overcome their basic shyness. Though 15 to 20 percent of children are born shy, one out of three infants lose their timidity by kindergarten.

why are you such a baby? Can't you play like the other children?" At this, Peter starts to whimper. His mother doesn't budge. Peter continues whimpering and looking lost; he makes no effort to play with the other child. Even if he does, it will be with duress: there's is no safety net to fall into should he need protection from his overwhelming feelings. His natural sensitivity to disapproval—recall how the inhibited infant gets easily distraught over even a mother's frown—gets intensified and prolonged by his mother's critical and disapproving manner. As this situation is repeated time after time, the belief that people are dangerously disapproving and rejecting becomes set in the child's mind and remains stubbornly hard to reset. Later, at the first sign of disinterest, his smile gets doused like an ash tray fire. Disapproved of by his mother, the child ultimately disapproves of himself.

Parents' behavior can be a precursor to later social phobia in other ways. Parents are role models. If they themselves behave with anxiety in social situations, their children might imitate this behavior. Likewise, if the parents possess inappropriate social skills, they will teach their children these same inappropriate social skills.

Learning the Wrong Lesson from Social Blunders

Having experienced what you perceive as a traumatic social faux pas in your formative years is another precursor for a social phobia. Yet all children make social blunders: misspelling a word in front of the class; falling down the stairs; spilling your pop all over your clothes. When this happens to inhibited children of supportive parents, they experience some discomfort and embarrassment but get over it. When this happens to inhibited children who lack parental approval and support, they experience intense unease and shame and the blunder looms in their mind as traumatic. Consequently, they may attempt to avoid the situation in which it occurred—like never raising their hand again in class.

Talking Yourself into Humiliation

Terry tells a joke and forgets the punch line. Humiliated, she wishes the earth would open up and swallow her, and she vows to never tell a joke again. Gina tells a joke and forgets the punch line. She says "Oh God—there goes my Alzheimer's again." Everyone starts laughing, tension is released, and the incident is quickly forgotten by all—including Gina, who soon tells another joke without memory lapse.

It's not what happens to us but how we interpret what happens that influences us. According to Dr. Aaron Beck, social phobics make two fundamental errors in how they perceive a social situation: they exaggerate the likelihood of something bad happening—disapproval.

Fear Forum

"What disturbs men's minds is not events but their judgment on events."
—Epictetus

And they exaggerate the consequences should this bad event occur—no one will like you. Later on in this chapter, I'll talk about ways to change these distorted perceptions.

Maladaptive Coping

If inborn temperament, childhood experiences and faulty perceptions create social phobia, maladaptive coping strategies, like the following, maintain it:

➤ Avoidance: Feeling awkward in a social situation, you avoid it. This prevents you from learning about your faulty perceptions, undermines your self-confidence and reinforces your phobia.

➤ Obsessing: You mull over in your mind everything you did and said to embarrass yourself and how others reacted to you. This increases your anxiety and the likelihood of the situation repeating itself and you expect the worst case scenario.

➤ Self-Preoccupation: Worried about your behavior with others, you monitor your actions. Any discomfort or negative sign and you point your finger at yourself: "He thinks I'm a dodo." or "I am so boring." These thoughts in turn increase your anxiety and self-consciousness and the likelihood that you will continue to behave awkwardly.

To sum up, the origins of social phobia are:

➤ Inborn reactivity to new situations and people, along with sensitivity to disapproval

➤ A non-supportive and critical early environment

➤ Misperception of threats as exaggerated

➤ Maladaptive coping styles, such as worry, avoidance and self-preoccupation that maintains the phobia

Social Phobia Self-Quiz

By now you have a good idea as to whether or not you are socially phobic. If so, your first step in recovery is to identify the situations in which this phobia occurs. Start by taking this self-quiz and rating your anxiety-inducing situations from 1-5 (mild discomfort, moderate discomfort, major discomfort, acute discomfort, panic). A high score suggests a corresponding high degree of social phobia.

Secret Weapons

Before going out socially, try some natural calming herbs like kava or valerian root (see Chapter 6) or calming amino acids (see Chapter 9). If these are ineffective and you wish to try a prescription tranquilizer, like Xanax, or beta-blockers, be sure and do so under a doctor's care.

Social Phobia Self-Quiz

___ Parties

___ Initiating conversation

___ Maintaining eye contact when conversing

___ Shaking hands

___ Engaging in conversation

___ Asking someone for a date

___ Meeting new people

___ Talking to someone in authority

___ Talking to someone older than yourself

___ Talking to someone younger than yourself

___ Talking to peers

___ Talking to someone of the same sex

___ Talking to someone of the opposite sex

___ Dancing in public

___ Eating in public

___ Drinking in public

___ Urinating in a public toilet

___ Defecating in a public toilet

___ Writing or signing your name in public

___ Creative writing

___ Public speaking

___ Public performing

___ Going out to dinner alone

___ Going to the movies alone

___ Going to a sporting event alone

___ Going to a lecture alone

___ Using the telephone when others are around

___ Crowds

___ Shopping centers

___ Standing in lines

___ Using public transportation

From Tiptoeing to Tap Dancing

Now that you have identified the situations that discombobulate you, how do you get un-discombobulated? First, have patience—years of social discomfort, faulty thinking, and maladaptive behavior can't be torn down overnight, but need to be chipped away gradually. You might need therapy in addition to self-help. Nevertheless, you can do much on your own to calm your body, quiet your mind, learn to assert yourself, and polish up your social skills, thereby helping you to reduce your anxiety to a more tolerable level.

Cooling Down

Since you are naturally reactive and easily excitable—a born nervous wreck—you must be reborn as a calmer person. To this end, relaxation techniques are essential (see Chapter 6 for relaxation exercises), as is proper nutrition to feed your overworked nervous system (see Chapter 9). Exercise and bodywork will help relax your tense muscles, which come from always being on guard, and offer an outlet for the over-abundance of stress chemicals streaming through your system.

Talking Yourself Out of a Corner

How do you feel if you see someone spill something in a restaurant, or flub up a punch line, or make noise while in a public toilet? You might feel momentarily embarrassed for them. Or you may be too busy with your own thoughts to give it a moment's notice. But you're unlikely to feel shocked and think this person a total buffoon.

To diminish your deep self-consciousness, you must become aware that few people care if you spill your coffee, have sloppy handwriting, spinach between your teeth, or take forever on the toilet. In other words, you have to change the maladaptive thinking pattern that feeds into your exaggerated concern for the opinions of others, and replace it with more realistic, positive, and constructive thoughts.

Here are some examples:

Situation: Drinking coffee in a public restaurant

➤ Destructive thought: I'm going to shake and spill my coffee.

➤ Constructive thought: I generally don't and if so, people are too pre-occupied to notice me.

Situation: Out to dinner with friends

➤ Destructive thought: If I tell people the funny story that happened to me at work, I'll only botch it.

➤ Constructive thought: If I botch it up, I can say something humorous about having botched it up and the moment will pass with everyone relaxed and enjoying themselves.

Situation: Dancing at a disco

➤ Destructive thought: I probably look like the biggest klutz.

➤ Constructive thought: Hell, not everyone is Barishnykov. I don't think any less of people because they can't dance well.

Imagine All the People

To overcome your people allergy, inoculate yourself one small dose at a time through a fantasy hierarchy of a fear-provoking situation—like asking someone for a date. Go through each step in your mind with a graded series of disturbing statements. Remember to stop if you feel anxious and relax before going on to the next step.

1. You pick up the phone and dial Jennifer's number.
2. Jennifer answers the phone.
3. You identify yourself.
4. Jennifer says, "Hi" enthusiastically.
5. Jennifer says, "Hi" indifferently.
6. Jennifer says, "Who did you say it was?"
7. Jennifer says, "Oh, hi. This isn't a good time."
8. Jennifer says, "Oh, hi. Can I call you back?"
9. Jennifer says, "You're kidding, right?"
10. Jennifer says nothing, but starts laughing out loud.

> **Fear Forum**
>
> "If I ever felt inclined to be timid as I was going into a room full of people, I would say to myself, 'You're the cleverest member of one of the cleverest families in the cleverest class of the cleverest nation in the world—why should you be frightened?'"
> —Beatrice Webb, British economist

When you can tolerate the worst case scenario without undue anxiety, write out a practice answer for each of Jennifer's greetings. When you feel prepared, do some deep breathing and make the phone call.

The Mouse That Roared: Assertiveness Training

Hand in hand with social phobia is non-assertiveness. You worry that expressing your feelings, asking for what you want, or saying no to something you don't want, may invite disapproval and rejection. Consequently, you yield to the desires, preferences, and needs of others, while at the same time discounting your own. This builds up resentment because you don't get your needs met, and tension because you've acted contrary to your own best interest.

Think back on the times that people have directly expressed negative feelings to you, made requests and said no. Though you may have felt a brief sting, it was over the next moment and no harm was done in the relationship. In fact, you felt more comfortable with this person: knowing that they wouldn't pull punches, you knew where you stood and didn't have to second-guess their thoughts and feelings.

To help build self-assertion skills, practice the following exercises—first by mentally rehearsing them, and then by an actual run-through:

Use "I" statements: "I" statements directly communicate what you're thinking or feeling. For example:

➤ "I'm happy that you asked me to have a drink with you."

➤ "I'm really too tired to go bowling this evening."

➤ "I'm annoyed at you for not calling when you said you would."

Make requests: You have the right to ask for something that you want. You can do this directly or indirectly. Some examples:

➤ Direct request: "I'd really appreciate it if you could take out the garbage for me."

➤ Indirect request: "Have you seen the new Sylvester Stallone movie? I'm dying to see it."

Refuse requests: Saying no can be tough but it's better than regretting saying yes afterwards. Listen to your feelings. If you feel hesitant, you either don't want to say yes or feel ambivalent about doing so. Here are the steps to saying no:

➤ Assess whether the request is reasonable: Do I really want to drive 45 minutes in the dark to meet someone at a movie theatre when we could both meet halfway?

➤ Get all the facts: Is the movie playing somewhere closer? Will it be coming soon to a local theatre?

➤ Refuse directly and succinctly with only a brief explanation: I really don't want to go. It's too far for me to drive alone.

Secret Weapons

To increase assertiveness, try assertiveness training groups or workshops. Some helpful books are: Manual Smith, *When I Say No, I Feel Guilty* (NY: The Dial Press, 1975); Herbert Festerheim and Jean Baer, *Don't Say Yes When You Want to Say No* (NY: David McKay, 1975); and Sharon Bower and Gordon Bower, *Asserting Yourself* (Reading, MA: Addison-Wesley, 1976).

Fear Forum

"The only man who is truly free is the one who can turn down an invitation to dinner without giving any excuse."
—Jules Renard

➤ Don't apologize: Apologies like, "I'm really sorry. I don't know what's wrong with me. I just hate to drive alone at night," only weaken your position and make you sound wishy-washy, as if you feel you should really be saying yes.

A Course in Social Skills

If you feel intensely socially awkward, you either lack social skills, or you have them but feel too anxious to use them: small talk is agonizing; one-to-one conversation is a near-death experience. Here are some ways to learn to improve your social skills or to use those you have more effectively:

Secret Weapons

For more information on acquiring better social skills, pick up *Talking with Confidence for the Painfully Shy* by Don Gabor (Three Rivers Press, 1997).

Learning small talk

➤ Think up subjects suitable for casual conversation, like the movies, theatre, new books, enjoyable restaurants, or hobbies.

➤ Practice in your mind what you would like to say.

➤ Think of an opener to a stranger.

Making the move

➤ In a one-to-one social situation, initiate the first move; waiting for the other to do so will only increase your discomfort.

➤ At a party, stand slightly outside a group of people so that you can listen and decide if you wish to enter. Glean who appears the most approachable person, go over in your mind an interesting comment relevant to the conversation, make eye contact with that person and make your move.

Other Tricks

➤ When told someone's name, repeat it so you can remember it and use it in conversation.

➤ Get the other person talking by thinking up open-ended questions—those that can't be answered in a single word. For instance, if you approach someone at a party, you might ask:

1. How did you find out about this party?
2. What do you think of the music they're playing?
3. What do you do?

➤ Get involved in interactive activities of shared interests—athletics, painting, sculpting, card playing, chess, backgammon, and so on. In this way, you are not forced to converse, nor made to feel the center of someone's attention. Involvement in a pleasurable task is relaxing and, when not put on the spot, conversation that does emerge will feel more spontaneous and natural.

➤ Arrange social events that involve two or more people so you are not forced to converse but can initiate conversation when you feel comfortable.

➤ Look for social events at which you have expertise and can converse with expertise.

➤ Seek out the company of extroverts who can help bring you out.

➤ Come armed with an excuse for your nervousness, should it become obvious. Blushing can be explained as being overheated; trembling hands from having had too much coffee or too many cigarettes; sweaty palms as a physical problem which, in many cases, it actually is.

A Little Help from the Medicine Chest

By giving you an inhibited disposition, biology may have dealt you a blow, but it can also be your ally by helping you alter your highly reactive biochemistry. Xanax or Klonopin, and beta blockers are all of value in beating social phobia, as are MAOIs and SSRIs, such as Prozac, Paxil and Zoloft (see Chapter 8).

The Least You Need to Know

➤ Social phobics are not just shy but acutely uncomfortable with people.

➤ Social phobics avoid situations where they feel at risk of public disapproval and embarrassment.

➤ Social phobics are often people born with a shy temperament and have disapproving parents.

➤ You need to learn to assert your right to express your feelings, ask for what you want, and refuse what you don't want.

➤ There are many ways to increase your social skills and feel more comfortable with people.

Chapter 13

Speaking When You're Afraid to Open Your Mouth

What do Barbara Streisand, Carly Simon and Luciano Pavorotti all have in common? Stage fright. In the case of Barbra Streisand and Carly Simon, it was enough to prevent them from performing for years. Fortunately, they both overcame their fears and returned to the stage.

Stage fright, or fear of public performance, tops the list of social phobias and strikes performers, athletes and public speakers alike. Few of us will ever know what it's like to suddenly feel terror while waiting in the wings, preparing to strut our stuff in front of thousands. Many of us, however, do know the fright of standing in front of an audience, even if only composed of three people to whom we're giving a sale presentation.

In this chapter, you will learn some helpful hints for quieting your butterflies when performing in front of others: as an entertainer or speaker; in front of millions, or only a few.

Butterflies Big Time

Stage fright! We all get it. As the curtain rises, or you step up to the podium, you may feel your heart pound, your stomach flutter, your hands sweat and tremble, a tightness in your throat, dizziness or chills—in other words, many of the physical effects of the fight-or-flight response.

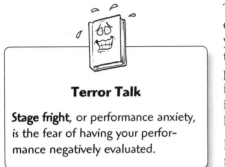

Terror Talk

Stage fright, or performance anxiety, is the fear of having your performance negatively evaluated.

These responses aren't unusual. After all, you are exposing your feelings and vulnerabilities, and setting yourself up for criticism. At a more primitive level, the performance situation, suggests Dr. John Marshall, probably activates dominant/submissive concerns. It is an open display of your goods and a bid for a boost in your status that, should you fail, carries the risk of losing some.

For many, this adrenaline surge enhances their performance. But if you're not used to performing, and if you've convinced yourself that you will fail, you can become frightened by what's happening to your body—in some people to the point where their symptoms balloon into a full-blown panic attack.

Here are some of the more vexing bodily experiences that accompany stage fright and what they mean:

➤ Brain Death: If you're going to speak to an audience or perform where you need to think, one of the most terrifying sensations is of your mind suddenly going blank. This happens because some of the blood normally found in the cranial cavity surrounding the brain has been pumped to vital organs, such as the heart. Rather than operating from the cerebrum—the center of conscious thought—your brain switches over to survival mode and the primitive part of your brain, called the brain stem, takes over. This is why you can't think: your blood supply to the thinking part of your brain has been temporarily cut off.

➤ Jelly Legs: When you perceive danger, your muscles tense to ready you for a quick departure. When you perform, this muscle tension can work against you. For dancers, muscle tension will restrict the flow and execution of movements. For singers and speakers, muscle tension can tighten the jaw muscle, the temporo-mandibular joint (TMJ), which is located where the lower jaw is fastened to the skull, and your throat muscles. Muscle tension also produces jelly legs, or uncontrollable shaking of your legs. Some people are afraid that if they move, their knees will buckle and they will collapse.

➤ Blurred Vision: The presence of too much oxygen in the bloodstream, relative to carbon dioxide, causes the pupils of the eyes to dilate. At the onset of the flight/fight response, you may actually see somewhat better because your senses are heightened and, therefore, may pick up audience facial expressions more easily.

Fear Forum

"The human brain starts working the moment you are born and never stops until you stand up to speak in public."
—George Jessell, 1998-1981

Fortunately, as you begin to concentrate on your performance, the red flag in your brain will lower, in most cases, and the symptoms will subside. But in some people, fears become excessive and take over, interfering with their performance.

Egg on My Face?

What makes some people panic when performing in front of people? The same concern that underlies all of social phobias: the fear of public disapproval. Nor, as the case of performers like Streisand, Simon and Pavarotti attest, does it matter how the public adores you. The fear comes from our inner critic, from our own perception that we may not be good enough to measure up to the audience's—or our—expectations. The more we predict that we will fail and the worse the consequences—loss of our career, our reputation, our self-respect—the more our knees buckle and our hands shake.

The sequence of stage fright looks something like this:

1. You worry that you may disappoint your audience.

2. These fear-provoking thoughts produce anxiety.

3. Your bodily symptoms create unease and you become afraid of feeling afraid, which only confirms your prediction that you will disappoint your audience.

4. You focus your attention on your uncomfortable overexcitation and your divided attention causes you to lose concentration.

5. Having lost concentration, you begin to make errors and your performance suffers, confirming your ineptitude.

6. Any sign of disinterest or disapproval from your audience further confirms your hypothesis that you're a failure, and increases your level of excitation and thus your anxiety. This further debilitates your performance and increases the potential of making future mistakes.

Angst Bulletin

Los Angeles Dodger second baseman Steve Sax was named Rookie-of-the-Year in 1982. During the season, he made a few bad throws and became increasingly focused on not making another mistake. The more he concentrated on not making bad throws, the more anxious he became. The more anxious he became, the worse he actually performed. By the following season, he found it difficult to make even routine throws to first base. More recently, New York Mets catcher Mickey Sasser developed a problem with throwing the ball back to the pitcher, an action that catchers generally do without thought.

Eyes of the Past on You

Sir Laurence Olivier, the famous English actor, was revered and respected as one of the greatest actors of our time. Yet, after almost fifty years of performing, "the terrors" struck him unmercifully at age 57 while on stage in *The Master Builder*. The panic attacks lasted unabated for five and a half years.

So terrified was Olivier when performing on stage, that he gave instructions to the other actors to not look him in the eyes: In spite of being revered by both the audience and his fellow actors, he expected to see disapproval and disappointment reflected in their eyes.

Why would an accomplished talent like Olivier have been plagued with such unrealistic fears? It goes back, in large part, to his childhood and his relationship with his parents, particularly his father. "My father...couldn't see the slightest purpose in my existence," he wrote in his autobiography.

We come to see ourselves as that which is reflected in our parent's eyes. If this is disinterest, we see ourselves as uninteresting. If it's disgust, we see ourselves as disgusting. Later, we view the world through the wounded eyes of the child; somewhere in the audience always lurks the disappointed or disinterested parental face that makes us feel shame, causing us to wish we could disappear. We lower our eyes to shut out the pain of the perceived rejection and, symbolically, to disappear from the other's sight.

Fear Forum

"Stage fright is an animal, a monster which hides in its foul corner without revealing itself, but you know that it is there and that it may come forward at any moment."
—Sir Laurence Olivier, *On Acting*

If you were born with a sensitive nervous system to boot, you experience double jeopardy: an expectation of rejection from others, and a heightened sensitivity that allows you to quickly and intensely pick up these cues. Such was probably the case with the sensitive Sir Laurence Olivier.

The Attack of the "What Ifs"

Before a performance, we all feel some stage fright and self-doubt. How many "what ifs" have floated through your mind before starting your act?

➤ ___ What if others notice I'm nervous?

➤ ___ What if my voice quivers?

➤ ___ What if my hands shake?

➤ ___ What if I get jelly legs?

➤ ___ What if I forget my lines?

➤ ___ What if I sound stupid?

➤ ___ What if I play the wrong notes?

➤ ___ What if I pee in my pants?

➤ ___ What if I faint?

➤ ___ What if someone asks me a question and I can't answer?

➤ ___ What if my mind goes blank?

➤ ___ What if I forget what I'm supposed to say?

➤ ___ What if I trip, or spill my water, or do something else humiliating?

➤ ___ What if I have a panic attack?

How badly these what-ifs trip you up depends on your perceptions and expectations, as well as on the nature of the situation: the characteristics of the place and the audience, your familiarity with the situation, and how much you are the center of attention.

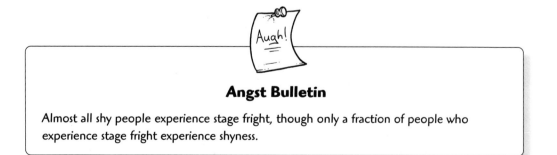

Angst Bulletin

Almost all shy people experience stage fright, though only a fraction of people who experience stage fright experience shyness.

Self-Perceptions:

➤ How much you risk to lose: The greater the consequences of your failure, the greater your stage fright.

➤ How well you believe you will perform: The worse you expect to perform, based both on real past failures and imagined present ones, the greater your anxiety level.

Personal characteristics:

➤ Sensitivity to others' reactions: The more you are bothered by and notice disapproval—a frown, a shake of the head—or disinterest—whispering, staring around the room, getting up and leaving—the greater your self-consciousness and anxiety.

➤ Introversion/extroversion: The more introverted you are, the more quickly and intensely you become overexcited and the longer it takes for you to calm down.

Fear Forum

"All the world's a stage."
—William Shakespeare

Audience characteristics:

➤ Size: Generally, the larger the audience, the greater the stage fright, since there are more people to scrutinize you.

➤ Power: The more important and influential the audience, the greater you perceive your risk.

➤ Competence: The more skilled or knowledgeable your audience, the greater their ability to detect flaws in your performance.

Nature of Performance

➤ Performing alone or in a group: The more you are the center of attention, the greater your jitters.

➤ Competition: The better the other performers relevant to your presentation, the worse you feel you may come across.

Degree of Unfamiliarity

➤ Place familiarity: The more a place differs from where you are accustomed to performing, the less predictable your performance and the more you worry about what could go wrong.

➤ Audience familiarity: If you know members of your audience, the more likely a poor performance may be remembered and discussed. On the other hand, familiar people may be more likely to root for you.

➤ Role familiarity: The more you find yourself in a new and unfamiliar role, the lower your confidence level and the greater your stage fright.

Face the Music and Dance

Now that you know what frightens you about performing or speaking in public, and now that you can identify the situations that exacerbate your fear, how do you overcome stage fright and knock them dead? As with other phobias, you need to attack stage fright on four levels:

1. Physical: You need to learn how to modulate physical excitation so you don't feel overwhelmed with anxiety.

2. Thoughts: You need to stop destructive thoughts.

3. Emotional: You need to learn how to quell your uneasy feelings and panic responses.

4. Actions: You need to learn techniques that make performing easier.

Calm Your Nerves

Stress builds upon stress. The higher your anxiety level leading into your performance, the more quickly it is likely to escalate during your performance. Therefore, use every trick in the book to calm your nervous system beforehand. By helping reduce your performance jitters and panicky feelings, you will begin to feel greater control over your anxiety level. This will help boost your confidence that you can do it—and succeed!

➤ *Herbal Darlings*: To get a good night's sleep the night before the big day and not wake up groggy, try a mixture of kava, valerian root and passion flower (see Chapter Eight) before going to bed. You may also like to try kava before the performance, to relax you. *Gotu kola* is another herb that has a mild calming effect and that improves mental alertness as well. You can mix it with gingko biloba, another powerful herb that clears the cobwebs out of your mind.

Secret Weapons

The herb **gotu kola** has been popular as a mild relaxant for thousands of years in India. It appears to help to vitalize a weakened nervous system, decreasing fatigue and depression, while increasing memory and intelligence. When taken in combination with ginkgo biloba, an herb that improves brain function by increasing cerebral blood flow and oxygenation, you should feel calmer and more mentally alert.

➤ *Relaxation Exercises:* Use progressive relaxation, visualization and meditation (see Chapter 6), to help lower your level of arousal and to keep your symptoms from escalating.

➤ *Breathing Exercises:* Do your deep breathing exercises. The alternate nostril breathing exercise, recommended in Chapter 11 for aviophobics before taking an airplane, helps to quickly quell those pre-performance butterflies and give you greater stamina during the performance.

➤ *Exercise:* A good workout the morning of your performance will help drain excess adrenalin and get your energy flowing outwards, as well as boost serotonin, and release endorphins, the "feel good" chemical, into your bloodstream. Afterwards, you will feel calm, focused, and energized, but not hyper.

➤ *Hypnosis:* Hypnosis has been effective in helping some people overcome their stage fright, but there are shortcomings. If you are a success, you might attribute it to the hypnosis and not to your own efforts, leaving you with the feeling that you have not gained control of this problem.

➤ *Prescription Drugs*: Anti-anxiety drugs help some people control their terror. Valium helped Sir Laurence Olivier eventually conquer his stage fright. Beta-blockers, such as propranolol (Inderal), block the receptors in the heart, muscle, throat, and so on that cause some of the unpleasant sensations associated with stage fright. But as with hypnosis, if you pre-medicate your butterflies away, you run the risk of attributing your success to the drug and to not taking personal credit for overcoming your fear.

Rewrite Your Script

Stage fright is, like all fright, the sense that somehow we are in danger. Our inner dialogue is telling us things like "I'm not good enough." "People will laugh at me." "I can't compete with the other speakers." Thinking is believing, thus the thought alone appears a fait accompli—as good as it having happened.

To rewrite your fear script and talk yourself out of fright, make a list of your destructive thoughts and replace them with constructive ones.

Here are some examples:

Situation: Public Speaking

➤ *Destructive thought*: "I will bore these people."

➤ *Constructive thought*: "I wouldn't have been invited to speak if I were boring."

➤ *Destructive thought*: "My mind will go blank."

➤ *Constructive thought*: "If my mind goes blank, I've got my notes to fall back on."

Situation: Dance Performance

➤ *Destructive thought*: "I'm going to fall flat on my face."

➤ *Constructive thought*: "If I fall, I fall. Even Nureyev fell at times while performing and look how much it harmed his reputation."

➤ *Destructive thought*: "What if my legs start to shake?"

➤ *Constructive thought*: "If my legs start to shake, it will pass as I concentrate on my movements and probably no one will know but me."

Situation: Tennis Match

➤ *Destructive thought*: "I'm never going to be able to return his serve."

➤ *Constructive thought*: "I've returned 90-mile-an-hour serves before and I can do it again."

➤ *Destructive thought*: "I'm going to freeze and lose my concentration."

➤ *Constructive thought*: "If I lose my concentration, I will take a few deep breaths and regain it."

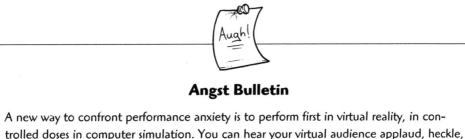

Angst Bulletin

A new way to confront performance anxiety is to perform first in virtual reality, in controlled doses in computer simulation. You can hear your virtual audience applaud, heckle, and see them walk out—a dress rehearsal for your actual performance.

Going Through the Motions

If you find yourself only going through the motions in replacing negative thoughts with constructive ones, and still believe it perfectly reasonable that you will bore your audience or fail to return the opponent's serve, don't be surprised. Changing the way you see the world doesn't happen over night. To help yourself further, try to identify the following logical flaws in your thinking process. These five are among several based on the work of psychiatrist Aaron Beck and identified by David Burns in his 1980 book *Feeling Good*:

Watch It!

Beware of absolutist thoughts that include words like *never, always, all, every, none, no one, nobody, everyone,* and *everybody.* They indicate overgeneralization of one bad experience to all future similar situations. "I'll never get a good job." "No one will ever want to marry me." "Everyone does better than I do."

1. Overgeneralization: You've had one bad experience in the present and assume all future events will repeat this failure. "I'll never be able to do this!"

2. All-or-nothing thoughts: You only think in terms of passing or failing, of succeeding royally or failing miserably. There is no middle ground. If you're not perfect, you're a failure. "This is all wrong."

3. Disqualification of the positive: You perceive yourself as inept and ignore evidence to the contrary. When people tell you how well you did, you tell them how badly you really did.

4. Magnification or Minimization: You blow out of proportion the negatives and then dwell on them, while minimizing your victories and strong points. Minor mistakes loom as catastrophic.

5. Mental Filter: You take an idea out of context and base a conclusion on it while ignoring other valid information. If someone compliments you on your performance and then suggests ways to make it more effective, you take this to mean your whole performance was a failure.

Write these logical flaws on a card and carry it around with you. When scary thoughts go through your mind before performing, write them down and see if they reflect any of these logical flaws.

Secret Weapons

In preparing for your speech or performance, remember that you were invited to perform. Others considered you an expert in the field, someone who has a meaningful experience to share with an audience, or a good performer.

Self Strokes

How do you feel about performing? Scared? Everyone does. Nervous? Everyone does. Terrified? Many people do. But, remember, you were asked to perform because you have something to offer people. If you don't believe it, make a list of self-affirming statements. Some examples:

➤ I got here because I'm good.

➤ I can do this.

➤ I'm going to give my all.

➤ I'm going to enjoy my 15 minutes of fame and milk it for all I can.

➤ How many people get to sing in front of a paying audience?

➤ I am well prepared and should do just fine.

Gradual Exposure

As with the other phobias, you can inoculate yourself against your fear by giving yourself little doses of fright at a time. Construct your own fantasy hierarchy and imagine in your mind each step along the way to the actual performance. Remember to stop and relax after each step before going on to the next. A dancer's fantasy hierarchy might look something like this:

1. I am walking up the theater steps.

2. I am in my dressing room putting on my tights and leotard.

3. I am putting on my make-up.

4. The stage manager comes in and announces 30 minutes until show time.

5. I am backstage doing warm-up stretches.

6. I hear the musicians warming up.

7. The stage manager announces ten minutes until show time.

8. The orchestra starts to play.

9. We take our places on the stage.

10. The curtain goes up.

11. I start dancing my heart out.

Next step—show time!

Practice Makes Perfect

Now that you've psyched yourself up for giving a good performance, what is your best strategy to ensure the least amount of nervousness during the delivery? The answer: Prepare and practice. Then prepare and practice some more. You don't want to learn your performance. You want to *over learn* it so that it just flows out of you. You want to become one with your audience and transcend self. The more performing skills you possess, the more you will think positively about your performance and the less about your stage fright.

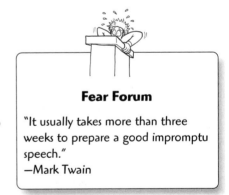

Fear Forum

"It usually takes more than three weeks to prepare a good impromptu speech."
—Mark Twain

Tricks of the Trade

In preparing your performance, identify what might throw you and then devise a game plan to diminish the likelihood of this happening. Here are some examples:

Public speaking

Fear: I will appear disorganized

➤ Make a comprehensive and well-organized outline of your speech, with a beginning, middle and end.

➤ Write or type words or phrases out large enough to be easily read.

➤ Color code key items, like your main points, to help you stay on track and to use as a reference should you lose your place.

➤ Continually connect the ideas and thoughts in your speech to the needs and interests of your audience.

➤ Prepare slides to highlight each point and number and name each one.

➤ Annotate by number and name the place of each slide in your outline and highlight it.

Fear: I will sound boring

➤ Begin with an amusing anecdote, an interesting quote, a shocking statistic, a personal story, or by asking a rhetorical question that your audience could identify with—"Did you ever get those superwoman blues?"

➤ Prepare colorful examples, facts, quotations, and anecdotes.

➤ Make up interesting slides that will highlight each point with information or humor. By amusing and impressing your audience, you gain their confidence.

➤ End your speech with a bang—a power quote or anecdote, for example.

Angst Bulletin

The Buddhist Roshi described the three great fears of the Japanese as dying, going insane, and public speaking—each of which involves entering the unknown.

Fear: I will sound inarticulate

➤ Write out the complete text of your talk in a conversational manner.

➤ Practice saying it slowly.

➤ Record it on a cassette tape. Play it back and see where you falter, or where thoughts don't flow easily. Keep recording it and playing it back until you've got it down pat.

Fear: I will be unable to answer questions

➤ Write out a list of potential questions and their answer.

➤ Should you be unable to answer a question, say you don't know and ask if anyone in the audience can help out.

Fear: The audience knows more than I do

➤ Picture your audience naked—that will cut them down to size.

➤ Use Self-effacing humor: Recounting a funny episode about how you handled an embarrassing or awkward situation builds quick rapport with the audience.

➤ Confide your nervousness—You may gain audience support. In 1981, while performing in front of thousands, singer Carly Simon's stage fright turned into panic. "I had two choices," Carly told a *New York Times* reporter. "I could either leave the stage and say I was sick or tell the audience the truth. I decided to tell them I was having an anxiety attack, and they were incredibly supportive. They said "Go with it—we'll be with you." This didn't stop her thumping heart, which she confessed to the audience. Two songs later, about 5 people came onto the stage and rubbed her arms and legs, and said "We love you." She was able to finish her performance.

Fear Forum

"Speak clearly, if you speak at all; carve every word before you let it fall."
—Oliver Wendell Holmes

Secret Weapons

While waiting your turn to perform or speak, you might eye the competition and find yourself intimidated by their talent, intelligence, and savoir fair. Don't let yourself get trapped in this deadly killer of self-confidence. Leave the room—physically or mentally. Imagine also what the competition might find intimidating about *your* performance.

Fear: When I'm introduced, I will freeze

➤ Take a few seconds to prepare yourself before you begin to speak.

➤ Have your opening lines memorized.

Mental Dress Rehearsal

After you've gotten your performance down pat, go over it in your mind, step by step, word by word, note by note. Then, when you feel ready, perform in front of a friend, a mirror, your children and spouse, or some colleagues.

Show Time

What should you do if you feel anxiety overcoming you during the performance? Refocus your thoughts away from your anxiety. Some suggestions:

1. Glance at your outline.

2. Look at someone in the audience and smile at them—they're bound to smile back.

3. Have something you can rub or fiddle with sitting next to your notes—a koosh ball, worry beads.

4. Snap a rubber band on your wrist.

5. Avoid looking at someone who appears disinterested.

The Least You Need to Know

➤ Everyone gets some stage fright before performing.

➤ The extent of your stage fright depends on how much you perceive you will fail, the severity of the consequences, as well as situational factors.

➤ When preparing for your performance, overlearn your script so that it just flows out of you.

➤ Do all you can to relax yourself the day of your performance.

➤ Use all the tricks of the trade for preparing an effective speech.

Chapter 14

Success or Failure: What's Worse?

In This Chapter

➤ Why optimism opens doors and pessimism shuts them

➤ All the ways success can be scary

➤ Self-efficacy: The key to successful success

➤ Walking yourself into success one step at a time

➤ When all else fails, look to your unconscious

When you think of stage fright, or performance anxiety, you think of fear of failure. But people can also be terrifically afraid of success or of the attaining of it, which can stop you from pursing your goals.

And stage fright happens not only when faced with a theater full of people peering at you but also when performing in front of just one person. In this chapter, we'll look at fear of failure or success during three common events performed for just one person:

➤ When you're being tested by an instructor

➤ When you're being appraised as a potential employee during a job interview

➤ When your masculinity or femininity is being sized up in a "performance of affections" in the bedroom

Fortunately, there are disarmingly simple ways to stop putting off your best work.

Doomed Before You Start

Do you have the "my-cup-is-half-full," optimistic outlook on life or the "my-cup-is-half-empty," pessimistic one? If you are an optimist, you are a hopeful person, tend to have higher self-esteem, and feel that things in life will basically turn out in your favor. For you, nothing succeeds like failure—it motivates you to evaluate your shortcomings and to work to overcome them. When you do succeed, you take credit and feel proud. It spurs you on to even greater conquests.

If you are a pessimist or a negative thinker, failure is devastating and confirms what you already believe about yourself: You are no good. Trying again is too chancy. You feel it's better to play it safe and protect what little self-esteem you possess. With so much to lose, it's not worth taking risks.

But what if you don't fail at your performance? What if you succeed? For the insecure, the sweet smell of success too often reeks of self-doubt, guilt, uncertainty, and anxiety. In spite of fame, fortune and power, you don't learn to own your success.

Do any of these concerns that underlie a fear of success sound familiar?

➤ Undeserving me

➤ Imperfect me

➤ I'm really a sham

➤ Do you love me or my money

➤ I'll be embarrassed in the limelight

➤ Success breeds rejection

➤ Success doesn't buy love so why bother

➤ I'll never beat this performance

➤ Success in sex requires too much risky intimacy

Undeserving Me

If you have low self-esteem, some part of you feels that you are too wretched a person to deserve to triumph. Sir Laurence Olivier attributed his stage fright to, "some overblown claim to pride in myself that would be bound to find the punishment that it deserved," as if he had no right to feel good about himself and his talent.

Imperfect Me

Underneath overblown pride, or narcissism, is the opposite feeling—that you are inherently flawed. To compensate, you strive for perfection and set unrealistically high expectations for yourself, others, and life. When, inevitably, things fall short, you become disappointed and self-critical. Even when enormously successful, you zoom in on the fly in the ointment and tend to discount and ignore what's good. You compare yourself to others, minimize your own achievements and feel like a failure—worse than nothing. And you project this self-hate onto others and assume that they too despise you for being so defective.

Fear Forum

"He who fears being conquered is sure of defeat."
—Napoleon Bonaparte

What drives people to perfectionism? Perhaps you had critical parents who expected perfection—"Only a B+ on your exam?"—and didn't understand the words "I can't." Regardless of your accomplishments, it was never enough to please them. Often these are parents who, like the quintessential stage mother, feel their child must become all they couldn't: "I sacrificed for you and you have to make-up for what I missed." Later, the whole world becomes a stage on which you play out your childhood longings for parental approval. If you give a perfect performance, you will be successful. Everyone will love you and your mother or father will finally come to see your worth. When you fall short of perfection, you see in your mind's eye that reflection of your parent's disappointment and feel like less than nothing.

Angst Bulletin

In the movie, *Shine*, piano prodigy David Helfgott was pressured by his domineering father, a man impassioned by music, to enter piano competitions, the first one at age nine. Living vicariously through his son, and acting as his tutor, mentor, and, ultimately tormentor, Peter Helfgott expected David to win and was personally wounded if he didn't. When David was offered a scholarship to study in London, which threatened the father's control of his son's career, Peter Helfgott became enraged and forbade it. The ensuing bitterness was apparently a catalyst in the nervous disorder that kept Helfgott in psychiatric institutions for over a decade.

The same need for perfection happens when you had a "perfect" parent or sibling and felt you couldn't compete. To make it worse, you were always compared. "Why can't you be smart like your sister Sue?" "Why can't you be a go-getter like your brother Brad?" In some cases, these perceptions were realistic: You were born with less talent than other family members; trying to compete is hopeless. In other cases, you falsely perceive your lack of abilities in light of the idealized parent or better sibling.

Patti, an undergraduate at a state college, had terrific test anxiety. Though exceptionally bright and always well prepared for an exam, she would convince herself that she would fail miserably and referred to herself as "the retard." The day of the test, she would wake up feeling nervous and worried that she had not mastered the material. By the time she sat down to take the exam, she had worked herself into a frenzy and froze. The page was a blur and her mind went blank. Often, she felt so nervous during an exam that she felt she would vomit.

Patti's mother was beautiful, charming, and an accomplished pianist, adored by everyone. Patti, in contrast, was quiet, a bit chunky and socially awkward. How could she ever do anything to match up to her perfect mother, who expected perfection, and her demanding father, who expected her to be like her perfect mother? "Why can't you be friendly and smile at people, like your mother does?" he would ask. "Why can't you care about your appearance? Look how well your mother puts herself together." No matter what success she achieved, it would fall short of what her exemplary and wonderful mother could do. Nor would her father ever love and adore her as he did her brilliant mother.

Watch It!

"I'm a sham blues" can keep the greatest from enjoying fame. Bob Fosse, Broadway's foremost choreographer during the late '60s and the '70s (*Chicago*, the movie *Cabaret*, and the musical *Fosse*, which celebrated his work on Broadway), viewed his successes as failures. In 1973, when he won a triple crown—the Oscar, a Tony, and an Emmy—he told his friends it was all a sham: "I fooled everybody."

I'm Really a Sham!

If you feel inherently inadequate, anything short of perfection makes you experience success as a sham—a cover-up for "a multitude of blunders," as George Bernard Shaw said. You have, as psychologists call it, the "imposter syndrome," and consequently, you feel guilty for cheating people who believe you to be better than you actually are. If they only knew! The only solution is to strive even harder for perfection.

Jacqueline sat staring at the man in front of her, the person with the power to give or deny her the job of a lifetime—an interior designer at one of the top firms. He looked carefully at her portfolio. "You're work is quite impressive," he said. She smiled coyly, squirmed in her seat and giggled nervously. "Do you really think so?" she said. "Yes," he responded. "Your work is good."

"Oh," said Jacqueline, "well, I mean…God, the girl before me had an incredible portfolio." "Shut up, Jacqueline," she told herself, "you're totally screwing up." He asked her what kind of salary she was looking for. "$50,000 a year," she blurted. $50,000! What possessed her to say that?

Out of a deep feeling that her work was really inferior, Jacqueline approached the interview undermining her competence by doubting her abilities. Then, to compensate, she over-inflated her worth and asked for an entry level salary that she knew was unrealistic at the ground level. Afterwards, she felt deeply ashamed and couldn't stop chastising herself for ruining an incredible career opportunity, financial independence and self-respect. All she could think of was how to make her work better and better so people would not find out it was really mediocre.

Do You Love Me or My Money?

What would it be like getting your fifteen minutes of fame, you wonder? So much attention. So much love. Wait! Is it love? Or is it the dinners you can buy? The people you know? The prestige of being with you?

Another frightening aspect of success is the uncertainty that people may not value you for who you are, or even know who you are, but rather for what you can do for them.

Angst Bulletin

Mark Schaller, Ph.D., of the University of Columbia, found that the constant attention that comes with fame made some acutely self-conscious. In the works of songwriters Kurt Cobain and Cole Porter and of writer John Cheever, he found that the use of first person singular, or self-reference, jumped after each became famous. The need to escape agonizing self-awareness may have led Porter and Cheever to become alcoholics and to the heroin addiction that eventually led Cobain to suicide.

I'll Be Embarrassed in the Limelight

Some people, especially those who are shy and introverted, feel embarrassed being the center of attention and balk at being in the limelight. The more visible you are, the more open you are to public scrutiny and the more obvious your blemishes. Larry, one of several singers in a rock band, felt this fear of visibility. Though his voice was good enough to sing solo, which the band encouraged, he preferred the less noticeable back-up position.

Talent can, however, overcome shyness with the right kind of support, as you may remember from Chapter 12. But Larry's mother, deeply worried about public opinion, appeared to have her own strong fear of failure, or success. Should your child succeed more than others, people might think that the parents have become too big for their britches. When Larry would burst into song for his friends, his mother would grimace and ask, "Must you be such a show-off?" She discouraged Larry from trying out for parts in the school musicals. What if he forgot his lines? What if he made mistakes? He might embarrass his father and her. Discouraged for his efforts, Larry felt guilty for doing well. Success brought not reward—it brought punishment.

What else might make a parent want to hold their child back?

Angst Bulletin

In the 1970s, Matina Horner, former president of Radcliffe College, found that women conceived getting ahead differently than men. Many women fear that success will bring social rejection.

Will You Still Love Me Tomorrow?

Success can punish in other ways: It can cause you to lose popularity contests—especially if you're female. Getting ahead of friends, co-workers, parents, spouses can be intimidating and threaten the other's self-worth. "There's always something about your success that displeases even your best friends," said Mark Twain. Your mother may feel threatened by your success if it reminds her of her own shortcomings. But it is surpassing your father and your spouse that really makes success costly, frequently bringing hostility, loss of love, and even abandonment.

It is this risk of losing "we" in the pursuit of "me" that is the core of the modern woman's dilemma. For most, the solution is at best a compromise: Keep your spouse and narrow your quest for self-fulfillment; or pursue your dreams at the risk of a lonely journey. Is it any wonder so many women sabotage their own success?

For men who get ahead of their own fathers, success may also come mixed with loss.

Fear of social rejection begins in childhood, when parents, who are threatened by children whose abilities and accomplishments may outmatch their own, unconsciously discourage their children from succeeding. The parent may react with disinterest to the child's accomplishments. Making the gymnastics team or getting an "A" on a spelling exam is met with an indifferent "that's good." The carefully designed

Valentine card is quickly tossed in the garbage, instead of being displayed on the refrigerator door. Or the child may get the high five and a seemingly proud smile but it is obviously phony and forced. When the child works hard, the parent might make comments like, "Don't study so hard. You'll tire yourself." Or, "I don't care if you win, only that you have a good time." Consequently, success carries a mixed blessing: pride mixed with guilt, as if their child has done something of which to feel ashamed. To not risk losing the parent's love, the child adopts a losing strategy: Failure buys love.

Fear Forum

"The deepest principle of Human Nature is the craving to be appreciated."
—William James

As a child, Hannah, a highly intelligent and deep thinking woman, only pleased her deeply insecure father if she behaved ineptly. When she spilled her milk, he laughed as if she were so adorable. When she brought home a highly creative paper Easter bonnet that she made and that won first place, he dismissed it as "nice" and "accidentally" sat on it. In seventh grade, she signed her best friend's yearbook "Goofy" because goofiness got you love; competence got you rejection.

Although Hannah eventually become an internationally recognized artist, it wasn't until she was in her 30s, and only then after five years of analysis, that she could even finish a painting. Freeing her imprisoned talents and abilities meant sacrificing her father's stultifying love—relinquishing the occasional twinkle in his eye and settling only for the usual long silences, interspersed with indifference and anger. It was a hard risk to take; her self-worth had depended on her father's approval. Only after she had strengthened and solidified her sense of self through analysis could she begin to understand and accept that the fault lay within him, not within her—that it was his own insecurities that prevented him from appreciating her strengths, not something inherently unlovable about her. When her self-worth no longer depended on his love, her muses broke free and took flight.

Success Doesn't Buy Love, So Why Bother?

Succeeding at something takes hard work and not everyone has Hannah's strong drive against all odds. Most expect some payoff: money, a smile, a word of congratulation. When you don't get it—your spouse didn't compliment you for getting an "A" on your exam; your boss, always quick to tell you when you've done something wrong, said nothing about how you handled that client with finesse—you may feel success is not worth the effort and not try again.

You tell yourself that it shouldn't matter—that your self-worth should not ride on the compliments of others. But that doesn't stop the hurt. If you had hard-to-please parents, nothing you ever did was enough to get that smile and gleam in their eye. When people fail to notice and comment on your successes, you feel that old sting of parental indifference or anger surface, and success, rather than make you happy, makes you feel anxious.

199

I'll Never Beat This Performance

Success is a two-edged sword. The more you succeed, the more people expect. Some people, especially performers and athletes, experience this as an overwhelming responsibility and worry; "Can I produce again? Will I disappoint?"

These fears surface as well in the bedroom, especially for men. Once you've exhibited sexual savoir-faire, you set up a standard that you believe your partner expects you to meet.

Success in Sex Requires Too Much Risky Intimacy

Bedroom success can also be scary for the intimate shy. Gabriel, a deeply avoidant person, is a good example. Though he had been dating Dorie for three years, the relationship had progressed little and they saw each other only two to three times a week, generally at Dorie's initiative. While she continually pressed for them to live together and eventually marry, he constantly protested that he needed his independence and space. Sex left much to be desired.

When Gabriel stayed over at Dorie's, he got into bed as late as possible in the hope that she would be asleep. Positioning himself at the edge of the other side of the king-sized bed, he turned his body away from her and said "good night"—no kiss, no pat, no hug. In the morning, he got up before her and did not touch her. During the infrequent times that they had sex, neither enjoyed it: Gabriel was too tense; Dorie was too disappointed in his "performance." Sex never began with kissing but with brief perfunctory foreplay that lacked passion. Then Gabriel would penetrate Dorie. His breathing tight and constricted and his movements fast and stilted, he would make a few quick thrusts, stop, then repeat this pattern. This erratic rhythm, which made it impossible for Dorie to enjoy intercourse, would go on for twenty minutes or so until finally he ejaculated, though he did not have a full, orgiastic feeling. Dorie went to bed frustrated, or snuck into the living room when he was asleep and masturbated to orgasm. Sometimes when Dorie got Gabriel very excited, he would take her hand away and masturbate to orgasm.

Gabriel equated enjoying sex with enjoying Dorie. But if he enjoyed her, he must care about her and, much worse, need her. To protect himself from such dangerous feelings, which threatened to overwhelm him with a powerful need for love and a catastrophic fear of rejection and loss of self, he felt compelled to behave toward

Dorie as if she were unimportant to him. To maintain this illusion, he denied all passion. When it emerged, he masturbated to orgasm, thus convincing himself that it wasn't Dorie that excited him but that he had excited himself.

The Approach/Avoid Trap

The uncomfortable feelings associated with failure or success create ambivalence, what psychologists call the approach-avoidance conflict: there's something we want but also fear and we cannot have one without the other. Gabriel wanted Dorie's love desperately (approach), but feared expressing this (avoidance), lest he open a Pandora's box of desires that would overwhelm him and scare Dorie away. You desire a master's degree to further your education (approach), but fear the anxiety of test taking (avoidance). You want a more challenging job (approach), but fear being turned down (avoidance).

The devil sitting on one shoulder, mouthing off about all the bad things that can happen to you, almost always has a louder voice than the angel sitting on the other shoulder, egging you on. This puts a real damper on your performance, as the rewards for performing get obscured by fear-provoking thoughts and their accompanying anxiety.

If that old devil fear has enough of a say, you may avoid performing altogether. This is perilous. Not only do you lose the satisfaction from performing, but the avoidance also feeds on itself. The relief you feel at not having to perform increases the likelihood of continued avoidance and you get nowhere.

Sometimes we cannot avoid and feel forced into a position where we must perform. What do we do? Procrastinate—a kind of avoidance. You put off studying for your exam until the night before and then arrive ill-prepared. You stall sex by playing computer games late into the night; by the time you get into bed, you only have time for a disappointing quickie. You get dressed for your job interview at the last moment and arrive late and missing a button on your shirt. Inadequately prepared, procrastination makes your performance worse and failures intensify.

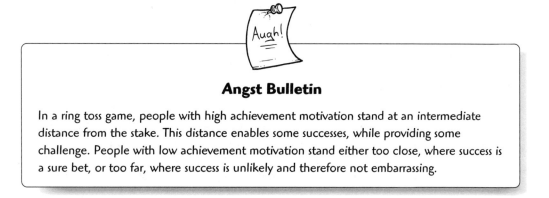

Angst Bulletin

In a ring toss game, people with high achievement motivation stand at an intermediate distance from the stake. This distance enables some successes, while providing some challenge. People with low achievement motivation stand either too close, where success is a sure bet, or too far, where success is unlikely and therefore not embarrassing.

Learned Helplessness

After a string of failures, you risk developing *learned helplessness*—the feeling that nothing that you do makes any difference so why continue to try. At this point, you become passive and give up pursuing your goal altogether. Rather than take another exam, you quit college. Rather than get one more job rejection, you stop sending out résumés.

The Crabby Gene

Once you get caught up in the rut of learned helplessness, you feel like a loser—a weak, self-destructive person who continually disappoints others and yourself. Why am I like this, you wonder? You may have been dealt some tough blows—a rough childhood, a rough life. But this is only a small piece of the puzzle. Actually, there's scientific evidence that suggests that optimism or pessimism is an inborn trait. If you're lucky, you inherited a cheery, hopeful disposition and approach life expecting good things. If you're unlucky, you inherited a crabby, gloomy one and approach life expecting the worst. Most of us inherit a disposition somewhere in the middle.

If it's not in your nature to look for the silver lining, don't give up. Though you have a bias to be crabby, hope can also be learned.

Fear Forum

"There is nothing either good or bad/ But thinking makes it so."
—Shakespeare, *Hamlet*

Learning Hope

What is the secret to learning to be more hopeful and upbeat? Building *self-efficacy*—the belief that you have mastery over the events in your life and can meet challenges as they come up. With it, you will feel safe enough to fail or succeed and persist in seeking your goal; without it, you will feel too vulnerable to risk the negative feelings associated with failing or succeeding and continue to procrastinate.

How do you build self-efficacy? This is a bit tricky. If you have high self-esteem, you possess an *internal locus of control,* meaning you naturally feel you can control your own destiny. Confident of your abilities, you choose moderately difficult tasks in which success is both attainable and attributable to your own skill and effort. Should you fail, you attribute it to something controllable, like not preparing sufficiently. In the future, you prepare better, which increases the likelihood of success and, in turn, confirms your belief in your own power to effect your destiny.

If you have low self-esteem, you have an *external locus of control,* meaning that you tend to feel that chance or outside forces determine your fate. Consequently, you choose tasks that are either very easy, making success likely, or very difficult, so that success is unlikely or failure is not embarrassing. When you succeed, you attribute it to luck—who wouldn't pass such an easy exam? Not taking credit for your accomplishments, success fails to increase self-efficacy and leaves you caught in a Catch-22: To increase your feeling of personal mastery, you need to experience success, but when you do, you don't take credit.

How do you break this negative feedback cycle and increase self-efficacy?

➤ Change the negative thinking that prevents you from enjoying success and taking credit.

➤ Build success one small step at a time so that it doesn't overwhelm you with responsibility, guilt, and fear of loss.

➤ Boost self-esteem so that you can feel a sense of self-worth that doesn't ride on the other's approval or on being perfect.

The question I'm sure you're asking now is "How?".

Talking Yourself Out of Failing Thoughts

Remember Patti? On the day of her child development midterm results, Patti sat at her seat with a cut-out paper "F" stuck to her forehead. The teacher looked at her and chuckled—she knew that Patti was, in fact, the only A in class. When she handed Patti her test score sheet, she expected a surprised smile of relief. Instead, Patti looked at it and mumbled disconcertedly, "I should have cut out a bigger 'F.'" Patti was too convinced that she had failed for the "A" to register.

When she found out her error, she expressed not relief at her A but more worry. "I'm really worried about my classroom presentation," she commented to the professor. Stuck in a negative thought pattern, success was only a brief, transitory way-stop on a failure track.

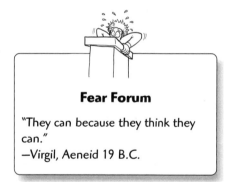

Fear Forum

"They can because they think they can."
—Virgil, Aeneid 19 B.C.

Patti was burdened with mistaken self-beliefs. Far from being a "retard," she was very bright, well read and able. But a strong fear of failure and success filled her with a broken recording of destructive, self-defeating thoughts, such as "I'm stupid" and "I'll never succeed." To increase self-efficacy, she needed to replace those destructive, self-defeating messages with those that are positive and constructive.

➤ Destructive thought: I am an idiot.

➤ Constructive thought: Idiots don't get A's on their exams.

➤ Destructive thought: I'll freeze and never be able to take the exam.

➤ Constructive thought: I won't freeze if I'm well prepared and I relax before the exam.

➤ Destructive thought: Even if I do pass, I'll fail the next time.

➤ Constructive thought: I have the ability to do well on these exams and I can do it.

➤ Destructive thought: If I don't pass this exam, people will think I'm stupid.

➤ Constructive thought: I'm not stupid and I generally only fail exams because I get too nervous. If I can calm myself down, I should do just fine.

Stopping old playbacks is not easy to do. If you've been anxious for a long time, these destructive, negative messages have been playing non-stop for years and become a well-established habit. Generally, it takes either short- or long-term therapy with a mental health professional to help learn a new script. But each time that you can stop a negative thought and replace it with a positive one, you will take a step in conquering your fears.

Fear Forum

"There is a luxury in self-reproach. When we blame ourselves we feel no one else has a right to blame us."
—Oscar Wilde

Starting with the Right ABCs

The ABCs of destructive thinking were outlined by Albert Ellis, the founder of *rational-emotive therapy*, and go something like this. Some *adversity* happens to us, which we think about. These thoughts turn into *beliefs*, which have *consequences*—they become part of how we view ourselves and influence future actions. If you can begin to see your thinking process in this way, you can learn to challenge your thoughts and change them. Let's look at how this might play out with Jacqueline, who worried that she messed up her job interview at an interior design firm.

➤ *Adversity*: Rather than toot her own horn during the interview, she tooted that of the previous interviewee. She then asked for an unrealistic amount of money for an entry-level position.

➤ *Beliefs*: "God, how could I have been so stupid. I'll never get anywhere."

➤ *Consequences:* She felt more miserable, more helpless, more inept, less-efficiency, and sidetracked from planning and deciding her next moves.

➤ *Disputation*: She blew things way out of proportion. Her denial of her talent could have come across as modesty, rather than awkwardness, and her request for $50,000 as an assertive, bold move that might come in handy to get clients to spend more money.

➤ *Outcome*: If she does not get the job, she need not feel discouraged from trying again. If she's concerned about her lack of self-confidence, she can take steps to increase it—by preparing a script ahead of time before the next interview, for instance.

To help dispute the negative thinking that fuels your fear of failure or success, see if you can identify the following logical flaws in your thinking process that were presented in the last chapter:

1. Overgeneralization—"I'll never get a good job."

2. All-or-nothing thoughts—"This is all wrong."

3. Disqualification of the positive—"Oh you're wrong. I am really stupid."

4. Magnification or minimization—"But I misspelled a word!"

5. Mental filter—"You're really telling me that I was lousy in bed, aren't you?"

Remember to write these logical flaws on a card and carry it with you. When you fail or succeed at a task and feel anxious afterwards, look at this card and ask yourself if your thinking reflects any of these logical flaws.

One Small Success at a Time

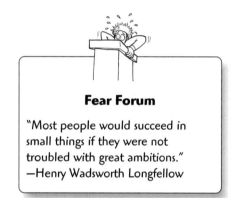

Almost any goal can be achieved if broken down into sufficiently small steps. It doesn't matter how small. Developing a competency of any kind strengthens your sense of self-efficacy and makes the next step easier. The more you succeed, the more willing you become to take more risks and seek out more demanding challenges. The secret is in setting goals that make failure less likely and success manageable.

Fear Forum

"Most people would succeed in small things if they were not troubled with great ambitions."
—Henry Wadsworth Longfellow

Here are some helpful goal-setting strategies:

1. Set realistic goals: Achievement-oriented people don't shoot for the stars unless they are certain they can capture the moon. In other words, before applying to medical school, make sure that you can ace a college chemistry course. Also, look carefully at the reality of issues such as time, energy, and resources. Remember, repeated failures are not only frustrating but can lead to learned helplessness, causing you to give up altogether. Accepting self-limitations and letting go of the need for perfectionism is the ultimate of self-acceptance.

2. Set goals over which you feel the greatest control: The more you can depend on your own actions rather that those of others when pursuing your goals, the more credit you will likely take for your success and as a result, you will feel enhanced self-efficacy.

3. Base goals on your destructive thoughts: The more direct steps you take to challenge your fears, the less they will control your life.

4. Be specific: Outline a game plan that is broken down into a time line and composed of small, discreet steps that will enable you to easily gauge your progress.

5. Give yourself lead way: The more time you have for each step of your journey, the more rewarding your trip. Ultimately, it is the doing, not the getting from which you reap the most rewards.

Succeed at Becoming Your Own Best Friend

People who feel unworthy of success generally have a distorted self-image. You may be smart, attractive and funny, but think of yourself as dumb, ugly and boring. To increase self-efficacy, you need to increase self-esteem—to take care of yourself as if you're worth it (forget those goofy commercials that trivialize this very important self-concept). Here are some suggestions:

Positive Reinforcement: Give yourself a gift for doing well. Patti aced that child development midterm because she promised herself a book for accomplishing her goal.

Self-care: Make a science of fawning over your body, the house of your soul, and your health.

➤ Keep your body and clothing clean

➤ Get enough sleep

➤ Do diaphragmatic breathing exercises

➤ Do relaxation exercises like progressive relaxation or meditation

➤ Engage in physical activity—exercise, cleaning house, taking a walk, yoga stretches

➤ Give up smoking and excessive drinking

➤ Go on a diet

➤ Wear comfortable clothes

Self-nurturance: Give yourself tender, loving care the way a mother does to a baby.

➤ Lounge in a warm, aromatic bath

➤ Take a sauna or steam bath

➤ Burn incense

➤ Buy fresh flowers

➤ Get a massage

➤ Have a manicure or pedicure

➤ Wear cologne or perfume

➤ Buy a desired item you can afford

➤ Buy or adopt a pet

➤ Organize your house and work space

Seek pleasurable activities: Spice up your life with pleasure as often as possible to lift gloom and doom.

➤ Listen to music

➤ Take a vacation

➤ Have sex

➤ Read a good novel

➤ Join a club

➤ Watch a funny video

➤ Sit in the sun or walk in the rain

➤ Take a walk along a lake or the ocean

➤ Watch wild animals

➤ Call a good friend

➤ Call a friend that you have lost touch with

➤ Engage in sports

➤ Attend a sporting event

➤ Rearrange your furniture

➤ Do puzzles

➤ Join a spiritual group

➤ Go for a weekend alone with your spouse

Fear Forum

"Failures are divided into two classes—those who thought and never did, and those who did and never thought."
—John Charles Salak

Set Self-Improvement Goals:

➤ Engage in creative activities

➤ Set an exercise goal and stick with it

➤ Attend a course in something you've always wanted to do

Assert yourself: Learn how to stick up for your rights and express your needs by taking a course, a workshop or buying a book on assertiveness training. Cognitive-behavioral therapy also offers exercises to increase assertiveness.

If at First You Don't Succeed...

Okay. You've done all you can to exorcise your fear of failure-and-success-demons but they still keep biting back and scaring your muses away. In spite of all your efforts, the poetry or song or dance within you stays largely untapped. Why, you wonder, are you such a wimp? Blame it on your unconscious.

If you don't believe Freud's notion that the power of the unconscious affects our behavior and shapes our personality, think back on times when you behaved contrary to your conscious aspirations. You told yourself that you would prepare all week long for your math test but it's ten o'clock the night before and you still haven't cracked the book. Or you decided to make the best impression at a job interview, but somehow mixed up the time and arrived 20 minutes late. Why must you keep behaving like you are your own worst enemy?

Failure Pays

If success doesn't pay off, failure might. As Freud taught us long ago, not succeeding can have important secondary gains or unconscious payoffs. If you have difficulty developing or sustaining motivation to succeed at your goal, ask yourself, "What am I gaining by failing?"

Here are some popular payoffs for not succeeding:

➤ *Failure is safe*: Success threatens loss. Failure to meet your goals or not pursuing them, on the other hand, keeps relationships intact, especially for women.

➤ *Success leads to independence:* As long as you appear helpless and dependent, people will take care of you, give you their attention, support you financially, and free you from having to deal with adult responsibilities. This secondary gain is often what keeps agoraphobics from going out into the world. If your spouse needs control over you to maintain self-worth, your continued dependence helps him feel confident that you won't leave.

Put Your Unconscious on the Table

Why are these conscious or unconscious rewards that so undermine motivation so hard to exorcise? Drew Westen, a psychoanalytically oriented Harvard psychologist and personality theorist, offers an explanation. When we purposely focus on conscious aspirations, they're activated. The problem is our attention only remains on a thought for seconds—at the most twenty to thirty. Most of the time our thoughts are automatic and under the control of our unconscious. That is why when you tell yourself to stand up straight, you do so for a brief period. When you glance in a mirror five minutes later, you notice yourself slouched. Or you tell yourself that you must pass your math exam and sit down, open the math book and do the first problem. Ten minutes later you find yourself staring at the book, lost in thought about the new dress you'd like to buy, and not even having begun the next math problem. And this goes on for hours!

What can you do to overhaul unconscious thoughts, feelings, memories, and motives out of the murky caverns of the psyche? Westen suggests bringing them onto the table, where they can be inspected, evaluated and modified—which, says Westen, is what psychoanalysis is all about. In other words, if you've found other therapies not to work and you have the money, time, and desire to try psychoanalysis, you may want to consider this long-term treatment. Although it doesn't work for all, it does work for some. And though it may take a long time to restructure your character and mine your inner talents and skills, don't become discouraged—after all, your personality wasn't formed overnight.

The Least You Need to Know

➤ Optimism, the key to success, is an inborn, and a learned trait.

➤ The need to be perfect interferes with the path to success.

➤ Success, especially for women, can lead to social rejection.

➤ To become comfortable with achievement, build self-efficacy.

➤ Most people can talk himself or herself into success one small step at a time.

Part 4
Anxiety...Panic... Obsessions...Trauma...

"In the midst of winter, I finally learned that there was in me an invincible summer."
—Albert Camus

Do you feel tense and worried all the time? If so, you might have GAD, or generalized anxiety disorder. Do you suffer panic attacks that come on out of the blue and live with fear of the next one? You might be one of the many Americans suffering from panic disorder. If you feel plagued by obsessive thoughts and forced to repeat ritualistic actions, you may you suffer from Obsessive-Compulsive Disorder (OCD). And if you've suffered a horrific trauma in your life and feel continually anxious, numb and filled with nightmares, you may suffer from post-traumatic stress disorder.

In Part 4, you will learn how to identify if you suffer from any of these anxiety disorders and ways to help you come to grips with them.

Chapter 15

Preventing Sudden Terror

In This Chapter

➤ What causes panic attacks

➤ Why you won't die during a panic attack

➤ Coping during a panic attack

➤ Preventing a full-blown panic attack

If you've never had a panic attack, it's hard to imagine the horror of one. Yet anyone can have one—from the burly football player to the meek computer nerd. Ninety percent of the population will have at least one panic attack in his or her lifetime, while forty percent will have one panic attack a year. And they happen "out of the blue," anywhere, anytime.

In this chapter, I describe how a panic attack feels, the frightening thoughts that accompany it, and what leads to panic disorder. If you suffer from panic attacks, you will learn strategies for reducing the likelihood of repeated attacks and how to dampen the effect when one occurs.

I'm Going to Die!

Twenty-two-year old Sarah, an aspiring poet, had her first introduction to panic when at the movies with a friend. While eating popcorn, her swallow reflex stopped dead; for an eternal moment the kernel of popcorn just sat in her throat. She thought she was choking. Finally, it went down. She had no idea why this happened, just that it terrified her and she felt sure she was going to die. After that, she was afraid to eat solid

Terror Talk

The word **panic** comes from Pan, the Greek god of the woods and fields, blamed for the inexplicable dread felt by travelers in lonely places.

foods. When she did, the same thing would happen again. She started to eat only high fat liquids. She was five foot three, and her weight went down to 98 pounds.

Three weeks after the popcorn incident, she had her first full-blown panic attack. Broke and about to be evicted from her apartment, she was on her way to an interview for a secretarial position in an ad agency, work that she considered demeaning. As she rode up the elevator to the thirty-third floor of an office high-rise building, she felt trepidation and a mounting sinking feeling in the pit of her stomach. By the time she got out of the elevator, she felt terrified, faint, and shaky. Her heart was racing, her hands were sweating and she was gasping for breath. She walked unsteadily into the ad agency, feeling disoriented and struck by how bright the lights seemed.

"Can I help you?" the receptionist asked. The room started to spin. The receptionist seemed fuzzy, as if her face couldn't be distinguished from the wall behind her. Terror shot through Sarah, like the horror felt in the brief second between feeling yourself losing your balance and starting to fall, and bracing your hand against the wall. She wanted to scream, "I have to get out of here!" but felt frozen in terror. Her legs seemed miles from her body. Finally, she stammered, "I'm sorry. I need to leave" and ran out the door, embarrassed and certain that she was losing her mind.

The elevator ride down seemed like an eternity. Sarah closed her eyes and sang inside her head, over and over, "Winds may blow over icy seas, I'll take with me the warmth of thee, a taste of honey..." When the elevator door finally opened, she ran out into the street, shaky but tremendously relieved to be out in the fresh air where she felt she could breathe again. Afraid to take a chance with the subway or bus—what if she needed to flee?—she took a taxi home, which meant no food for two days. Over the next few days, she found herself often gasping for breath, as if she couldn't inhale enough air. But the worst was the sinking feeling in her stomach.

Two weeks later, she had another panic attack. This time it happened while waiting on the platform for the subway train. Although the tracks were a good twenty feet away, they seemed dangerously close. She felt as if a magnet could pull her onto them or if she got any closer, she would fall onto them or someone might push her. Sweating and shaking in terror, she waited until the attack subsided and then forced herself to get on the next train. When she got home, she called a friend, and asked for the name of her therapist and then called her father who, after a "just get over it" lecture, reluctantly agreed to lend her some money for therapy.

The sight of the therapist, a small kindly looking older man, brought immediate relief. At last there was someone she could talk openly to about her strange attacks of fright. He listened patiently. "What you're experiencing is not unusual," he said. "You can get over it. You're having panic attacks but they're not dangerous and you're not going to die. Should you stop breathing and faint, which you won't, you would automatically start breathing again." What a relief! She wasn't going to die. She could fight this thing.

Miscued Survival Instinct

When Sarah told the therapist of her panic attacks, the most important thing that he said to her was that she wasn't going to die.

During a panic attack, many people feel as if in mortal danger. This is how you're supposed to feel. What you're experiencing, as you may recall from earlier chapters, is your body's spontaneous fight/flight survival reflex that, within the context of a real danger, is an entirely natural bodily reaction. In fact, your body goes through the same physiological flight reaction as it would were you facing a charging bull.

If you were facing a bull, your concentration would be focused entirely on saving yourself from peril. But since a panic attack doesn't occur in the face of a real threat, your bodily symptoms absorb your attention and you misperceive their exaggeration as perilous and even life threatening. In the midst of a panic attack you might feel:

Fear Forum

"O lift me from the grass! / I die! I faint! I fail! / My cheek is so cold and white, alas! / My heart beats loud and fast."
—Percy Bysshe Shelley

This poem from *Indian Serenade*, sounding very much like a panic attack, would likely have been diagnosed in Elizabethan times as love sickness, a physical malady or "the vapors," a depressed or hysterical nervous condition.

➤ A pounding heart that feels like you are having a heart attack.

➤ Breathing difficulties that lead you to believe you will stop breathing, even suffocate.

➤ Vertigo, or dizziness, making you feel like you will faint.

➤ Buckling knees that make you fear you will be unable to walk or you're going to fall.

➤ General disorientation that makes you feel you are losing your mind.

None of this will happen. In his very helpful book, *The Anxiety and Phobia Workbook,* Edmund Bourne debunks each fear.

1. A panic attack cannot cause heart failure or cardiac arrest. Although frightening, rapid heartbeat and palpitations during a panic attack are not dangerous. During a true heart attack, people commonly experience continuous pain and pressure, not a pounding heart, or a missed or few extra beats. If you move around, the pain and pressure intensifies, while during a panic attack movement may ease a racing heart.

Secret Weapons

During a panic attack, you are not damaging your heart. A healthy heart can beat 200 beats per minute for days—even weeks—without sustaining any damage, wrote Claire Weekes, Australian pioneer in the treatment of phobias and panic disorder and author of *Peace from Nervous Suffering*.

Watch It!

If, at the onset of a panic attack, you experience dizziness, vertigo, spaciness, or the feeling that you are about to lose your balance, you may want to consult an otolaryngologist to check for possible inner ear dysfunction, which can mimic panic-like symptoms or exaggerate them from other causes (see Chapter 8).

2. A panic attack will not cause you to stop breathing or suffocate. Under stress, your neck and chest muscles tighten and reduce your breathing capacity. Though scary, there's nothing wrong with your breathing or lungs, and the tightening sensations will pass. When deprived of oxygen, your brain has a built-in reflex mechanism that will eventually force you to breathe. You'll automatically gasp and take a deep breath long before reaching the point where you could pass out from a lack of oxygen. If you did pass out, you would immediately start breathing again, as Sarah's therapist assured her.

3. *A panic attack cannot cause you to faint.* Light-headedness is common at the onset of panic since you are breathing more rapidly, which slightly reduces the blood circulation to your brain (see the section on hyperventilation in Chapter 6). This leads some to fear fainting. But this is extremely rare. Actually, since your heart is pumping harder, you're increasing your circulation. Don't fight this sensation by breathing even more rapidly, but try to breathe slowly from the diaphragm, preferably through your nose, and try to walk around a bit.

4. *A panic attack cannot cause you to lose your balance.* The dizziness or vertigo, which are among the first sensations of panic (recall how Sarah felt the room was spinning), come from hyperventilation or from balance-related problems. It is normal and will pass.

5. *You won't fall over or lose your ability to walk when you feel "weak in the knees" during a panic attack.* "Jelly legs" comes from the adrenaline released during a panic attack, which can dilate the blood vessels in your legs and cause blood to accumulate and not fully circulate. Although you may feel that you can't walk, you can and the trembling and weak sensations will pass.

6. *You can't "go crazy" during a panic attack.* The sometime feeling of unreality and depersonalization during a panic attack comes from reduced blood flow to your brain, and is due to arterial constriction, a normal consequence of rapid breathing. Although it feels eerie, it is harmless and has nothing to do with losing your mind. This too will pass.

7. *A panic attack cannot cause you to "lose control of yourself."* During a panic attack, you may feel as if your body has taken control of your mind. But you lose neither your mind nor your body during a panic attack, though in the desire for quick escape you may speed up your movements. When the receptionist asked Sarah if she could help her, Sarah felt a terrifying second in which she was unable to talk or move. But it passed; she did talk and walk out the door, albeit quickly.

What Causes Panic

No one is quite sure what causes the first panic attack. Apparently, something bio-chemical, or perhaps some dysfunction in your inner ear system, triggers exaggerated alarm to something seemingly innocuous, but to which your brain registers as danger-ous (see Chapter 8). Sarah felt threatened by taking a job grossly out of tune with her self-image and level of talent. Though she was going "up" to the job interview, in her mind she was going "down," symbolized by the sinking feeling in her stomach.

Whatever ignites this false flight/fight panic response, cumulative stresses create the tinder. When the pile gets high enough, it takes little ignition to set it off. Stress can come from real life survival threats, like loss of a loved one, a job and financial secu-rity, or the insecurity of a new move, marriage, and so on. Or it can emanate from symbolic loss, like the fear of dependency, helplessness, and the inability to live your life in accord with your basic essence—all of which threaten loss of self.

For Sarah, both kinds of stress had been mounting for a long time. Introverted, sensi-tive, intelligent and introspective, she always felt different and outside the main-stream. At college, her friends were planning teaching careers, joining sororities and dating fraternity boys. None of this resonated with her deep thinking and highly creative sense of self, intensifying her feelings of discomfort and of not belonging.

She quit college and fled to Greenwich Village to pursue a writing career, much to the horror of her unsupportive and conventional parents. Although in New York she met fascinating writers and artists with whom she felt greater camaraderie, she felt lonely, isolated, depressed and intensely insecure about her lack of finances and of her future. Walking three miles home one day from lack of bus fare, she decided she must get an office job. On this note, she had her first panic attack.

Understanding what precipitated your panic attack can help avert future attacks. Make a list of how you were feeling before it began.

➤ Were you tired, anxious, tense, depressed, uncomfortably hot or cold?

➤ Did an overstimulating environment overwhelm you?

➤ Had you consumed too much caffeine, or smoked too many cigarettes?

➤ Were you under the influence of drugs or alcohol?

➤ Were you ill?

➤ Were you alone or with someone with whom you felt uncomfortable?

➤ Were you under stress or worried about something?

All these factors can add up and ignite the fire.

Watch It!

If you experience panic attacks, you are more sensitive to caffeine, nicotine, marijuana, and carbon dioxide.

The Self-Fulfilling Prophecy

The sheer terror of that first panic attack, for no immediate or apparent reason, is petrifying. You don't understand what's happening to you, or why. Catastrophic thoughts—I'm going to die, I'm going insane, this will never end, I'm having a heart attack—exacerbate your fright and sense of danger and further the likelihood of another dreaded attack.

Thereafter, you become sensitive to internal signs of autonomic overarousal and tend to overreact. Perhaps an external cue sets off your anxiety. Your husband walks in and doesn't kiss you hello, or your teenager stays out past curfew, and you immediately feel your stomach churning, your breathing quickening, your heart speeding up. Or perhaps the trigger is internal: hyperventilation, hypoglycemia, muscle tension, vertigo, or reaction to a drug like caffeine or marijuana. Once set in motion, you associate bodily overarousal with the fear that another attack is imminent. This escalates your level of anxiety, sometimes into a full-blown panic attack.

Panic Attack Does Not Equal Panic Disorder

Having a panic attack doesn't mean that you have panic disorder. Some people experience one or two attacks and then never again. The following are the criteria for panic disorder without agoraphobia as established by the *Diagnostic and Statistical Manual of Mental Disorders* (DSM-IV, American Psychiatric Association):

➤ You have experienced four or more of the following symptoms at the same time:

1. Shortness of breath or smothering sensations
2. Heart palpitations or accelerated heart rate
3. Trembling or shaking
4. Sweating
5. Choking
6. Nausea or abdominal distress
7. Numbness or tingling sensations
8. Dizziness, unsteadiness, or faintness

9. Feeling of detachment or being out of touch with yourself

10. Hot flashes or chills

11. Chest pain or discomfort

12. Fear of dying

13. Fear of going crazy or being out of control

➤ While disturbed, one or more panic attacks have occurred unexpectedly and were not triggered by you being the focus of attention.

➤ You have experienced two or more panic attacks, and the attacks have been followed by at least a month of persistent fear of having another.

➤ During at least some of the attacks, at least four of the listed symptoms developed suddenly and increased in intensity within ten minutes of the beginning of the first symptom noticed in the attack.

➤ Any organic cause of the attack has been ruled out.

Watch It!

Once you have a panic attack, you can get stuck in a negative feedback cycle. You notice intense bodily symptoms, like a fast heartbeat or clammy hands. You begin to fear the worst, which intensifies your symptoms and elicits the flight/fight response. This exacerbates your bodily symptoms further, along with your catastrophic thoughts and, in some cases, leads to a full-blown panic attack.

Angst Bulletin

Twenty percent of people with panic disorder have attempted suicide.

Body *and* Mind Push the Panic Button

If you have panic disorder, the first step towards recovery is knowing that your panic attacks do not mean that you're crazy, that you're going to die, or that you will always be like this. To help reinforce this confidence, and to better understand the relationship between your bodily experience and your thoughts, fill out the Panic Attack Worksheets 1, 2 and 3. This will give you insight into how the mind and body collude to exacerbate your anxiety and increase the likelihood for further panic attacks.

PANIC ATTACK WORKSHEET 1: BODY SYMPTOMS*

Evaluate the following symptoms, any of which can occur during a panic attack, according to their effect when you are having an attack, using the 0-5 scale.

Key to Worksheet 1

0 = No effect

1 = Mild effect

2 = Medium effect

3 = Strong Effect

4 = Severe Effect

5 = Very Severe Effect

	0	1	2	3	4	5
1. Sinking feeling in the stomach	0	1	2	3	4	5
2. Sweaty palms	0	1	2	3	4	5
3. Warm all over	0	1	2	3	4	5
4. Rapid or heavy heartbeat	0	1	2	3	4	5
5. Tremor of the hands	0	1	2	3	4	5
6. Weak or rubbery knees or legs	0	1	2	3	4	5
7. Shaky inside and/or outside	0	1	2	3	4	5
8. Dry mouth	0	1	2	3	4	5
9. Lump in throat	0	1	2	3	4	5
10. Tightness in chest	0	1	2	3	4	5
11. Hyperventilation	0	1	2	3	4	5
12. Nausea or diarrhea	0	1	2	3	4	5
13. Dizzy or lightheaded	0	1	2	3	4	5
14. A feeling of unreality, as if "in a dream"	0	1	2	3	4	5
15. Unable to think clearly	0	1	2	3	4	5
16. Blurred vision	0	1	2	3	4	5
17. A feeling of being partially paralyzed	0	1	2	3	4	5
18. A feeling of detachment or floating away	0	1	2	3	4	5
19. Palpitations or irregular heartbeats	0	1	2	3	4	5
20. Chest pain	0	1	2	3	4	5
21. Tingling in hands, feet, or face	0	1	2	3	4	5
22. Feeling faint	0	1	2	3	4	5
23. Fluttery stomach	0	1	2	3	4	5
24. Cold, clammy	0	1	2	3	4	5

PANIC ATTACK WORKSHEET 2: Catastrophic Thoughts*

Catastrophic thoughts play a major role in aggravating panic attacks. Using the scale below, rate each of the following thoughts according to the degree to which you believe that the thought contributes to your panic attacks.

Key to Worksheet 2

1 = Not at all   3 = Quite a lot

2 = Somewhat   4 = Very Much

1. I'm going to die.	1	2	3	4
2. I'm going insane.	1	2	3	4
3. I'm losing control.	1	2	3	4
4. This will never end.	1	2	3	4
5. I'm really scared.	1	2	3	4
6. I'm having a heart attack.	1	2	3	4
7. I'm going to pass out.	1	2	3	4
8. I don't know what people will think.	1	2	3	4
9. I won't be able to get out of here.	1	2	3	4
10. I don't understand what's happening to me	1	2	3	4
11. People will think I'm crazy.	1	2	3	4
12. I'll always be this way.	1	2	3	4
13. I'm going to throw up.	1	2	3	4
14. I must have a brain tumor.	1	2	3	4
15. I'll choke to death.	1	2	3	4
16. I'm going to act foolish.	1	2	3	4
17. I'm going blind.	1	2	3	4
18. I'll hurt someone.	1	2	3	4
19. I'm going to have a stroke.	1	2	3	4
20. I'm going to scream.	1	2	3	4
21. I'm going to babble or talk funny.	1	2	3	4
22. I'll be paralyzed by fear.	1	2	3	4
23. Something is really physically wrong with me.	1	2	3	4
24. I won't be able to breathe.	1	2	3	4
25. Something terrible will happen.	1	2	3	4
26. I'm going to make a scene.	1	2	3	4

WORKSHEET 3: Connecting Body Symptoms and Catastrophic Thoughts*

In the left-hand column below, list body symptoms you rated 5 or 4 on the first Panic Attack Worksheet, describing your most troublesome body symptoms, one at a time. Then list catastrophic self-statements from the second worksheet "Catastrophic Thoughts" which you rated 4 or 3 that you would be most likely to make in response to each particular body symptom. For example, "Rapid heartbeat" is a body symptom that might elicit self-statements as, "I'm having a heart attack," and "I'm going to die."

Body Symptom	Catastrophic Thoughts
_____	_____
_____	_____
_____	_____
_____	_____
_____	_____
_____	_____
_____	_____
_____	_____
_____	_____
_____	_____
_____	_____

*(*From The Anxiety and Phobia Workbook by Edmund J. Bourne, Ph.D.. Copyright © 1995 by New Harbinger Publications, Oakland, CA; www.newharbinger.com. Reprinted by permission of the publisher.)*

Catch Your Panic Before It Catches You

Stop for a second and scan your body for tension. Are you completely relaxed? Slightly anxious? Considerably anxious? The following scale will help you identify your present anxiety level:

0   Relaxed: Calm and alert; at peace

1   Slight anxiety: Passing twinge of anxiety; slight nervousness

2	Mild anxiety: Butterflies in stomach; muscle tension; definitely nervous
3	Moderate anxiety: Feeling uncomfortable but still in control; heart starting to beat faster; chest tight and breathing more rapid; palms sweaty
4	Marked anxiety: Marked tension or feeling "out of it"; heart beating fast; muscles tight; breathing tight and constricted; beginning to worry about losing control
5	Early panic: Heart pounding or beating irregularly; constricted breathing; spaciness or dizziness; clear fear of losing control; compulsion to flee
6	Moderate panic attack: Palpitations; difficulty breathing; feeling disoriented or detached (feeling of unreality); panic at thought of loss of control
7-10	Major panic attack: All of the symptoms of Level 6 exaggerated; terror; fear of going crazy or dying; compulsion to escape

(Adapted from The Anxiety and Phobia Workbook by Edmund J. Bourne, Ph.D.. Copyright © 1995 by New Harbinger Publications, Oakland, CA; www.newharbinger.com. Reprinted by permission of the publisher.)

Use this scale to help you become adept at recognizing your rising state of tension so you can take action (explained below) to stop it from escalating. Since anxiety is omnipresent in your life, you take it for granted. You, like many anxious people, are probably out of touch with your body and ignore physical symptoms of stress, like fatigue, headaches and head pressure, nervous stomach, tight muscles, cold and sweaty hands, which you experience as "normal." Consequently, you may be unaware how stressed you are until it's too late and you become completely overwhelmed.

The scale may not necessarily correspond exactly to your felt experience of tension. What's important is that you identify what constitutes your level 4—the point at which your anxiety level is sufficiently high for you to feel you might start losing control. At this time, you want to cease what you're doing and take action. If you can recognize your pre-panic state, the following coping strategies should help you abort a full-blown panic attack:

Secret Weapons

If you cannot stop yourself from catastrophic thinking, try imagining the worst case scenario. For example: You couldn't breathe, and you fainted and were taken to the emergency room. When you came to, the emergency room doctor sends you home with a prescription for a tranquilizer. You called a friend and the two of you laughed about it.

1. If you can, leave the situation until your anxiety subsides. If you're driving on a freeway, pull your car over to the side until you resume control.

2. Try to talk to someone. If no one is there, get on the phone to a significant other. This will help refocus your attention away from your symptoms.

3. Get moving. Activity will help release the extra energy and adrenaline surging through your bloodstream that's creating the need to flee.

4. Focus on your surroundings to try to divert attention away from your vexing physical symptoms and catastrophic thoughts.

5. Do something repetitive, like repeating words or a song over and over, as Sarah did—"Winds may blow..." Or try repetitive movements like rocking, chewing gum, shaking a foot—anything to take your mind off your symptoms. Repetitive movement increases the serotonin level in your brain.

6. Try something that requires concentration, like a crossword puzzle.

7. Take out your anger on an object: pound on a pillow; scream into one or scream while in your car alone with the windows rolled up; throw a dozen eggs into the bathtub (the remains wash away easily); hit a punching bag.

8. Indulge yourself to something immediately pleasurable—a snack, a snuggle, sex, a hot shower or relaxing bath.

9. Visualize a comforting person or scene.

10. Refocus attention away from catastrophic thoughts by snapping a rubber band on your wrist and yelling, "Stop!"

11. Use positive self-talk like, "I'm going to be okay." "I'm not going to let this get out of control."

12. Practice diaphragmatic breathing and muscle relaxation.

Secret Weapons

Hyperventilation during a panic attack prolongs the attack. An old treatment for hyperventilation is pressing your lips firmly together, forcing you to breathe through your nose and making it very difficult to hyperventilate.

Fright Foes for When Hell Breaks Lose

Sometimes, in spite of all your efforts, your anxiety hits its peak and you have no choice but to ride out your moments in hell. If this happens and you experience full-blown panic, try the following:

1. Don't fight your symptoms—keep telling yourself that you're not in real danger, that the wild bodily fluctuations that you're experiencing are the result of the adrenaline rushing through your body and that this will subside as your anxiety level drops, generally within a few minutes.

2. Try to leave the panic-provoking situation.

3. Try to find a safe person and express your feelings to them.

4. Get moving to dispel the stress chemicals from your system.

5. Try to divert your thoughts by focusing on a constructive thought, or on simple objects around you.

6. Touch the floor, the physical objects around you, or "ground" yourself in some other way.

7. Put your hands under hot or cold running water—whatever works for you.

8. If you are in a place where you can do so, discharge tension by pounding your fists, crying, or screaming.

Watch It!

Panic is believed to be caused by a sudden surge of adrenaline, much of which will metabolize and be reabsorbed in three to five minutes. Fighting the attack will trigger more adrenaline and increase the terror. If you can, try to slow it down with proper breathing.

9. Breathe slowly and regularly through your nose to reduce possible symptoms of hyperventilation.

10. Squelch your destructive thoughts like, "This panic attack will never go away" with supportive statements like: "I'm okay," "This will pass," "I'm not going to let this control me," "I've survived this before."

11. If you can, try diaphragmatic breathing.

12. Take a quick dose of kava (you may want to keep some on you at all times). Or take an extra dose of a minor tranquilizer (with the approval of your doctor).

Voluntary Panic

David Barlow, Ph.D., a noted psychologist and leader in the field of anxiety disorders, has devised another means for teaching people how to cope with panic. He has the therapist teach patients how to re-create the fearful sensations experienced during a panic attack right in the office. If you hyperventilate during a panic attack, you might be asked to breathe forcefully and deeply for a minute or two to bring on the dizziness and other physiological sensations of over breathing. At this point, you would be told to close your eyes and breathe slowly until the physical sensations subside.

Or you might be asked to spin around in a chair to re-create the sensations of extreme dizziness or to stare in a mirror to bring on the feelings of unreality. In this way, you learn that even when the physical symptoms that you experience during a panic attack are exaggerated, they are not in any way harmful.

The Least You Need to Know

➤ You need to learn how to monitor your inner level of tension to stop it from getting out of control and culminating in a panic attack.

➤ If you feel your tension building up, stop what you're doing and employ some coping strategies.

➤ Once a panic attack begins, fighting it will only intensify the symptoms.

➤ Catastrophic thoughts of what might happen if you have another panic attack increase the likelihood of its reoccurrence.

Chapter 16

First Aid for Nervous Wrecks

In This Chapter

➤ Anxiety versus "*anxiety!*"

➤ Life as chronically anticipating disaster

➤ Worriers are both born and made

➤ Reboot your nervous system

Do you feel constantly restless and on edge, your thoughts, speech, breathing and heart rate speeded up? Do you worry, and worry—about the future, loved ones, even your possessions? If this sounds like you, you may be among those chronically anxious; you may have GAD, or *generalized anxiety disorder*.

Be careful. Chronic anxiety is bad for your health—mental as well as physical. In this chapter, you will learn how you joined the ranks of the nervous wrecks and the many measures you can take to reboot your nervous system into a calmer, less anxious mode.

Worry as a Way of Life

Adam, a 29-year-old architect, can't concentrate on his work. His mind is constantly racing, jumping from one worry to another: whether he can compete with the other architects in his firm; whether his wife will leave him; why she hasn't gotten pregnant yet; whether his mother and father will die. High-strung and jumpy, he suffers from heart palpitations, hyperventilation, clammy hands, and light-headedness. He experiences a ringing in his ears and sometimes finds himself shaking. This perpetual tension has scraped his nerves raw and leaves him often at once exhausted and keyed up. At night, it's hard for him to drift into sleep.

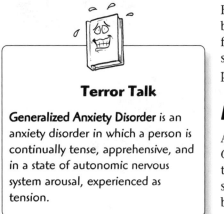

He's been a nervous type for as long as he can remember. But lately his nerves have gotten the best of him; frequently, he feels as if he's going to jump out of his skin. To make things worse, depression, colitis, back pain and constant colds plague him. All this at 29!

Life as Chronic Anxiety

Adam and other classic nervous wrecks suffer from *Generalized Anxiety Disorder (GAD)*. Constantly tense, they live in an inner fast lane, where thoughts, bodily sensations and movements are all accelerated and fueled by excessive worry—by an omnipresent feeling that the world is unsafe. And the anxiety doesn't have to be set off by a specific situation. It is free-floating—a general feeling that life is haphazard, unstructured, unpredictable and, along with your internal turmoil, beyond your capacity to control and organize.

Worry in and of itself isn't bad. It is a natural part of the human condition—a mild form of fear that nags us to take necessary action to survive in the world. When we think of all the things that can go wrong, we take steps to prevent them. But people like Adam see the world through a glass darkly and worry without necessary cause. They worry about money when financially secure; about a child who's healthy getting leukemia; about—well, most everything.

Are you concerned that you may be a GAD sufferer? If so, see how much your behavior matches the following symptoms.

➤ Feeling keyed up

➤ Irritability

➤ Restlessness

➤ Muscle tension, strained facial expressions, furrowed brows, deep sighs, visibly shaky

➤ Autonomic overdrive: sweating, dizziness, pounding or racing heart, hot or cold spells, cold and clammy hands, upset stomach, lightheadedness, frequent urination or defecation, lump in the throat, high pulse and respiration rates

➤ Incessant and rapid speech

➤ Racing thoughts

➤ Apprehensive about the future

➤ Easily distracted

➤ Sleep difficulties

➤ Feeling fatigued

➤ Mind going blank

➤ Hard to control worry

➤ Excessive anxiety and worry for more days than not for at least six months

Fear Forum

"Worry is interest paid on trouble before it is due."
—William Ralph Inge

Inner Rumblings

How anxious are you? Take this anxiety self-test to find out.

Anxiety Self-Test

Put a check next to each nervous symptom that you experience.

____	Constant exhaustion	____	Impotence
____	Restlessness	____	Tight chest or throat
____	Irritability	____	Shaking
____	Attention-seeking	____	Light-headedness
____	Flying off the handle	____	Dizziness
____	Rapid speech	____	Diarrhea
____	Constant worry	____	Gas
____	Poor concentration	____	Bloating
____	Tinnitus (ringing in ears)	____	Aching all over
____	Hyperactivity	____	Insomnia
____	Loss of appetite	____	Palpitations
____	Weight loss	____	Breathing difficulties
____	Impatience	____	Frequent urination
____	Keyed up	____	Startling easily to noise
____	Compulsive behavior	____	Jitteriness
____	Obsessive behavior	____	Headaches
____	Excessive sweating	____	Swallowing problems
____	Gloomy feelings	____	No interest in life

Add up your score: 1–10 = anxious, 11–20 = very anxious, 21–35 = extremely anxious

Roots of High Anxiety

Did you score in the high anxiety range? If so, you might wonder why. Perhaps you have overwhelming challenges in your life. Perhaps you were mistreated as a child. Actually, though these variables get factored into the GAD pool, the primary underlying reason that you are a nervous wreck comes from the gene pool.

Nervous Genes

As we've discussed in previous chapters, some people are born destined to live with thorny anxiety. Sensitive and emotional, negative signals are picked up sooner and elicit stronger reactions. If you're born with this trait, called behavioral inhibition, emotional sensitivity or harm avoidance, incessant fret and worry are hard-wired into your brain and you are naturally apprehensive, fearful, prone to worry, nervous, tense, and jittery.

You are not a wimp or a loser. Through no fault of your own, you live at the mercy of a nervous system set to jump at the slightest provocation:

Watch It!

The brain appears to make its own benzodiazepine substances. Some speculate that their deficiency, at a biological level, may make you vulnerable to generalized anxiety.

➤ Physical: You may startle easily to noise and feel bothered by bright or flashing lighting, odors, crowds, heights, certain textures on your skin, or light or unexpected touch.

➤ Emotional: You may be quick to perceive others as hostile, disapproving, or disinterested.

➤ Mental: You excessively worry about your own safety and that of those close to you.

When you tell people your worries, they often tell you to just "Chill out," "Get over it," "Stop worrying so much." Unfortunately, this is not easy. Once agitated, nervous types are less able to self-soothe than hardier, less excitable people.

Psychic Wars

Inborn sensitivity and harm avoidance does not necessarily make for an unhappy life. If you were born into a protective environment, of sensitive parents who wiped your tears away and made you feel safe from danger while at the same time nudging you forward, your tendency to react strongly was dampened and you didn't get as easily out of control. Eventually your mother's soothing was internalized, enabling you to wipe your own tears and to protect yourself from overwhelming anxiety. As a person, you remain slow-to-warm to new people and situations and prone to negative emotions, but feel inwardly secure and able to enjoy life and healthy relationships. Moreover, your ability to discern greater nuances in your world makes you more creative, in tune with others, and deep thinking.

But if you were born into a toxic family environment, in which your anxiety was not quelled but accentuated, then your distress and perception of the world as threatening was intensified and your level of agitation increased to uncomfortable levels. Since your parents were unable to make you feel better, you developed a sense of hopelessness about depending on others for comfort, support, and guidance. With this attitude, combined with inborn sensitivity, later stressful situations often exceeded your capacity to cope, and hit you with that much more of a wollop, further intensifying your stress.

Angst Bulletin

When a monkey who is bred to be nervous is reared by a bold, easy-going foster mother, the youngster takes on her easy-going ways and even her low-norepinephrine (one of the chemicals released during stress) chemistry, so discovered primate researcher, Steven Suomi, of the National Institute for Child Health and Human Development.

Here are some common situations that exacerbate the child's level of anxiety and hopelessness:

➤ Child abuse: Physical or sexual abuse realistically intensifies the belief that the world is a dangerous place.

➤ Physical or emotional neglect: Ignoring the child's basic survival needs, or failing to take an interest in the child, or not hugging or holding them, leaves the child to care for and nurture themselves. Such overwhelming responsibility exacerbates the child's view of the world as threatening and unsafe.

➤ Psychological abuse: Name-calling or belittling, threats of abandonment, or refusal to provide emotional comfort also intensifies the child's anxiety and view of the world as perilous.

➤ An alcoholic parent: Parents under the influence of alcohol often abuse and neglect their children, physically, sexually and emotionally.

➤ An anxious parent: Anxious parents provide an anxious model for the child to emulate. They also leave children stuck with two problems: calming themselves and calming their parent. The consequence is either two "screaming mimis," or a child who suppresses his own emotions and assumes the parental role and quiets the parent.

231

➤ A critical, angry parent: To avoid incurring parental criticism or anger, children suppress and deny their feelings and feel increased anxiety as a result.

➤ A depressed parent: When faced with a withdrawn parent, children deny their own needs and behave falsely cheerful to make the parent happy and thus have the parent minimally available to protect them.

➤ An overprotective parent: Parents who overprotect their children intensify a view of the world as dangerous and risky. This not only engenders greater insecurity and anxiety in the child, but by not allowing their children to take chances, the parent prevents the child from learning how to handle and overcome fears.

➤ A seductive parent: When parents behave seductively toward their children, they overstimulate the child to an uncomfortable level. Later in life, erotic feelings evoke tension, and are therefore experienced as overwhelming.

➤ Rigid family rules: Rigid rules ignore the child's individual needs. Children behave to please their parents and become hypervigilant to avoid incurring parental anger and punishment.

➤ Suppression or denial of feelings: When parents discourage emotional expression, either by discounting it as unimportant, as in ignoring the child's cries, ridiculing it—"Don't be a crybaby"—or punishing it, children learn to bury these feelings. In their place emerges a general state of unease: anxiety. When emotions do seep out, they feel painfully raw.

➤ Separation or loss: Separation from a parent, whether because of illness, divorce or death, creates feelings of sadness, anger and anxiety. The child may feel helpless to control and undo the bad things that happen to her.

➤ Lack of information about the interconnection of bodily sensations and emotions: Anxious people tend to be out of touch with their bodies and do not recognize bodily sensations that signal anxiety or emotional states. A sense of body awareness, body functions, and body activities originate in infancy and provide the foundation for a psychological sense of self. When a parent fails to comfort the infant, especially fussy, sensitive babies who get easily out of control, the infant experiences uncomfortable anxiety and bodily sensations. This overexcitation interferes with establishing healthy body awareness and clear-cut boundaries. Later, uneasiness gets mixed with bodily sensations of tired, sick, excited, scared, joyful, sad, making them hard to tease out.

Stress!

If you are chronically anxious, you are perpetually in the flight/fight mode. This is why you feel so tense and keyed up: Your brain, aware of danger, has released stress hormones and activated your sympathetic nervous system to ready your body for quick action. This explains your pumped up heart rate, which energizes your body, your fast breathing, which gives you more oxygen, your sweaty hands, which help to cool your body, and your tense muscles, which ready you for running or punching.

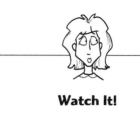

Watch It!

Physical illness, mental duress and self-destructive habits are all red flags. Your body, which has built-in mechanisms for preventing its own self-destruction, is giving you a warning sign: slow down.

But, since you are generally responding to threats elicited by stressful or disturbing thoughts, rather than any real physical danger, there's no one to punch and nowhere to run and therefore no way to release all this energy. It is this pent-up adrenaline that triggers the feeling of anxiety and creates stress. Eventually, this stress drains you and wears you out, as Hans Selye, the "father of stress research," first outlined in what he called the general adaptation syndrome.

Selye described three stages of physiological change set off by stress:

➤ Alarm: An alarm reaction mobilizes the body and prepares it for flight-or-fight.

➤ Resistance: If the stress is not removed, your body continues to cope with it by sympathetic nervous system activation and hormonal release, though not at levels as high as when in the alarm reaction. In this stage, the body attempts to restore energy, repair damage, and bolster resistance to noxious stimuli and illnesses, such as infectious diseases.

➤ Exhaustion: If the stressful stimuli or responses are not diminished, your body becomes overworked and depleted of its normal energy reserves. Resistance to disease decreases and you become vulnerable to "diseases of adaptation"—from allergies and hives to ulcers and coronary heart disease— and, ultimately, to death.

Fear Forum

"When you suffer an attack of nerves, you're being attacked by the nervous system. What chance has a man got against a system?"
—Russell Hoban, b.1925, US writer and illustrator

Stress wears you down both physically and mentally, and you become more vulnerable to depression, GAD, panic attacks and phobias. Stress also makes you more prone to self-destructive behavior. When keyed-up and agitated, people feel as if in danger and take immediate self-protection to lower their level of autonomic arousal or anxiety. You let off steam by screaming at your child or kicking your dog. You reach for a cigarette, a candy bar, a beer or a joint—habits that can, in excess, further compromise your health. It is only after you calm down that you can examine your behavior and its long-term consequences; while agitated, your only concern is getting through the next ten minutes. Thus, as long as you remain stressed, the self-destructive behavior continues.

See if you can identify your stress:

Life Stress

Physical Stress	Environmental/Sensory Stress
___ Anxiety	___ Noisy neighborhood/home
___ Panic attacks	___ Noisy work environment
___ Insufficient or poor sleep	___ Overly bright home
___ Eating poorly	___ Overly bright office
___ Smoking	___ Unpleasant odors at work
___ Weight problems	___ Unpleasant odors at home
___ Alcohol or drug problem	___ Daily hassle of crowds
___ Caffeine excess	___ Daily hassle of traffic
___ Sensory overstimulation	___ People in your space
___ Muscle tension	___ Chemical overexposure at home
___ Illness	___ Chemical overexposure at work
___ Physical disability	___ Too hot, too cold, too stuffy at home
___ Heavy physical work	___ Too hot, too cold, too stuffy at work
___ Chronic pain	___ Bothered by feel of clothing on your skin

Emotional Stress	
___ Depressed and worried	___ Feeling under someone's control
___ Feel worthless	___ Unable to say "no" to requests
___ Loneliness	___ Find life meaningless
___ Fear of confrontation	___ Overwhelmed with responsibility (especially for children)
___ Difficulty in expressing thoughts and feelings	___ Fear of danger, like rape or being mugged
___ Lack of recognition or approval from others	

Change Stress

___ Loss of relationship	___ Getting a divorce
___ Moving (house, work relocation)	___ Death of a loved one
___ Empty nest as children leave home	___ Changing jobs
___ Moving out of the family home	___ Getting married
___ Having a baby	___ Divorce
	___ Getting old

Family and Relationship Stress

Financial Stress

___ Taking care of the elderly	___ Poverty
___ Taking care of the young	___ Unemployment
___ Taking care of the sick	___ Making ends meet
___ Relatives or best friends moving away	___ Can't pay bills
___ The crying baby	___ Insufficient funds for basic maintenance
___ Problem with children or adolescents	___ Poor housing
___ Marital stress	___ Winning the lottery
___ Isolation	
___ Insufficient supports	
___ Sexual problems	

Work or School Stress

___ Loss of employment	___ Long hours
___ Stress at work	___ Poor work environment
___ Burn out	___ Not enough responsibility or autonomy
___ Too much work	___ Constant travel
___ Work not challenging	___ Conflict with boss
___ Retirement	___ Long commutes
___ Learning difficulties	___ Exams
___ Promotion	___ Meeting deadlines

Defusing the Panic Button

The core of our behavior is the functioning of our nervous system: The better tuned, the less likely we are to experience unmanageable anxiety and fright. If you suffer from GAD, it takes a lot of effort to manage your nervous system and interrupt the chronic flight-or-fight mode that leaves you living with perpetual anxiety.

Chill Out

Relaxation exercises are essential for learning to calm your nervous system, but they're also not a magic bullet, though the media and many self-help books would lead you to think so. First, you have a naturally sensitive, easily out-of-whack nervous system to contend with. Second, the exercises take time and perseverance. Since impatience is a characteristic of GAD, your tendency may be to give up easily if you don't see instant results. To overcome this, change your expectations and don't expect too much too soon. Rather, think in terms of small term gains that will build up over the long-term and daily relaxation practice as necessary a part of your daily health routine as brushing your teeth.

➤ Breathing: Since the chronically anxious tend to be over-breathers (see Chapter 6), you must learn to change your breathing pattern. If not, whatever relaxation you achieve will be quickly lost as you resume hyperventilating.

➤ Progressive relaxation: Muscle tension, which gets in the way of relaxing, can be relieved at least somewhat through progressive relaxation and body scanning (see Chapter 6).

➤ Meditation has repeatedly been found to reduce chronic anxiety and the use of pharmaceutical tranquilizers.

Angst Bulletin

What is the difference between worry and panic? The two states reside in two different cerebral hemispheres, found University of Illinois psychologist Wendy Heller. Anxious apprehension (worry) sparks more left brain activity because the left hemisphere controls speech production and worrying is primarily a verbal activity. Anxious arousal (panic) sparks more right brain activity, which plays a greater role in regulating panic's physical effects: increased heartbeat, sweating, and production of stress hormones.

Sweat Away Anxiety

Exercise is the best anti-anxiety and anti-worry antidote that we have. An antidepressant as well, it massages the brain with "feel-good" chemicals, drains off excess energy and frustration, relaxes your body and helps you sleep. If you start off your day with some kind of strenuous aerobic exercise, your nervous system will be more kind to your throughout the day. Check it out. Do vigorous exercise for several mornings in a row and then skip a day. You'll find yourself more edgy, impatient, agitated, less able to concentrate and, ironically, more fatigued. If lacking time, try starting your day walking up five to ten flights of stairs.

Exercise also helps build a healthy, strong body that is better able to tolerate stress.

Rock Around the Clock

You know how rocking stops babies from crying? That's because it reminds babies of being in the womb. Mothers spontaneously rock their babies at precisely the walking rhythm during the later stages of pregnancy and at the heartbeat of the average resting adult. You never forget this primitive calming device. Simply moving your body rhythmically and repetitively—side-to-side, up and down, back and forth—or nodding or shaking your head can lock you into that primitive sway and quell your nerves. One reason may be that repetitive motion boosts your serotonin level.

Secret Weapons

If you work at home on a computer, try sitting on one of the new large exercise balls as a chair. They allow you to bounce up and down, sway side to side and rock back and forth—while you're working.

Knead Away Tension

Nothing quiets, relaxes and reassures like human touch. And in this low-touch society, few of us get enough. Massage can help compensate some. In addition to relaxing muscle spasms, relieving tension, and decreasing inflammation and swelling of the joints, massage stimulates the tactile system, as well as the proprioceptive (our sense of space) and vestibular (our sense of balance) systems, and helps restore the nervous system. Any kind will do—Swedish, shiatsu, trigger point, sports massage. For best therapeutic results, try to get two one-half-hour massages weekly.

In addition to massage, there's a host of other bodywork that oils your nervous system, including:

➤ Trager: Involving a sequence of softly rocking and rhythmic movements that induces deep states of relaxation, Trager work re-educates the body's movements back to a pre-injury or pre-tension state.

➤ Feldenkrais: Utilizing a system of movements, floor exercises, and body work designed to retrain the nervous system, Feldenkrais helps open new pathways around any areas of blockage or damage.

237

Fear Forum

"A healthy body is a guest chamber for the soul; a sick body is a prison."
—Francis Bacon

Secret Weapons

Trager, which involves a sequence of softly rocking and rhythmic movements, is a kind of rocking massage that induces deep states of relaxation that continue for an extended time.

➤ CranioSacral Therapy: Through the interchange of the electromagnetic energy from one person to the other, the CranioSacral therapist uses gentle touch manipulations to remove the obstacles that block the free flow of fluids and energies in your body. Afterwards, you feel greater relaxation, enhanced mobility and less pain. You continue to experience your body changing and readjusting for several days following treatment.

Don't Let Thinking Be Dangerous to Your Mental Health

Mistaken beliefs and habitual thinking patterns fuel your on-going anxiety. If you don't learn how to turn down the volume when erroneous thoughts start screaming in your head and at least attenuate their control over your behavior, relaxation exercises will offer a temporary relief of symptoms at best.

Eliminating these thoughts is a challenge. Since people who suffer from high anxiety tend to have creative minds and imagine things vividly, you can let your imagination soar and picture graphically all the many frightening things that could happen to you. And since you are highly aware of your world, you may easily interpret ambiguous stimuli as threats or overestimate the likelihood that a negative event will occur.

When relaxed, write down your erroneous and destructive, negative self-talk. Practice replacing them with constructive, positive thoughts until they become automatic and available for you in troubling situations.

Here are some examples:

➤ *Destructive thought*: I am so nervous, I can't stop talking.

➤ *Constructive thought*: I'm uptight and need to talk. This will change when I become more relaxed.

➤ *Destructive thought*: I'll never stop feeling anxious.

➤ *Constructive thought*: It takes a long time to change behavior. I will be patient with myself.

➤ *Destructive thought*: I can't stop myself from feeling tense.

➤ *Constructive thought*: I need to pay closer attention to what builds up my tension before it gets out of control.

Pills Can Help

Although medication is not going to cure GAD, the benzodiazepines, such as Xanax and Klonopin, help take off the edge. When you feel things starting to get under control, you can discontinue use or, if you've been on them for awhile, wean yourself off gradually. BuSpar is an effective anti-anxiety drug that, though not offering instant relief, makes you feel gradually better and without the usual side effects. Since GAD is a long-term problem, and since drug use should only be a short-term solution, you should not rely solely on prescription medication. Remember that the gains achieved can be lost when the anti-anxiety drug is discontinued. Furthermore, you may attribute improvement to an external agent rather than to your own coping efforts—the drug did it, not me. Thus, you continue to believe that your anxiety and worrisome possibilities remain uncontrollable.

Herbs like kava, and amino acids like 5-HTP can reduce anxiety naturally without harmful side effects and the herb St. John's Wort is effective in reducing the depression often accompanying GAD (see Chapter 8).

Connectedness

When you are in trouble and stressed, you need to feel that something or someone is looking out for you. The more supports or connectedness you have in your life, the better your emotional state and your ability to handle stress. Edward Hallowell in his marvelous book *Worry* (Pantheon, 1997) outlines six different domains of connectedness:

Fear Forum

"It's no use putting up your umbrella until it rains."
—Alice Caldwell Rice

1. Familial connectedness
2. Historical connectedness between you and your past
3. Social connectedness to your friend's, neighbors, and colleagues
4. Connectedness to information and ideas, the feeling of being at home with the very wide and complex world of what is known and thought
5. Connectedness to institutions and organizations, your feeling of belonging to where you work, play, or learn
6. Connectedness to what is beyond knowledge—a sense of being a part of nature or in the hands of God

The more meaningful connections you make to something larger than yourself, the less your anxiety will overcome you.

Can't Relax!

So, you've done everything and you still can't relax? Why not? If you're chronically tense, your efforts at self-calming can get short-circuited by your easily excitable nervous system: You tell yourself to "relax" but it comes out as "RELAX! RELAX!" Or you may manage to relax some, but it's short-lived. Sometimes the pressure is just too great. After all, if you feel like jumping out of your skin, it's hard to focus on anything but escape.

©*PEANUTS reprinted by permission of Newspaper Enterprise Association.*

The secret is to not let your nervous system get to this point—to avoid roadblocks to balancing your nervous system. Here are some common ones:

➤ Letting anxiety get out of control

➤ Overexposure to toxic people and situations

➤ Sensory defensiveness

➤ Adrenal exhaustion

Dont't Ignore Anxiety

Your body and you are wedded for life; if you take good care of it, it will take good care of you. To do so, you need to learn not only what stresses you, but to not ignore it when this is happening. This isn't always easy. If chronic anxiety is a steady state and you are out of touch with your body, you may miss the physical symptoms of stress, which you've come to experience as "normal." In fact, when "flight-or-fight" is activated often enough, you can unknowingly send your body this command. If this happens frequently, your anxiety can escalate past the point when you can control it and lead to panic attacks, exhaustion, or illness.

Be kind to yourself and learn to recognize the early signs of stress and to take appropriate action at that time. Stop and do deep breathing, progressive relaxation, body scanning, meditation, rocking, self-massage, aromatherapy—whatever works to help you self-calm and regenerate.

Be sure to follow these suggestions as well:

➤ Since stress depletes your body of resources, eat nutritiously and make sure to feed your nervous system with the necessary supplements outlined in Chapter 9.

➤ Get enough sleep.

➤ Delegate as many responsibilities as you can.

➤ Set aside quiet time to unwind at the end of the day.

➤ Simplify your lifestyle to minimize daily hassles and unnecessary responsibilities.

A good resource for learning to manage the details of your household and of your life is *The Complete Idiot's Guide to Organizing Your Life.*

Avoid Overexposure

Since you get easily overwhelmed, take steps to avoid or minimize people and situations that rile you:

➤ As much as possible, keep toxic people, such as negative parents, co-workers, or friends at a physical and emotional distance.

➤ Say "no" to stress-inducing situations—parties you don't want to attend, meetings you can successfully avoid, baseball games that bore you, and so on.

➤ Avoid toxic environments that in some people trigger or exacerbate allergies and chemical sensitivity.

➤ Avoid sensory overstimulation.

Secret Weapons

If being with your parents is a negative and destructive experience that evokes powerful uncomfortable feelings, keep your visits infrequent and short. Try to avoid "heart-to-hearts" by not being alone with them and see them within the context of an event that takes the focus off of you.

Beware of Sensory Overkill

Our buzzing, humming, flashing, and vibrating world keeps all of us more revved up and prone to stress. If you are a nervous type, you might get easily irritated and overwhelmed by the on-going sensory onslaught. If so, you may be sensory defensive. As you recall, people with this syndrome perceive harmless stimuli as threatening and overreact with the primitive survival response. The sound of that jackhammer, or the sight of those flashing neon lights, or the smell of someone's pungent perfume registers in your brain as "danger" and evokes the flight-or-fight response. Since unpleasant and annoying stimuli are all around, you feel constantly keyed-up and anxious.

Relaxation techniques and drugs, though helpful in reducing defensiveness, don't eliminate this state. Although you may feel less irritated by noxious stimuli, you will still find loud noise or bright lights or strong odors or tags in your clothing vexing and hard to ignore. Consequently, in spite of all your efforts, it's hard to find your comfort zone.

Here are some suggestions to help reduce sensory defensiveness:

➤ Identify what sensations in your environment bother you: noise, bright lights, odors, the taste or feel of certain foods, open space, heights, rough textures on your skin, light or unexpected touch, crowds or violation of your space. Make every effort to avoid or at least minimize exposure to annoying stimuli.

➤ Create the most nurturing sensory work environment that you can. For instance, if overhead fluorescent lights bother you, buy a desk lamp with a full spectrum light bulb for your workspace.

➤ Create a pleasing and nurturing sensory home environment to which you can take refuge.

➤ Set aside a quiet, dark place for your relaxation exercises and add pleasant sensory stimulation, such as burning incense, aromatherapy, candlelight, and soft music.

➤ Learn what sensory integrative interventions reduce sensory defensiveness and, in some cases, eliminate it altogether. For more information, contact Sensory Integration International (see Appendix B).

Watch Out for Adrenal Exhaustion

If you are under constant stress, your adrenal glands work overtime to keep you ready to fight all your perceived enemies. Prolonged stress on the adrenal glands results in a state of chronic under-functioning or exhaustion, a condition developed over a series of stages as described by Hans Selye.

➤ In the first stage of combating stress, the adrenal glands tend to hyperfunction, producing high amounts of adrenaline and noradrenalin, as well as steroid hormones such as cortisol.

➤ As stress becomes prolonged, the glands become overtaxed and go into a state of temporary under-functioning. If you are relatively healthy, the glands will try to compensate, actually rebuilding themselves to the point of hypertrophy (growing larger).

➤ If high levels of stress continue, the glands will eventually exhaust themselves again and then remain in a chronic state of underfunctioning. At this stage, they overproduce adrenaline some of the time, causing anxiety or mood swings, while under producing adrenaline the rest of the time. With insufficient adrenal resources, you will tend to have a difficult time handling any stressful situation without overreacting or becoming unglued. In short, your capacity to manage stress is exhausted.

Symptoms of adrenal exhaustion include:

➤ Chronically low-stress tolerance

➤ Frequent fatigue

➤ Depression

➤ Insomnia

➤ Light and noise sensitivity

➤ Worsening allergies or asthma

➤ Craving for caffeine, sugar, tobacco, alcohol, and recreational drugs

Angst Bulletin

A long-standing addiction to caffeine, sugar, nicotine or alcohol worsens adrenal insufficiency and exhaustion. Continuing stress, inadequate sleep, sudden trauma, severe physical illness, prolonged exposure to heat or cold, exposure to toxins, pollutants, and substances of which you are allergic, as well as prolonged taking of cortisone, all aggravate adrenal exhaustion.

Overcoming adrenal exhaustion takes effort but is possible. Here are some guidelines to reduce overwhelming stress:

➤ Get as much sleep as you need to feel alert and productive.

➤ Substitute herbal tea for caffeinated beverages.

➤ Stop smoking, drinking alcohol, or using recreational drugs.

➤ Find out if you suffer overgrowth of the *Candida albicans* fungus (see Chapter 3), and explore diets that could eliminate this problem.

➤ Eat natural food, preferably organic, fresh vegetables, and fresh fruits, protein in the form of beans and grains, organic poultry or fish.

➤ Take B-complex, vitamin C, calcium, magnesium and chromium as outlined in Chapter 9. Try raw adrenal extract, 50 to 200 mg per day, preferably under the supervision of a doctor or nutritionist experienced in using glandular extracts.

➤ Get plenty of fresh air and sunshine.

➤ Do daily exercise to slough off excess adrenaline.

➤ Simplify your lifestyle.

Light Up Your Life

If you live in a northern climate, and you are of the anxious type, your nerves can feel especially exposed during the winter months when days become shorter. If, in addition, your moods reflect the surrounding gray skies and colorless bleak terrain to the point of lifeless-ness, depression and despair, you may suffer from *seasonal affective disorder* (SAD), a cyclical depression that occurs from lack of sufficient light exposure. Daily exposure to full spectrum lighting dramatically reduces depression for SAD victims.

Secret Weapons

For information on light therapy for the treatment of SAD, contact the National Organization for Seasonal Affective Disorder (NOSAD), P.O. Box 40133, Washington, D.C. 20016.

Are We Happy Yet?

If you are born with that old pessimistic gene, don't expect all these interventions to bring happiness. Apparently, we have a set point for happiness based largely on inborn temperament; if you are sensitive and fear prone, your set point is higher than your more upbeat counterparts. Both wonderful things that happen to people, like getting married or having a baby, and terrible things that happen to people, like losing some-one or a serious illness, seem to have short-term effects. We become happier or sadder for a few months but then return to our baseline state of being. Lottery winners, for instance, are no happier a year after hitting the jackpot than they were before.

With conscious effort, you can move above your set point. Grand achievements will give you a more secure base from which to work. But, advises psychologist David Lykken, who has studied the genetics of harm avoidance, it is a steady diet of simple pleasures that keep you above your set point—a walk along the ocean, your favorite CD, a gourmet meal, your favorite perfume, talking to an old friend.

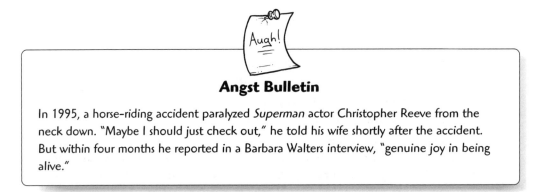

Angst Bulletin

In 1995, a horse-riding accident paralyzed *Superman* actor Christopher Reeve from the neck down. "Maybe I should just check out," he told his wife shortly after the accident. But within four months he reported in a Barbara Walters interview, "genuine joy in being alive."

Summing Up

To combat anxiety, make yourself a list of reminders:

➤ Slow down *before* you go into overdrive.

➤ Use breathing exercises.

➤ Get plenty of fresh air and sunshine.

➤ Exercise—outdoors if possible.

➤ Don't allow yourself to get exhausted.

➤ Get eight hours of sleep.

➤ Set aside quiet time to unwind.

➤ Keep an arsenal of stress busters, like wooden hand massagers and aromatherapy paraphernalia.

➤ Use positive self-talk.

➤ Watch out for sensory overstimulation.

➤ Simplify your lifestyle.

➤ Unclutter and organize your house.

➤ Stay connected.

The Least You Need to Know

➤ People who suffer from GAD feel constantly anxious and overworry.

➤ People who experience chronic anxiety were generally born more sensitive and nervous.

➤ If you are a nervous type, exposure to stress smites with much more of a blow.

➤ Too much stress can lead to adrenal exhaustion, when your body can no longer fight stress or disease.

➤ A syndrome called sensory defensiveness, in which you overreact to sensory stimuli as threatening, can prevent you from learning to relax.

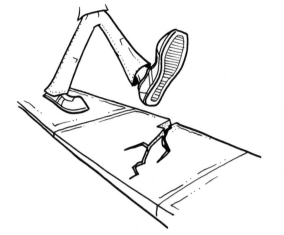

Chapter 17

Avoiding Sidewalk Crack "Crack Ups"

In This Chapter

➤ "Obsessing" and "compulsing" vs. Obsessive-Compulsive Disorder

➤ Why people engage in bizarre repetitive rituals

➤ What causes the repetition compulsion to take over

➤ Treatments that control this "idée fixe"

"Stop obsessing about him," we tell our friend who cannot stop jabbering away about her new boyfriend. "You're so compulsive," we tell another friend who shops till she drops and spends money she doesn't have.

Most of us obsess and act compulsively to some extent. Some of us do it excessively and are obsessive/compulsive types. But few actually suffer from *Obsessive-Compulsive Disorder* (OCD), a debilitating disease in which repetitive thoughts and rituals control the person's life.

In this chapter, we will learn about this bizarre disorder—its symptoms, its proposed causes and how to treat it. And you will learn how to tell if you suffer from OCD or are merely an obsessive-compulsive type.

The Repetition Compulsion

On her way to work, Marisol had some doubt about whether she had locked her door. She turned around and went back home to check her locks. Though she found all three locks bolted, she re-locked them seven more times and rubbed the door

Terror Talk

Obsessive-Compulsive Disorder is an anxiety disorder characterized by the inability to control a preoccupation with specific ideas and/or prevent yourself from carrying out compulsive rituals.

Fear Forum

"Sufferers from this illness (OCD) are able to keep their affliction a private matter. Concealment is made easier from the fact that they are quite well able to fulfill their social duties during a part of the day, once they have devoted a number of hours to their secret doings, hidden from view."
—Sigmund Freud

handle seven times. Still, the thought nagged her all morning that she might not have securely locked her door. At lunchtime, she again returned home to repeat the whole ritual. Worry that her house was unlocked and being burglarized plagued her the rest of the day.

Once home, she stood outside her door and carefully checked the outside door locks for tampering. She then cautiously unlocked and opened the door and stood in the doorway. The sight of one of her cats mildly reassured her that no one appeared to be lurking in the house, and she gingerly walked in the door and went through the ritual of locking the three door locks seven more times and rubbing the door handle seven times. She turned on all the lights in the house and then checked all windows for entry, then checked under all the beds, in all the closets, in the shower stall and even in the dishwasher, washing machine and dryer for a possible burglar. She repeated this routine at least ten more times before going to sleep, eating up most of her precious evening time. And she woke twice during the night to recheck everything again. Marisol does this routine daily—with little variation.

Marisol is among the more than four million people in the United States who suffers from Obsessive-Compulsive Disorder (OCD). She and others live under a dictatorship, an inner tyrant who fills their heads with persistent and unwanted thoughts—fear of being burglarized, fear of being poisoned, fear of someone kidnapping their child, fear of sleeping walking and murdering their spouse are but a few. To prevent these unwarranted and frightening worries from happening, they repeat endless "magical" rituals. They continually check the locks, or wash their hands, or repeat the Lord's Prayer 20 times out loud, or avoid stepping on cracks in the sidewalk—"Step on the crack, break your mother's back."

This devastating disorder can begin in childhood or later, during adolescence or adulthood. If you are intelligent and in an upper income bracket, you are a more likely candidate for OCD. Your gender, however, doesn't matter—it attacks men and women alike. Sometimes the onset is sudden: you wake up one day and find yourself unable to leave the house without first taking four showers. For others, the onset is gradual and insidious.

Until recently, OCD was considered a rare condition. But in the last twenty years, the number of cases has increased alarmingly. In fact, around 2 to 3 percent of the population may suffer from OCD. It's unclear whether the increase relates to greater incidents or greater awareness. And there may be more, since many manage to keep their preoccupations and rituals a secret and appear to lead a reasonably normal life. Talk show host Howie Mandel is a germ freak who has been living with OCD for years and avoids shaking his guest's hands lest he catch some illness. Seeking neither therapy nor medication, he describes himself as "happy" and accepts OCD as part of who he is and has no wish to change. His family and he merely make adjustments to accommodate his peculiarities. At the first sniffle from his wife or children, for instance, he immediately seeks shelter in a separate small house he built to avoid contamination.

The Face of an Idée Fixe

Many people are superstitious. They don't walk under ladders, or let a black cat cross their path, and keep umbrellas closed in the house. For luck, they carry around a rabbit's foot and knock on wood. Likewise, many people find that unwanted, horrifying, and bizarre thoughts pop into their head. You may momentarily see your child at the bottom of a swimming pool, or picture part of your body cut up and defiled. But these thoughts are infrequent and the rituals driven by superstitions mild, and take up little of your daily routine. But thoughts of the "obsessors" (those who mostly ruminate) and the rituals of the "compulsives" (those who mostly ritualize) consume most of their lives.

You know that your haunting ruminations are senseless and that you have done nothing harmful—that nothing *is* wrong. But you feel that something *is* wrong and feel compelled to check and count. The usual flap in your brain that says, "my hands are now clean" doesn't get shut. Your hands and arms become red and even bleed from continual washing, but your battle with invisible germs continues unabated and you can't stop yourself from washing and from wasting hours of precious school, work, or personal time every day.

Angst Bulletin

It is likely that French composer Eric Satie (1866–1925) had OCD. Obsessed with numbers, his works were frequently conceived in threes, like the three "Gymnopédies," which musicologists refer to as his "trinitarian obsession." He was an eccentric who dressed fastidiously and allowed no one in his room while he was alive. When he died, his wardrobe was revealed to contain a dozen identical suits, shirts, collars, hats, and walking sticks.

249

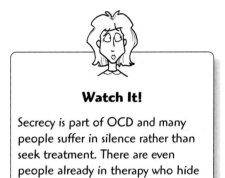

The ritual serves to temporarily chase away your foreboding concerns and relieve the anxiety they produce. Yet, because you are too anxious to concentrate on what you are doing, you cannot be absolutely sure that you *did* lock all the locks, or wash all the germs off your hands, or miss all the cracks in the sidewalk—that you did these rituals *perfectly*. Thus, relief from the constant battle with your urges is short-lived and you resume worrying that you still have germs on your hands or your house will burn down, feeling compelled to repeat the ritual.

You are fully aware of the absurdity and irrationality of your thoughts and of your behavior—you know that the doors are locked, that your hands are not dirty, and that your child is not in imminent danger. Yet, if you try to resist, ignore or suppress these uninvited cerebral intruders and not follow through with the rituals to banish them, you feel acutely anxious. Thus, the script repeats itself day in, day out. Greatly embarrassed by your behavior, you go to great lengths to hide it from family, friends, and co-workers.

The best coping tactic you can muster is to avoid situations that trigger discomfort, like not going out of the house if you fear it will burn down while you are gone. But avoidance only leads to more avoidance and greater fear, tightening the rule of your tyrannical intruders on your behavior and adding to your problem. Though your behavior seems crazy and you worry that you are crazy, you are in every other way sane. In fact, once symptoms are controlled by medication, many OCD patients seem amazingly normal and lacking in psychological conflicts.

Here are the symptoms of Obsessive-Compulsive Disorder:

➤ The obsession or compulsion intrudes insistently and persistently into your awareness.

➤ You feel anxious dread if the thought or act is prevented for some reason.

➤ You recognize that the obsessional thought, impulses, or images are a product of your mind (not imposed from without as in thought invention).

➤ You recognize the absurdity and irrationality of the obsession or compulsion.

➤ You feel a need to resist it but feel helpless to do so.

Living with an Emotional Tic

Obsessions are ideas, thoughts, images, and impulses that dart through your mind repeatedly. They are distasteful, shameful, and acutely distressing. The most common are worries about contamination, harming yourself or others, disasters, swearing, becoming violent, or sexual and embarrassing concerns.

Common Obsessions:

➤ Contamination: "I have E-coli all over my hands," "That telephone is contaminated with germs," "That wine might be poisoned."

➤ Harm to self or others: "A burglar is going to kill me," "Someone is bludgeoning my daughter."

➤ Disasters: "My house is burning down," "My mother is dying," "I have cancer."

➤ Swearing: "I'm going to tell my boss to f*!## off."

➤ Violence: "I'm going to impale my husband," "I'm going to kill the cat."

➤ Sexual concerns: "I'm homosexual," "I'm a child molester," "I'm a pervert," "I'm going to have sex with my cat."

➤ Embarrassment: "I'm going to take off all my clothes in public," "I'm going to soil my pants."

➤ Miscellaneous: (fear of not saying things right) "I'm going to make a Freudian slip"; (intrusive nonsense sound, words, or music) "I'm Henry the Eighth I am, Henry the Eighth I am, I am"; (Lucky/unlucky numbers) "Seven is heaven; six is nix."

Often your thoughts appear so real that you avoid picking up any knives for fear of stabbing your husband, or don't use matches lest you set your house on fire.

Compulsions are repetitive or stereotyped behaviors that you perform to prevent your obsessions from happening and to relieve your tension. Washing is the most common and, not surprisingly, more prevalent in women. Checking, repeating and ordering are also common.

Common Compulsions:

➤ Washing, cleaning, or decontaminating: Hands must be washed over and over for fear of contamination; you may shower repeatedly throughout the day. Dr. Judith Rapoport (*The Boy Who Couldn't Stop Washing*) has found that at least 85 percent of her patients have performed excessive, compulsive washing at some point in their illness. Cultures less obsessed with cleanliness than ours, such as rural Nigeria and rural India, also have patients preoccupied with contamination and ritual purity as their most common form of OCD.

➤ Checking: You repeatedly check for safety such things as: closets, drawers, appliances, light switches, doors, locks, gas, water taps, irons, a burning cigarette.

➤ Repeating: You count, touch objects in a certain way or repeat certain words, numbers or prayers to yourself to avoid some feared disaster or repeat behaviors like going in/out doors, up/down from chair, and so on.

➤ Ordering: You arrange objects in a particular way or according to some set of rules. Shoelaces must be exactly even; eyebrows must be identical to a hair; furniture never an inch out of place; dressing and undressing, brushing your teeth, and using the toilet done in a precise, unvarying order.

Angst Bulletin

Obsessive thoughts and impulses appeared to plague many religious figures, including John Bunyan, author of *The Pilgrim's Progress*, and Martin Luther. From 1517, when Luther first celebrated mass, he became obsessed with worry that he had omitted something trifling, which would be a sin. His mind became clouded with blasphemous thoughts that he wished, several times a day, to confess.

You may not be only a washer or only a checker, but combine these rituals. Or you may start out primarily a washer and become primarily a checker. These thoughts and rituals may torment you daily without letting up. Or you may find your obsessive-compulsive behavior waxes and wanes. During times of stress, over fatigue, or physical illness, your rituals will likely intensify.

Although rituals generally follow your thoughts, like washing to avoid contamination, sometimes there's no logical link between your intrusive thoughts and your ritualistic actions. For instance, you avoid stepping on cracks to prevent your daughter from being harmed. A few people experience obsessional thoughts without compulsive behavior, though may engage in mental rituals. In rare cases, people engage in compulsive rituals without obsessional thoughts.

Normal Anal Retentives and True OCs

If you are an obsessive or compulsive type, you are a brooder and non-stop worrier. Thoughts get stuck in your head like gum on the bottom of your shoe and stop you from moving on until you clear up the problem. Worried about the nutrition of the school's meals, you get up at 5 o'clock every morning to juice organic fruit as part of your children's healthy, natural breakfast and pack a nourishing, organic, homemade lunch. Worried that your husband will forget his doctor appointment, you write reminders and insert them in his pant pockets, his jacket pocket, on his car visor and call his secretary to have her remind him. Meticulous and organized, your house is spotless, your clothes hung by category and your canned food shelved by type; all activities are carefully written in a daily calendar that you check off when completed and your day runs smoothly with little confusion.

After reading this chapter, you might worry that you too have OCD. There are, however enormous differences between healthy people with compulsive streaks and those with Obsessive-Compulsive Disorder.

If you suffer from OCD, your behavior is extremely disabling:

➤ Your obsessions and compulsions interfere with normal daily life, are acutely distressing, occupy a great deal of your time, are hard to resist, and control your thoughts and actions.

➤ You are wracked with self-doubt and filled with guilt in how your behavior may be affecting your family.

➤ You find yourself unable to make even simple decisions.

➤ Although you are careful to enact your rituals exactly, your life otherwise might be disorderly and you may be personally slovenly.

➤ There may be histories of psychiatric difficulties in your family.

➤ You may have learning disorders or other problems that indicate neurological compromise, like tics and twitches (often indiscernible to other people).

Watch It!

Not all OCD patients fit Freud's conception of the obsessive-compulsive person as fastidious, perfectionistic, punctual, cold, and neat. Dr. Judith Rapoport found that this description fits only around 20 percent of OCD patients. Some patients who incessantly wash will at the same time look slovenly and throw their clothes on the floor.

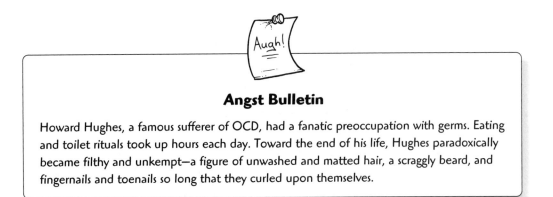

Angst Bulletin

Howard Hughes, a famous sufferer of OCD, had a fanatic preoccupation with germs. Eating and toilet rituals took up hours each day. Toward the end of his life, Hughes paradoxically became filthy and unkempt—a figure of unwashed and matted hair, a scraggly beard, and fingernails and toenails so long that they curled upon themselves.

Your symptoms can run from ordinary checking, like in the case of Marisol presented at the beginning of the chapter, to more extreme and bizarre behavior:

➤ One man, when taking a shower, uses a yellow glycerine soap to wash both legs up to his knees, a green glycerine soap to wash his thighs, a red glycerine soap to wash his genitals, a purple glycerine soap to wash his chest, and an orange

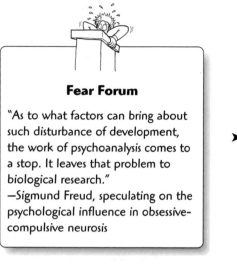

Fear Forum

"As to what factors can bring about such disturbance of development, the work of psychoanalysis comes to a stop. It leaves that problem to biological research."
—Sigmund Freud, speculating on the psychological influence in obsessive-compulsive neurosis

glycerine soap to wash every other area of his body. He can only use the soap once and discards them after each shower. If he doesn't do this ritual exactly, he feels dirty and has to take another shower immediately, until he washes himself "correctly." To ensure that he always has enough soaps on hand, he keeps an entire closet full.

➤ One college student has to tap her foot ten times when she comes across a word in her reading with a double "ee," as in "sweet." Not only does stopping to enact this ritual interrupt her concentration, but she feels compelled to reread each page five times lest she missed a word with this magical double vowel. Reading ten pages of text can take her four to five hours and leave her exhausted from the effort. Yet, if she doesn't do this ritual, she feels somehow in danger. She has considered just dropping out of college.

➤ In his book *Worry*, Dr. Edward Hallowell described treating a patient who had to count to a thousand before he left a bathroom. And he had to wipe out and then lick any ashtray he saw, including large ones in airports and public buildings. Imagine how embarrassing and, talk about germs, how unhealthy! Yet, if he didn't do it, he thought he would go mad and kill himself. How did he solve the problem? He didn't go to places where he might pass an ashtray. That meant he hardly ever went out!

The Why and Wherefore of OCD

Before the 1980s and the advent of tools to eavesdrop on the human mind, OCD was considered a disease of the psyche. Psychoanalytic theory posited that obsessive-compulsives are fixated at the anal stage. The urge to soil makes you compulsively neat, for instance. Washing symbolizes the need to wash away forbidden thoughts.

Learning theory viewed obsessions and compulsions as learned behavior through conditioning, and cognitive theorists explained OCD as a thought disorder, where people overestimate the likelihood that harm will befall them. The cognitive theorists also noted some memory deficit. Compulsive checkers, for instance, have poorer recall of prior actions.

But the notion that OCD is buried in the unconscious psyche or is learned behavior has lost momentum. Today, the response of this disorder to drugs and the discovery of abnormalities in brain scans suggest strong biological underpinnings. If you suffer from OCD, you no longer have to feel weak, crazy, immoral or shameful. Your bizarre behavior is no more your fault than shaking is to the Parkinson's patient.

The first hints that OCD was a biological disease surfaced in the early 1900s, when Europe was struck by an epidemic of viral sleeping sickness. After the epidemic passed, many previously normal survivors experienced OCD symptoms. This led researchers to the possibility that biological changes, brought on by the virus, could be the underlying cause of obsessive-compulsive behavior.

Angst Bulletin

A man, extremely distraught by OCD, put a bullet in his brain. He didn't die. But it cured his OCD! Somehow, the bullet disrupted the abnormal activity in the part of the brain that triggered his obsessive-compulsive behavior.

Today, we have further evidence of a link between OCD and a viral infection. About half of OCD cases start in childhood. Some of these children are like any other normal child and then wake up one day counting and recounting all their stuffed animals and avoiding sidewalk cracks or other senseless rituals. Such was the case with eight-year-old Eli. Your average kid, suddenly he was unable to touch anything in his house that might have germs—door knobs, faucets, clothing, and on and on. This behavior began right after a common childhood infection: strep throat. Apparently, streptococcal antibodies find their way into the brain and attack a region called the basal ganglia, causing characteristic clumsiness and arm-flapping along with obsessions and compulsions. It's unknown how many childhood cases, or adult cases, may be a result from complications of this infection.

Our newfound ability to peer into the brain has also confirmed the biological connection. Picture this. During a brain scan, a technician offers an OCD patient a benign object, such as a clean rubber glove; there is no change in brain activity. Then the technician gives the patient a dirty rubber glove. The patient's brain shows a sudden burst of activity in the caudate nucleus, one portion of the basal ganglia in the human brain that controls instinctive, repetitive behavior such as grooming and nesting, just as its counterpart in animal brains triggers repetitive, ritualistic behavior.

Treatment with antidepressant medications that raise serotonin levels in the brain appear to normalize this activity and buttress support for the notion that OCD is largely a medical problem. Dr. Barry Jacobs of Princeton University, who discovered that repetitive movements, like chewing or licking, boost serotonin level, suggests that the repetitive motions involved in much ritualistic behavior in OCD may be a form of self-medication via the serotonin system.

Steadying That Emotional Tic

In the 1960s, when OCD was considered an incurable disease of the psyche, people stayed in psychotherapy for years trying to uproot the conflicts underlying their bizarre behavior, which continued. Today, armed with the knowledge that OCD is best understood in genetic and biological terms, it can be successfully treated through drugs and behavioral therapy. Though not a cure, these interventions drastically reduce the severity of the symptoms.

Secret Weapons

Psychological treatments clearly produce biological effects on the brain. Dr. Jeffrey Schwartz and others at the University of California at Los Angeles Medical Center has recently shown that a form of cognitive-behavioral therapy can correct abnormalities in the brain metabolic rates of OCD patients in the same way as psychotropic drugs like Prozac.

Magical Pills Control Magical Thinking

If you want to see the face of many OCD sufferers light up, the buzz word is "Anafranil." Introduced a decade ago, Anafranil (clomipramine) is a highly effective drug treatment that quickly became the drug of choice to treat OCD and was found to work well in around two thirds of cases; in just a few weeks of treatment, ritual behavior was reduced by 80 percent. Today, Prozac, Zoloft, Paxil and Luvox have also been found highly effective treatments that reduce symptoms of OCD.

Mind Inspection

What if you don't like taking medication? Are you doomed to a life of washing and checking? Not necessarily. A recent study found that cognitive-behavioral therapy with OCD patients altered excess brain activity in those that responded well to treatment in the same way as antidepressants like Prozac and Anafranil. Before treatment, subjects demonstrated excess activity or hypermetabolism in the caudate region. After either medication *or* behavioral treatment, the activity in the caudate region dropped to normal.

In other words, if you alter the thoughts that drive your symptoms, and, through systematic desensitization, reduce and even eliminate the compelling ritualistic behavior, you can change brain chemistry without drug intervention. In a typical session, you may be asked to rephrase the thought that your hands are dirty. If you feel compelled to wash your hands, you will be asked to tolerate not doing so for a minute or as long as you can. You then increase this toleration time gradually, as your level of anxiety allows. By preventing the ritual response and, instead, practice going through the obsessive anxiety calmly, the obsessive thoughts eventually stop.

This does not mean that OCs should not use medication. Many in the field believe the most effective treatment for OCD is a combination of medication and therapy. What's more, not everyone wishes to be in therapy nor succeeds at it.

Other Ways to Steady the Tic

In addition to drugs and therapy, relaxation helps you feel less fearful and less likely to have fear provoking thoughts. Meditation, for instance, has been found to break up obsessional mental patterns and helps you restructure your thoughts more productively. The problem is that many obsessive people find it hard to relax—to stop their intrusive and disturbing thoughts from racing. And so relaxation may be ineffective until your symptoms are under control.

Since OCD symptoms appear related to the level of serotonin in the brain, you should also try to boost serotonin level naturally. Here are some ways to do this, as suggested by Dr. Michael Norden in *Beyond Prozac*:

1. Exercise

2. Repetitive motions like chewing gum, licking, rocking, walking, bicycling, running

3. Sleeping well

4. Exposing yourself to negative ions, like walking in the rain, taking a walk along the beach, or buying a home ionizer

5. Vitamin, mineral and amino acids supplements (see Chapter 9)

The Least You Need to Know

➤ There's a substantial difference between obsessing and acting compulsively, and suffering from Obsessive-Compulsive Disorder.

➤ Although the symptoms of this disorder seem bizarre and crazy, the sufferers are quite sane and, when relieved of the symptoms, often normal and non-conflicted individuals.

➤ OCD, which until recently was viewed as a disorder of the psyche, is now assumed to have a strong biological basis.

➤ Though incurable, OCD can be effectively treated by antidepressant drugs and cognitive-behavioral therapy.

➤ Both drug treatment and successful cognitive-behavioral therapy correct brain abnormalities associated with OCD.

Trauma Ward

Chapter 18

Help Relieve Your Living Nightmare

In This Chapter

➤ What happens when trauma strikes

➤ The signs of post-traumatic stress disorder

➤ How different people cope with the shock

➤ Cultivating your survival skills in the short-term

➤ What to do when the pain doesn't go away

It's scary enough to imagine horrors happening to you. It's an unbelievable devastation when horrors become real events. When you see a loved one murdered. When you are raped. When you experience the ravages of war in live combat.

These and others traumas "outside the range of usual experience" tax every coping strategy you have within you and strip you of your basic concepts of safety. Suddenly, there could be danger lurking everywhere and anywhere.

The lucky ones manage to bounce back and return to their normal selves. Others are not so lucky and experience long lasting *Post-Traumatic Stress Disorder* (PTSD). In this chapter, you will learn its symptoms, its effects and some ways to help yourself or other victims of PTSD to bury the past and get on with your life.

Unimaginable Real Fear

For two months, Cicily, a 31-year-old, unmarried elementary school teacher dreams nightly of unfamiliar scary men in red T-shirts trying to rip her clothes off. She struggles furiously, tries to scream and then awakens—panting, sweating and petrified. To avoid the nightmares, she delays going to sleep. She scrubs her floors and bathrooms from top to bottom and douches repeatedly, trying to rid herself of the dirt that defiles her body and being.

Two months earlier, Cicily had been raped. After shopping in the mall, she returned to her car in a dimly lit indoor parking lot and started to unlock the door. Suddenly, a large young, white man, with filthy, scraggly blond hair, came out of nowhere, grabbed her and threw her forcefully into the back seat of her car. She tried to push him away but he overpowered her and forced her down on her stomach. She tried to scream but no sounds came out. He tore off her clothes and forcibly penetrated her from the back. She felt as if knives were tearing her up inside and sobs started to rack her body. "Shut up or I'll kill you," he said. She froze as he continued to rape her. Then he got up, zipped his pants and fled. The whole incident took no longer than five minutes, but seemed an eternity. Five minutes, and her life was irrevocably changed.

Afterwards, Cicily could barely remember his face. But she couldn't get that red T-shirt out of her mind. It haunts her. Every red object that she glimpses—a red car, a red dress, a child's red barrette, a red door—seems to jar flashbacks of the incident, causing her to feel crazy and sick to her stomach. If one of the children at school brushes past her or comes up from behind and taps her unexpectedly on the shoulder, she flinches and her eyes open so wide that the children look at her as if she were crazy.

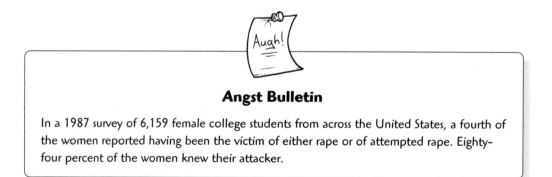

Angst Bulletin

In a 1987 survey of 6,159 female college students from across the United States, a fourth of the women reported having been the victim of either rape or of attempted rape. Eighty-four percent of the women knew their attacker.

She feels emotionally numb and has lost interest in her boyfriend, with whom she's been unable to have sex. When he embraces her, she stiffens and feels panic. Initially, he was sympathetic but lately he has lost patience and tells her it's time to "just forget it." At this, she often bursts into tears and begins to scream like a madwoman, which is very unlike her. She would like him to move out but is terrified of being alone, especially at night. At school, she often "spaces out," as the children say, during a lesson. She feels constantly jumpy and terrified and has been unable to drive her car unless accompanied and cannot drive into a parking lot, even when with someone. When she walks down the street, she feels she's being followed and looks furtively around. Lacking appetite, she has lost twenty pounds and feels constantly tired. She cannot look at herself in the mirror and has become slovenly in her appearance and feels that she hardly knows herself.

Tortured by Memory

Cicily is one of many who have experienced an event of such horror that they live tortured daily by the memory. For some, the memory lingers for months, for others, the torment lasts years, or even for the rest of their lives. They suffer from Post-Traumatic Stress Disorder (PTSD), an anxiety disorder that happens to people who experience, witness, or are confronted with an event or events that involve actual or threatened death or serious injury to themselves or to others, especially loved ones. Terrifying experiences such as:

Fear Forum

"Once you've been bitten by a snake, you are very cautious even of a coiled rope."
—The Dalai Lama

➤ Combat or prison camp experiences

➤ Natural disasters

➤ Accidents—industrial and automobile

➤ Rape or assault or other threats to personal safety

➤ Witnessing harm to or the death of loved ones

Evoking intense fear, helplessness, and often horror, the event lives with you. After returning from combat, a soldier experiences flashbacks of watching his best friend blasted to bits in front of his eyes. A woman who was raped hears a noise and wakes up screaming from a nightmare in which a strange man is creeping towards her. A child who was repeatedly screamed at and slapped without provocation and who felt helpless to stop the parents' abuse, lives constantly on guard. She retreats inward into numbness, an emotional freeze, and flees the here-and-now by hiding in her room with her nose in her books, which is both a distraction and an acceptable means of ignoring her parents.

If you've ever suffered from PTSD or do now, you've experienced most if not all of these symptoms:

Secret Weapons

The average person who seeks treatment following exposure to a traumatic event will recover twice as fast, in approximately six months, than those who don't seek treatment.

➤ You relive the event daily in images, dreams or flashbacks.

➤ You avoid thinking about the traumatic event and anything that reminds you of it.

➤ You live with intense anxiety and agitation when exposed to cues of the trauma; anniversaries of the event are unbearably painful.

➤ You feel numb and emotionally dead, yet flare up at little things.

➤ Anxious and tense, you have difficulty sleeping, concentrating, or even remembering things.

➤ You are hyper-vigilant and constantly on the lookout for danger and startle easily at noise or sudden movements.

➤ You feel depressed and may have even contemplated suicide.

➤ You may find yourself turning to drink and drugs to numb your pain and memories.

Although we recognize these as predictable patterns following exposure to a trauma, PTSD has only recently been accepted as a psychiatric or emotional disorder that needs treatment. First described during WWI as "shell shock," and then later in World War II as "combat fatigue," or "war neurosis," it was considered a sign of psychological instability and evoked contempt and pity. To avoid being stigmatized, soldiers did their best to keep their fear and trembling and nightmares secret, leaving them to lick their own psychological wounds in silence. Until the 1970s, many mental health professionals continued to believe that "normal" people could endure any atrocity. It took the suffering of Vietnam veterans, haunted long afterwards by their combat experience, to open the eyes of the psychological community and to establish PTSD as an official diagnosis.

Right After the Shock

If you've ever experienced trauma, which is an amazing half of all women and a little over half of all men, you know that you initially go through at least short-term trauma. During the event itself, you probably felt:

➤ Intense fear

➤ Disbelief

➤ Numbness

➤ Anger

➤ Confusion

➤ Pounding heart

➤ Trembling or shaking

➤ Fast breathing

➤ Sweating

➤ Nausea

In the days following the trauma, you may have felt anxious or fearful of being alone and worried about another catastrophe happening to you or those you love. Though you tried to not think about what had happened, you found yourself preoccupied with it—reliving it, or experiencing quick flashbacks or images. You felt tense, trembly, and had diarrhea or constipation, nausea, headaches, sweating and tiredness.

Depressed and anxious, you lost interest in your usual activities, including food or sex, and you couldn't think or concentrate on your work. Mostly, you walked around feeling sad, lost, alone, numb or unreal—in shock and disbelief. At night, you found it hard to sleep and awoke with nightmares. Though others tried to help, you felt isolated or detached from other people.

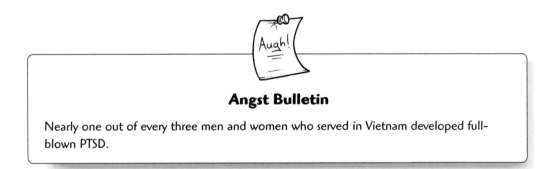

Angst Bulletin

Nearly one out of every three men and women who served in Vietnam developed full-blown PTSD.

Consumed with guilt and self-doubt, you mulled over in your mind how you could have acted differently and prevented the trauma, and felt "responsible" for another person's injuries or death. Why, you wondered, did you survive and/or come out of the ordeal better off than they did? You felt angry and irritated at what had happened, at what caused the event, and the senselessness of it all. "Why me?" you asked.

Why Me?

Not everyone experiences all of these reactions to the same degree and some people cope better than others. Fortunately, most people get past the trauma within hours, days or weeks. With the exception of rape, with whom 80 percent of victims will experience PTSD, less than 25 percent of people exposed to a typical PTSD trauma will go on to be diagnosed as having PTSD—that is, to continue for more than a month to re-experience the trauma, to avoid anything that reminds you of it, and to feel anxious and remain on guard for possible danger.

Though more men are exposed to trauma, more women develop PTSD following trauma, as the statistics following rape indicate—women obviously being the majority of rape victims. The real numbers of PTSD sufferers are probably higher, as not all victims seek psychological help. And of those that do, some therapists may diagnose them as having clinical depression or GAD, rather than PTSD.

What makes a person vulnerable to developing PTSD? Several factors:

➤ How intense and severe was the trauma? Someone who lost their home in a fire will get on with their life more easily than a person who saw their child murdered.

➤ Is this your first experience with trauma or does it get piled on top of other horrific experiences? Clearly the more on your plate, the harder it is to digest new pain.

➤ Do you have a prior history of anxiety and depression? If you are already emotionally unbalanced, life can knock you off your feet that much more easily.

➤ Are you sensitive and fear prone with a harm avoidance personality? If you are, you will experience the trauma more intensely and weather the storm with more difficulty than those hardy and resilient.

➤ How much do you exaggerate expectations that the trauma may recur and that your anxiety will never go away? The more so, the more fearful and troubled you will continue to feel.

➤ How many people, if any, do you have in your life available to comfort you, to listen to you, to aid you and to take your pain seriously? The more people to turn to, especially a significant other, the easier it will be to work through the nightmare and get on with your life.

➤ Do you have the financial resources for treatment and recuperation? Financial security may not buy happiness but it does buy psychological therapy, massage therapy, vacations, lawyers and other ways to get your life in order.

About 30 percent of people recover a year after the traumatic event. But about one-third of people who experience trauma never recover from it, even with professional treatment. Why is a traumatic memory so hard to blot out of your mind? Following trauma, the brain mobilizes all its forces and sends out various hormones, neurotransmitters and other substances that surge through the brain, actually changing the brain's physical structure. The more extreme and long-lasting the trauma, the more permanently it alters brain chemistry and a formerly outgoing, cheerful person can become a jittery, guarded, despondent person within a few months. Some pain can last forever.

Angst Bulletin

Psychiatrists J. Douglas Bremner, Dennis Charney, and colleagues reported that some trauma victims, including Vietnam combat vets and victims of child abuse, may experience physiological brain changes—specifically, a shrinkage in the size of the hippocampus, a structure important to memory and learning—as a result of the "toxic" levels of stress they've endured.

Abusive parenting and other trauma also seriously deplete the brain of serotonin and set the stage for potential serious psychiatric illness. Dr. Michael Norden (*Beyond Prozac*) suggests that the following problems arise directly from low serotonin levels:

➤ Increased irritability, aggression, impulsivity, violent suicide, alcohol and drug abuse, eating disorders, and sexual activity

➤ Greater likelihood of chronic pain, seizures, hypoglycemia, and insomnia

Coping with Trauma's Aftermath

Right after the shock, what can you do to help yourself? Here are some suggestions:

➤ Don't be alone and especially not at home. If you live alone, try and get a friend or relative to stay with you.

➤ Talk about the event with others. This will help you get over the initial reactions.

➤ Try to do strenuous physical exercise to burn off some tension and anxiety.

➤ Avoid or at least restrict stimulants that will further agitate you, like cigarettes, tea, coffee, chocolate, and cola.

➤ Try to eat even if you have no appetite.

➤ If you are tossing and turning and unable to sleep, get up and do something relaxing, like reading, knitting, computer games and the like, until you feel tired. Try an herbal combination of kava and valerian root, which you can buy at the health food store, to ease you into sleep.

Watch It!

Though sedatives, sleeping pills or alcohol may be initially necessary to help you get over the initial shock of your experience, try not to build a reliance on them. They will dull your experience and not allow you to deal properly with your feelings, which is necessary for recovery.

The few days following the trauma are rough. To help you cope, remind yourself that your reactions are a normal result of trauma and that you just have to ride it out until they pass. If you can, try to get back into your normal routine as soon as possible. Have patience with yourself and ease slowly back into taxing and difficult tasks.

When you feel afraid, anxious or uncomfortable, sit down, close your eyes, take some slow breaths and remind yourself that you are safe—that the trauma is over. Delegate as many responsibilities that you can and try to do things that are relaxing and enjoyable.

Work on your general stress level:

➤ Try to get adequate sleep.

➤ Eat a good diet.

➤ Do regular exercise.

➤ Do breathing exercises.

➤ Practice relaxation to help reduce nervous tension.

➤ Take long, relaxing baths.

➤ Get a massage.

➤ Listen to soothing music.

Secret Weapons

What doesn't kill you makes you stronger.

Breaking the Silence

Some people deal with trauma by not dealing with it—by denying its power and trying to bury it as soon as possible and not talking about it. This can happen if you are an emotionally inhibited person and don't share your feelings and experiences. It happens as well because some people are uncomfortable hearing of horrifying experiences; they feel awkward and don't know what to say or how to comfort you.

But denying the impact of the trauma will only prolong its effect. To get over your feelings and come to some resolution or closure, you have to allow yourself to go through a normal mourning period of loss. Therefore, it's essential to deal with the memories and to try to continue to talk to your family, friends, and colleagues about the trauma. Even if you feel a bit detached from other people, try to not reject their support.

Coming to Grips

If over time your wound only festers, rather than heals, you should seek out professional help. If you do, you have double the chance of coming to grips with the event and moving on. While the memory of the trauma almost never goes away, it need not always torment you and dominate your thoughts.

What balm seems to work best to soothe and detoxify the hurt? A combination of drug treatment, and cognitive-behavioral therapy. Some people have also found that innovative new treatments like EMDR and light therapy can help.

Drugs to Ease the Pain

Following a trauma, it's best to try and quickly ease the pain and shock in any way possible. Sedatives like Xanax and Klonopin can be helpful.

Once past the initial acute phase of the trauma, and you feel more stable and reassured that the danger is over, you may consider antidepressants, like Prozac, Zoloft, and Paxil, to help reduce the frequency and intensity of upsetting symptoms.

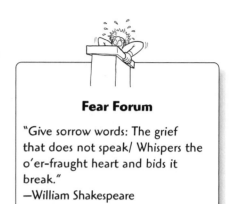

Fear Forum

"Give sorrow words: The grief that does not speak/ Whispers the o'er-fraught heart and bids it break."

—William Shakespeare

Reliving the Horror from a Safe Place

In cognitive-behavioral therapy, you will be asked to do that which you so ardently avoid—to re-experience the event. However, you will do so with a therapist trained to know how to support your pain. Although it's painful to relive the horror, if you stay with it, your anxiety peaks and then starts to decline. Why does this happen? The flight-or-fight response to stress cannot stay in red alert for much longer than forty-five minutes. After that, your brain runs out of the chemicals that fuel extreme alarm. And then something quite extraordinary happens. You can visualize the trauma *sans fear*. This experience teaches you that the original trauma need not overpower you with terrifying feelings. You have debrided your wound and washed away the hurt. In its place, you can insert into your brain new thoughts and memory structures. Thoughts like "It was not your fault," "You did all you can do to protect yourself or others," "You don't have to feel guilty for surviving."

EMDR

Picture this. A woman walks into a therapist's office and collapses in sobs, unable to let go of the memory of coming home and finding her husband's head splattered all over the bathroom floor from a self-inflicted gunshot wound. The therapist asks the woman to recall the events of that day, and to simultaneously follow with her eyes the therapist's finger, which is waving rapidly from side to side twenty or so times in front of the patient's face. The woman immediately feels less anxious. By the end of the first session, she feels relief for the first time since the incident eight years earlier. By the end of ten sessions, she is no longer haunted by the memory.

The treatment, devised by Francine Shapiro, is called *EMDR (Eye Movement Desensitization and Reprocessing)*. To date, no one is quite sure how it works—but, for some PTSD sufferers, it does appear to.

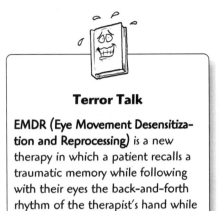

Terror Talk

EMDR (Eye Movement Desensitization and Reprocessing) is a new therapy in which a patient recalls a traumatic memory while following with their eyes the back-and-forth rhythm of the therapist's hand while it moves across her field of vision.

Something about the eye movements occurring simultaneously with the remembered trauma activates something in the brain and drains the poison from the memory. Shapiro suggests that the EMDR eye movements are akin to those in dream sleep, known as rapid eye movement (REM) sleep, which helps the brain digest, process and integrate troubling experiences. When deprived of REM sleep, people become irritable, disoriented and anxious. This, however, is a theory not supported by dream researchers and EMDR also appears effective if you substitute finger tapping or auditory tones in one ear, while speaking into the other.

A more plausible explanation is one of dual attention. You conjure up the memory and then distract your attention from it with the eye movements. Somehow, this helps the right and left hemispheres of the brain chat with each other and, in effect, negotiate how to better process the traumatic event.

Secret Weapons

For trauma victims, Dr. John Downing, an optometrist in Santa Rose, California, and a pioneer in the field of light therapy, has found the use of colored filters successful in relieving painful memories. He has found blue light to work consistently 90 percent of the time. For more information on light therapy, see Appendix B and *Light Years Ahead* (Berkeley, CA: Celestial Arts, 1996); *Light, Medicine of the Future,* Jacob Liberman (Sante Fe, NM: Bear and Co., 1991).

Light at the End of the Tunnel

In Chapter 16, I talked about how light therapy alleviates winter depression for people who suffer from SAD. For some people, colored light therapy also appears to help cleanse the brain of traumatic memories of physical, sexual, and emotional abuse.

Light is not something that just allows us to see. It goes directly from the visual cortex into two different pathways into the brain: the cerebral cortex and the limbic system. When it hits the cerebral cortex, we think about it, organize it, interpret it and make sense of it. When it hits the limbic system, it jars our emotions. Some trauma victims have found that the use of colored light therapy with selective filters triggers old painful memories that literally gush out and are often accompanied by the bodily symptoms associated with the original experiences. Afterwards, it's as if the stress was literally squeezed out of the mind. Different colors have different impacts and it is up to the therapist (usually an optometrist, physician, psychiatrist, psychologist, or a chiropractor) to determine the appropriate color (or colors) for each patient. The sessions last for about 20 minutes, four to six times a week, over a period of weeks or months.

The Least You Need to Know

➤ Three fourths of those who experience a trauma get over it within days, weeks or a few months.

➤ People who don't get over trauma within a month suffer from Post-Traumatic Stress Disorder (PTSD) meaning that they continue to re-experience the trauma, avoiding anything that reminds them of it, and remain hyper-vigilant and on guard for possible danger.

➤ People with PTSD have double the chance for recovery if they seek treatment.

➤ Research has demonstrated that cognitive-behavioral therapy is the most effective treatment for PTSD sufferers.

Part 5
Childhood Fears

"Mommy, there's a bear under my bed." "Daddy, there's a monster in the closet."
What parent has not heard this cry at one time or another from their young child?

When you meet these witches, wolves, and bogeymen of childhood head on with your
support, empathy and protection, these fears tend to get buried along with the blankey
and your children, feeling secure and safe, grow up better equipped to face life's
challenges. But if ignored, minimized, exaggerated or teased about, the normal fears
that should come and go—separation anxiety, barking dogs, the dark, ghosts, burglars,
staying alone, getting hurt—fester, strengthen and spread, and the world feels generally
unsafe. By adolescence, they might rear their ugly head as fears of dating, taking tests,
giving a speech, and by adulthood, of flying, going out of the house, or failing.

In Chapters 19 through 22, you will learn how to distinguish normal from abnormal
childhood fears and how to create a haven of safety for your children that will help
circumvent later fears and anxieties from doggedly pursuing them.

Chapter 19

Lions, Tigers, and Bears...Oh My!

In This Chapter

➤ Why some children stay afraid of the "big bad wolf"

➤ Fright is normal, phobic avoidance is not

➤ Teaching your child to outfox the foxes

➤ When it's time for professional ghost busters

I was a very fearful child. At five, I was certain that Frankenstein had taken up residence in my closet and was only waiting for me to close my eyes so he could attack me and squash out my young life. Petrified, I kept a careful watch for hours. Once I closed my eyes, they stayed shut, lest I opened them to find him looming over me. At age seven, I saw my first monster movie—*The Creature from the Black Lagoon*. At the first sight of the black claws creeping out of the water, I fled down the theater aisle. After that, I avoided monster movies. Childhood was frightening enough.

Childhood is fraught with deep, dark, penetrating fears. After all, it's all new, and who knows what might happen the first time you're left with a babysitter, your first day of school, your first dance recital, your first date? Little wonder that ninety percent of children aged two to fourteen express a wildly exaggerated and irrational fear of dogs, cats, snakes, thunderstorms, vacuum cleaners, or faucets. Children aged two to six average four fears; those aged six to twelve average seven. Your daughter, however, is likely to have more fears than your son, or at least she will admit to having more.

Most of their fears are developmental in nature, and should disappear as your child gains independence, self-control, and can think more logically. When he learns that he won't disappear down the bathtub drain, the fear no longer has a reason for being. When he learns that ghosts and the bogeyman belong in the land of fantasy, he no longer buys into monsters—or Santa coming down the chimney.

Angst Bulletin

Fears of animals, weather, accidents, heights, enclosures, the dark, doctors, and medical procedures often begin in childhood. Fears of transportation, public speaking, meeting people, and other social fears generally begin in adolescence as unresolved earlier fears.

But some children live imprisoned in a dungeon of terror that doesn't abate with time. Stealing joy, hope, security, and comfort from them, these out-of-control fears become the stuff from which phobias, panic, anxiety and depression are made. The four-year-old's fear of monsters becomes the eight-year-old's panic of robbers; the toddler's separation anxiety becomes the six-year-old's school phobia and, in the adult, agoraphobia; and the infant's stranger anxiety becomes the adolescent's social phobia. At the very least, unresolved fears can make us timid or bitter, and cause us to procrastinate and avoid.

In this chapter, you will learn how to identify if your child's fears have become phobias and everyday fright anxiety. You will discover ways to bust your child's ghosts and keep the fears from resurfacing during times of stress, and to know when he needs a professional ghost buster to do so. If freed of these taunting psychic demons early on, your child will be better equipped to cope with life in general—which never ceases to be scary.

Locked in the Dungeon of the Imagination

Four-year-old Perry, an active and easily excitable child, hates to go to sleep. He's certain that a monster lurks in the dark, ready to grab him by the throat and take him to Never-Never Land as soon as he closes his eyes. Every night his parents go through the ritual of looking under the bed and in the closet for any hiding ghouls. Yet Perry still doesn't feel safe enough to sleep alone in his room and cries until his parents take him into their bed, tucked safely between them. This has been going on for over a month, since his preschool teacher, whom he adored, got married. Now he has Miss Monique. When that bully, Jordan, hits him and he hits Jordan back, she puts both Jordan and him in time-out. At school, he's become uncharacteristically quiet and has also recently become highly allergic—to mold, bananas, peanuts, wheat products and to his cat.

Seven-year-old Tali refuses to be in the bathroom alone or to even close the bathroom door. A bright, sensitive and imaginative child, she pictures monsters oozing out of the faucet and crawling creepily up her arms and sucking her blood out. When doing her business on the toilet, she imagines something slithering up and biting her. If mom or dad do not wait outside the door until she's finished, she starts crying and screaming for the parent. In school, she will only use the toilet during bathroom break, when several girls are in there at once. At other times, she will hold it in and has, more than once, peed in her pants. She is constipated all the time which, ironically, means *more* time spent in the dreaded bathroom.

Watch It!

When normal childhood fears mushroom into abnormal intensity, disrupt your child's life, and stick around for more than a month, they're a cause for concern.

At night, she tries to sneak into her parent's bed and has begun to suck her thumb, a habit she gave up at four. In addition to constipation, she complains of headaches. Her parents try to convince her that nothing will ooze out of the faucet or wiggle out of the toilet, but to no avail. This behavior began a few months ago, shortly after viewing *The Blob*, a horror movie where a monster emerged from a bathroom spigot.

Are Perry and Tali's monsters the normal childhood fears and frights or are they the phobic avoidance of an overly anxious child? If you answered the latter, you are right. Their fears have all the signs of psychological disturbance. They are intense and preoccupy the children's lives. And the children's anxiety is spilling out into physical symptoms.

This doesn't mean the children won't resolve their fears on their own. But even if they do, the monster's demise may be superficial: It may take refuge underground to incubate, ready to pop up later in another form. For instance, a six-year-old might be afraid of swings. If unresolved, this can spread to a fear of heights in general and as he grows, he may feel anxious when climbing steep stairs, taking escalators, driving across a bridge or looking out the window in a high-rise.

Terror Talk

Night terrors, which occur during deep sleep, are different from **nightmares**, which occur during dreaming or REM sleep. When a child has a night terror, they scream or talk loudly in fear but cannot be awakened, eventually go back to sleep, and don't remember the occurrence. Night terrors appear to be primarily physiological and generally disappear by age six or so.

How do you recognize that your child's fears have gone beyond the norm and present either a clear anxiety disorder or the seeds of one? It's not always easy. Even in Tali's case, which is extreme, some parents lack the right information and may believe that she is just going through a stage that she will get over. The older the child, the harder it is to recognize when fears have become phobias,

Watch It!

By five to eight years of age, some fearful children show mild obsessive-compulsive behavior. The child may dwell on a morbid thought, such as being killed or of the parent dying, and in response, enact rituals like straightening out each stuffed animal before going to sleep, or pushing something under the bed so there's not enough room for a monster, for instance.

anxieties, and obsessions and compulsions. Children are poor at putting their fears into words. As they mature, they become more secretive about their concerns and, if they have them, ritualistic behaviors. They worry that you might think them crazy. They themselves may not recognize the true nature of their worries and fears. So you need to play detective.

To find out if your child's fears are a cause for concern, look over the signs that indicate that fears have gone beyond the normal, expected terrors of childhood:

➤ Disruption of child's life: friendships, schoolwork, appetite, sleeping, going to new places or even familiar ones

➤ Avoidance: of places, people, or objects, such as school, water, elevators, dogs, and so on

➤ Persistence: regardless of reassurance, fear lingers or even worsens for more than a month

➤ Sleep disturbances: insomnia, nightmares, night awakenings, and *night terrors*

➤ Age-inappropriate behavior: an eight-year old unwilling to separate from the parents; a teenager fearing monsters

➤ Out of character behavior: a bubbly child suddenly becoming serious; a child who loved to go swimming suddenly becoming afraid of water; a child who has always slept in a darkened room suddenly becoming hysterical about the dark

➤ Extreme reactions: trembling, sweating, fidgeting, crying, weight loss/gain, diarrhea, vomiting, insomnia, hysteria, or panic

➤ Psychosomatic complaints: constant stomachaches, or headaches or similar ailments without apparent physical cause

➤ Denial of all fears: behaving as if unafraid of anything

➤ Change in activity level or concentration: sluggish and withdrawn or hyperactive; sudden short attention span

➤ Regression: bed-wetting after a long period of staying dry at night; suddenly not wanting to leave the parent; loss of intellectual gains

➤ Mild obsessions and compulsions: checking and rechecking locks on windows; placing and drawing curtains so burglars can't come through; closing the closet door so the monster can't come out—or leaving it open so the monster can't go in; checking under beds once or twice a night; covering up in the dark even when warm

Planting the Seeds of Terror

What makes a child vulnerable to abnormal fears? Barring serious trauma, such as child abuse, it begins with a fear-prone temperament. Experience then reinforces it by:

➤ A parent who fails to buffer the child's high reactivity

➤ Real life events like a dog bite, witnessing someone close who is also afraid of dogs

➤ What the child reads in a book or sees on television

➤ Our cultural practice of separate sleeping

➤ The secondary gains of maintaining fears inherent within the family system

Angst Bulletin

University of Maryland psychologist Nathan Fox, who has measured brain activity by electroencephalogram (EEG) in inhibited and outgoing children, found two characteristic patterns. Inhibited, or fearful children show greater right-brain activity, which plays more of a role in negative emotions, while bold children show left-brain patterns, which plays more of a role in positive emotions. These patterns hold true not only under stress, but even when the children are resting, and continue into adulthood.

Born Scared

If you have a fearful child, she's likely a girl—high strung and quick to react with trepidation to strange or threatening situations. At first, you may have wondered what you did wrong to make her so easily frightened of the most innocuous things—a sudden, loud noise, a clown face popping out of a box. But, as you've learned in previous chapters, she was probably born with a panic button set to go off easily. In fact, a high heart rate—the physiological marker of the shy, inhibited child—is evident even in the womb. Sensitive and alert to nuances, she more easily notices noises or shadows in the night that could mean a lurking monster under the bed. And while your bold son, with his low heart rate, interprets the loud noise as interesting, she instantly interprets it as scary. Children who have vivid imaginations are also more prone to develop a variety of fears.

Being born fear-prone does not mean she will develop phobias, anxieties, or obsessions and compulsions. But it does mean that you will have to work overtime to make her feel safe and relaxed in the world.

Watch It!

If you're wishy-washy, and "no" means "yes, if you nag me enough," there's a good chance you will fail to instill in your child the confidence that you are strong enough to protect them should danger arise. Instead, your child feels left to his own devices and this is scary.

Who's in Charge? Nature or Nurture?

Sensitive, loving parents take their children's fears seriously and respond to them with cookies and sympathy, with nurturance and understanding. At the same time, they neither overreact with hysteria, which increases the child's anxiety, nor diminish their meaning, which makes the child feel unprotected and her feelings invalidated. Structuring and organizing their child's life with consistent and fair rules, supervision, schedules, and an environment that neither over- nor understimulates, they maximize certainty, predictability, safety and protection. Fears don't get out of hand because what the monsters symbolize—being abandoned, overpowered, disapproved of, helpless, a failure, or losing "me" and being annihilated altogether—is not perceived as a direct threat. The barking dog is not what is likely to hurt the child. It is the power of the barking, angry father who might hurt or desert you. Fear of monsters also symbolizes the child's own monstrous behavior—the monster within—that makes fathers irate.

But when parents, for whatever reason, don't create a warm, nurturing, organized and secure environment, biology dominates and the child becomes even more reactive, fearful and easily overwhelmed by stress. This is especially true for the fear-prone child.

Secret Weapons

Dr. Joel Feiner, author of *Taming Monsters, Slaying Dragons*, believes that when a child's fear doesn't go away, it's not just the child's problem. It's the problem of the whole family because deeper, less obvious family difficulties are probably at the root of these lingering terrors. The best way to treat them is to treat the whole family unit.

If a six-year-old has to feel humiliated the day of the school picture because her mother forgot to dress her up, or feel afraid to give her mother the carefully drawn Mother's Day card because it will go straight into the garbage—if she has to worry about love, it's hard to just concentrate on being a six-year-old. Instead, she will begin to worry about how to behave to avoid the frown on the mother's face and the edge in the mother's voice. Inside, she will be so twisted with fears and terrible consequences that it's hard to learn or have fun or feel confident that people will like you.

She might also learn that fears come in handy: they force parental protection. A child may begin to fear the dark, for instance, if it means an otherwise distant mother holds her while she falls asleep. Or she may begin to fear swimming in water if the ignoring, distant father lets her ride the waves on his back.

All in the Family

Children are part of a family. And families behave like mobiles: when one part moves, the whole configuration is changed. In other words, the behavior of each family member affects everyone else. If childhood fears linger or intensify, the underlying cause, according to Dr. Joel Feiner, author of *Taming Monsters, Slaying Dragons,* may be their use as a ploy to divert attention away from the parent's own unresolved marital, job, or emotional conflicts.

In the ideal family situation, the strongest bond is between the two parents and this helps sustain each to have the emotional wherewithal for their children. Family roles are flexible, communication is open—people really *listen* to each other—and the outlook is positive and upbeat. All of this makes fear less likely to settle in and grow out of proportion.

But if this bond is shattered, by marital friction or divorce, mother or father may instead turn to the child for support and the stronger bond develops with the child. Roles become muddied, as the child assumes the responsibility for meeting the parent's emotional needs. And this is fertile ground for fears. The fear might be used as a coalition between mother and child to exclude father. For instance, daddy won't let the frightened child snuggle into the family bed so mommy snuggles with the child in the child's bed. But since life is really shaky without daddy's involvement, fears might intensify to force an alliance between the parents and greater parental protection. The child might, for instance, develop a fear of water since his screams get both mommy and daddy concerned and working together to calm him.

In Bed Alone

In a *Dennis the Menace* cartoon by Ketcham, Dennis stands at the foot of his half sleeping parents' bed and says, *"It's easy for you to say, 'Don't be afraid of the dark'... You got somebody to sleep with!"*

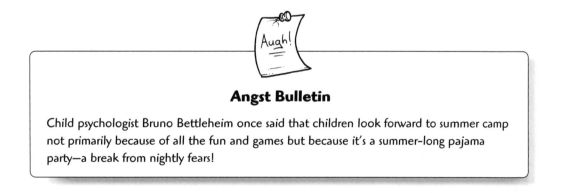

Angst Bulletin

Child psychologist Bruno Bettleheim once said that children look forward to summer camp not primarily because of all the fun and games but because it's a summer-long pajama party—a break from nightly fears!

Of all childhood memories, few are more frightening than those long nights alone, and few are more poignant than slipping into sleep locked safely in your mother or father's arms? Solitary sleeping can be a time of separation, loneliness, anxiety, and fear of sleep that breeds uncertainties and insecurities in children and explains why many behave at bedtime as if banished to a dungeon.

To what extent might our children's fears in this society be exacerbated by sleeping alone in a room, which is unheard of anywhere else in the world? Though our childcare experts caution that co-sleeping creates dependency and advise parents to not sleep with their children, most children in the world sleep in bed with their mother or in the same room, and always have. These cultures do not report the sleep problems common here—the endless rituals and "lovies" to get a child to sleep, fear of the dark, frequent night awakenings and nightmares. As for our fear of dependency, that stems not from co-sleeping but from the nature of the parent-child relationship. In healthy families, children generally leave the family bed on their own by age three to four, returning only during times of high stress.

You've Got to Be Taught to Be Afraid

Fears are as catchy as colds. If you are afraid of something and convey it, your children will pick it up. Tony Dorsett, one of football's giants, is a good example. As a child, he was taught that spirits walk a house left in complete darkness and so his parents always left the doors open a bit to allow a crack of light to come through. Even as an adult, he cannot sleep in the dark. "In my house," says Dorsett, "you see lights on everywhere."

Fear Forum

"Now there is one place where you can meet a ferocious beast on your own terms and leave victorious. That place is the imagination. It is a matter of individual taste and preference whether the beast should be slain, maimed, banished or reformed, but no one needs to feel helpless in the presence of imaginary beasts when the imagination offers such solutions."

—*The Magic Years*, by Selma Fraiberg

Terror on the Tube

For the first time in human history, parents are not in control of what influences their children: the media has taken over that role. In days of yore (pre-television!), children did not confront the likes of animated witches, King Kong or Freddie Kruger. They met their monsters mostly in their imagination, through nursery rhymes or scary stories, like fairy tales, that were told or read to them from books that had few or no pictures. This allowed the child to conjure up his own image of ghosts and witches in terms of what he could handle. How many children do you know who become frightened when hearing the nursery rhyme "Three Blind Mice, They all ran after the farmer's wife, She cut off their tails with a carving knife?"

In fairy tales, which start with "Long ago and far away," children are reassured that there is no imminent danger. This is also why they so like dinosaurs: Before the movie Jurassic Park, they were confident they would never run into one! And the frightening symbols of monsters in fairy tales are often gotten rid of by the children themselves, who slay the dragon, fell the giant, and burn the wicked witch. This increases the child's confidence that they themselves can learn to tame their own fears.

Television, in contrast, often portrays horrifying images beyond what children can manage and exacerbates their view of the world as scary and dangerous.

First Steps in the Monster Mash

As a parent, you can't stop your child from feeling afraid. But you can do much to tame the monsters and prevent them from taking residence. First, though, you need to identify your child's fears.

Using the list on the following page, check off the category or categories in which your child displays fears. In the blank space, fill in your child's specific fears. Mark with an asterisk those that are strong enough to constitute a phobia—those that are unusually intense, persist over time and cause avoidance that disrupts your child's life. For instance, if your child reacts fearfully to strange men, underneath strangers write "men." If your child reacts phobicly to getting a shot, underneath medical, write "getting a shot*".

Watch It!

Pronounced stranger anxiety that does not end sometime in the second or third year can lead to acute shyness and later social phobia. Children, reluctant to socialize with peers and others, will retreat into themselves or behind their mother's apron strings.

Augh!

Angst Bulletin

Young children, unable to conceive of the finality of death, rarely dream of being killed or of a loved one dying. But by six to eight, children are likely to describe scary dreams in which they or loved ones were killed.

Childhood Fear Survey

1. Strangers
   Examples: _____

2. Separating (going to sleep, to school or to a babysitter's house)
   Examples: _____

3. Noises
   Examples: _____

4. The Dark (ghosts and monsters, burglars and kidnappers, nightmares)
   Examples: _____

5. Fantasy characters (clowns, Halloween masks, characters from scary movies)
   Examples: _____

6. Animals
   Examples: _____

7. Insects
   Examples: _____

8. Nature (thunder, lightning, wind, tornados, hurricanes, earthquakes, floods, water)
   Examples: _____

9. Transportation
   Examples: _____

10. Medical
    Examples: _____

11. Dental
    Examples: _____

12. Germs
    Examples: _____

13. Social (meeting new people, making friends, going to parties)
    Examples: _____

14. School
    Examples: _____

15. Enclosed spaces (bathrooms, closets, elevators, back seat of cars, crowds)
    Examples: _____

16. Heights (swings, slides, ladders, bridges, glass elevators, roller coasters)
    Examples: _____

17. Death or serious injury
    Examples: _____

Teaching Children to Outfox the Foxes

Now that you've identified your child's fears, what are the best fear-busters? That which increase your child's feelings of the world as safe—a place where, for the most part, she will not encounter threats that she cannot manage or that she cannot rely on her parents or other caring adults to manage. The magic formula?

> **Secret Weapons**
>
> When children were confronted in a room with a toy gorilla, those who were able to control it and had realistic knowledge about it were unafraid.

➤ Self-efficacy—the feeling that her actions have the power to get her needs met, that she has the ability to create a favorable outcome for herself

➤ Internal control—the capacity to organize events and to reasonably predict a favorable outcome

➤ Trust—the perception that she can depend on caregivers to safeguard her from harm, both physical and psychological, and to not abandon her

How do you help your child, when faced with fears, to feel greater self-efficacy, internal control, and trust in people to safeguard her?

➤ Recognize and respect her fears

➤ Structure her world to minimize confrontation with them

➤ Stay cool

➤ Expose her gradually to feared objects and situations

➤ Give her information about what frightens her

➤ Encourage mastery of feelings through play and imagination

➤ Tell her stories

Monsters Are Serious Business

Take your child's fears seriously. Don't downplay them and don't ridicule, scold or punish your child for expressing them. Comments such as "that's silly, you know there isn't a bear under your bed" "don't be such a scaredy-cat" "there's nothing to be afraid of in the dark" "don't make a mountain out of a mole hill" erodes trust in you as a protector and makes her feel ineffective in getting what she needs—your understanding and protection.

> **Watch It!**
>
> By age three or so, when children are able to imagine danger, there's no telling what lurks in the dark, which is why so many children are afraid of sleeping without a light on. The shadow on the wall could be daddy checking on you, but it could also be the big bad wolf who's come to eat you up.

She will now feel that she has to hide her feelings from you and face her fears alone, which is a daunting task for a child. Later, fears will re-emerge as full-grown phobias or, in the least, anxious behavior.

Underlying these fears is a concern that the world is unsafe. And this is what needs to be addressed by reassuring your child that you will always be there to protect her: "Daddy wouldn't let a bear hurt you," "If you don't find any friends at the new school, mommy will be your friend." Communication with your child is key. For the preschool child especially, remember that fantasy is real: Big Bird is as much a person as everyone else she knows.

A Stitch in Time...

Become aware of the most common childhood fears (see Chapter 5), so you can predict what might frighten your child and prepare her ahead of time for a potentially scary event. At the very least, your quick and appropriate response can minimize many childhood fears.

Secret Weapons

One of the best ways to help latch-key children feel less fearful about coming home to an empty house is to get your child a pet, especially a dog with a loud bark.

➤ If you know that eight-month-olds often show stranger anxiety, you won't hand your baby over to the open arms of someone new until he has gotten used to that person.

➤ If you know that three-year-olds often get the "creeps" in the dark, you will leave on a light, which allows a view of familiar surroundings.

➤ If you know that a five-year-old still can't distinguish fantasy from reality, you won't take her to see the movie *Halloween Three*.

➤ If you know that your six-year-old takes awhile to get used to new situations, you won't just drop her off in front of school the first day of kindergarten.

Tame Your Own Monsters

When you feel afraid, try to remain calm, or at least appear so in front of your child and avoid focusing too much on the fear. If a loud barking German Shepherd scares you, you won't be able to calm your child's fear of dogs. And you give your child the message that the world is truly dangerous and you aren't strong enough to protect them.

Your own fears may also lead you to become overprotective and discourage your child from facing his own fears. This only reinforces them. Moreover, your over-protectiveness, not the dog, will come back to bite you: If you keep him from playing with children who have dogs, for instance, you may find yourself your child's constant playmate.

Catering the fear has another danger: secondary gains. If your child feels that being afraid is the best way to get your attention, his fears take on a reward and like catered guests, stick around.

You cannot protect your child from all danger and worry. You can, however, teach him how to worry wisely.

Once Upon a Time

"Tell me a story," says the child. Do. It is one of the best ways to reach a child. If he's sitting in your lap while you tell of once upon a time, love of the stories becomes intertwined with your love for each other. That kind of strength can slay any dragon.

Children love fairy tales and other stories not just for their entertainment value, but because the characters and plots contain meanings that speak directly to their inner-most concerns: parents who turn into witches and abandon overdemanding children, who try to eat them out of house and home, to forests; little girls who show up one day and usurp your spot as number one, eating your porridge and sleeping in your bed; kindly grandmothers who sometimes yell and turn into ferocious wolves; the giant that mothers must continually appease so he won't find and punish little boys. And then there are those stories that carry helpful hints on how to deal with a variety of situations: going to the doctor, the first day of school, the big brother who does everything better.

Read or tell your children stories as much as possible, rather than letting them watch fairy tales and other stories on TV or at the movies. Remember, your child will imagine only as scary an image as he can manage. When stories become visual, some of the images are pretty gruesome and frightening to young children.

Angst Bulletin

For more information on children's books, see *The New York Times Parent's Guide to the Best Books for Children*, by Eden Ross Lipson, and *Choosing Books for Kids*, by Joanne Oppenheim, Barbara Brenner, and Betty Boegehold. Also ask your local librarian or bookseller for helpful suggestions.

Just the Facts

Children can let their imaginations run away with them. Often, they picture themselves in dangerous situations that overpower them—like Frankenstein looming over my bed. But just as your child's imagination can create fears, so can it, with the power of knowledge, dispel them. To help your child better grasp a situation and realistically calculate the risks, correct their misconceptions with facts, while at the same time being careful to not deny their feelings. Then teach them how to use this information to give themselves a fear pep talk. Work out strategies to increase personal safety and give them lots of stories to read, or be read, on the subject. All this will enhance their feelings of mastery and control and trust in you as a protector.

Here are some specific examples abstracted from the book *Monsters under the Bed and Other Childhood Fears* by Stephen Garber, et. al.:

Thunderstorms

➤ Information: If your child understands that thunder and lightning, though scary, are highly unlikely to harm him, he will have less reason to fear danger. Explain what causes them and why people are unlikely to get hit by lightning.

➤ Plans: Talk about the precautions that you've taken in case of a severe storm, like a ready flashlight and batteries and a battery-powered radio.

➤ Pep Talk:

 1. Lightning hits the highest place and I am safe inside.

 2. Most storms do not cause any harm.

 3. Storms pass very quickly and this one will be over soon.

 4. I saw the lightning ____ seconds before I heard the thunder, so it was ____ miles away.

➤ Some helpful books to read:

 1. *Flash, Crash, Rumble, and Roll*, Franklyn M. Branley

 2. *Forces of Nature*, Anita Ganeri

 3. *Thunderstorms*, Mary Szilagyi

Dentists

➤ Information: Explain to your child all about teeth, what causes cavities, why the dentist must do some drilling to get rid of them.

➤ Plans: Take your child with you when you make the appointment to introduce him to the office. Go over with him each step of what will happen.

➤ Pep Talk:

1. The dentist will help teach me how to care for my teeth so they will be strong and pretty and I won't get cavities.

2. It does not hurt when the dentist looks into my mouth.

3. The novocaine shot only hurts a little and makes all the big pain go away.

➤ Some helpful books to read:

1. *Alligator's Toothache*, Diane DeGroat

2. *The Bear's Toothache*, David McPhail

3. *The Berenstain Bears Visit the Dentist*, Stan and Jan Berenstain

4. *Going to the Dentist*, Fred Rogers

Water

➤ Information: Give your child the basics about water. For instance that, though our bodies are about two-thirds water, we are lighter than water, which is why we can float. Show your child how. If he closes his mouth in water, it can't come in. Teach him water safety rules.

➤ Plans: Do water experiments to show how different objects float.

➤ Pep Talk:

1. I am lighter than water, so I can float.

2. A little water in my face cannot hurt. Even swallowing some cannot hurt.

3. Water is fun if I relax.

4. If I follow the rules, I will be safe.

5. If I should feel myself in danger, a lifeguard will immediately spot me.

➤ Some helpful books to read:

1. *Let's Go Swimming with Mr. Sillypants*, M. K. Brown

2. *The Magic School Bus at the Waterworks*, Joanna Cole

3. *Water is Wet*, Penny Pollack

Angst Bulletin

" The King of Beasts shouldn't be a coward," said the Scarecrow.

"I know it," returned the Lion, wiping a tear from his eyes with the tip of his paw. "It is my great sorrow, and makes my life very unhappy. But whenever there is danger, my heart begins to beat fast."

—L. Frank Baum. The Wizard of Oz

Watch It!

Each child's fears are unique and require a different gradual approach. Some children may be able to be in the same room with a chained dog, while others may find even that too frightening. Tailor your child's gradual exposure to fit their particular fear level and tolerance.

Avoid "Sink or Swim"

Don't force your child to confront her fear all at once, like by diving into the dreaded swimming pool or petting the barking dog. This "in the face" approach may only aggravate the fear and make it worse. Fear-prone children especially need to get used to something gradually or they will feel quickly overwhelmed. To help her feel greater control and confidence, that she can manage her fears, and trust in your ability to structure her world to reduce danger, break down confrontation of a scary situation into a series of steps.

When developmental psychologist Megan Gunner of the University of Minnesota observed how children reacted to stress by presenting a friendly clown, she found pace to make all the difference for the initially frightened, inhibited, anxious child. When mothers ignored or denied their child's discomfort and pushed them toward the clown, the child's stress level rose, as measured by the amount of the stress hormone cortisol in their saliva. When mothers accepted their child's caution and calmly helped them feel more comfortable, the child's stress response subsided and soon they might approach the clown.

Here are some helpful suggestions:

Dogs

➤ Have your child stand at whatever distance from the dog that he feels comfortable, making sure the dog is held or on a leash.

➤ Move up to the dog and pet it.

➤ As you hold the dog down, ask your child to touch an innocuous spot, like the dog's tail.

➤ If he becomes afraid, have him back off. If not, ask him to pet another "safe" part of the dog, like his back.

➤ As long as his fear doesn't escalate, continue in this manner until he begins to lightly stroke the dog.

➤ Continue in gradual steps to have him walk the dog, play with the dog, feed and give a treat to the dog.

Strangers

➤ Inform your child that she is about to meet someone new.

➤ Explain to the stranger that your child is slow to warm and to maintain a bit of distance, to not touch your child and, for an extremely fear-prone child, to not look directly into her eyes until she initiates and sustains eye contact.

➤ Allow your child to remain close to you until she begins to feel more comfortable and then slowly try inching away from her, eventually leave the room for brief periods.

➤ Practice social skills with her ahead of time, like saying hello, giving appropriate answers to questions, like "how old are you," and ways to open up conversation with a stranger.

➤ Help her slowly approach strangers on her own, like paying for something at a cash register or asking the librarian for a book.

➤ Give her a pat on the back for each step she takes to interact with new people—making eye contact, smiling, speaking, staying alone in a room with a stranger.

Power Play

Child's play is serious business. Similar to the adult joke, it allows children to express their full range of fears, confusions, and uncertainties, and deal with them in a safe way. To cope with death, the child plays "bang, bang, you're dead," but no one dies. To cope with daddies who scream and hit, the child becomes superman, who can fly away at will. In this way, the child feels in control. Anna Freud, a well known child psychoanalyst and Freud's daughter, reported a case of a little girl who was able to cross the dark, scary hall by pretending to be the ghost she was afraid of. By choosing the role of the ghost, the child could switch from the passive to the active role. This accounts for a great deal of the healing power of play.

Angst Bulletin

In the Italian film, *Life Is Beautiful*, a Jewish father protects his little boy from the horrifying reality of life in a Nazi concentration camp by pretending that the routines of the camp are no more than an elaborate game staged for his son's benefit.

If you want to know what makes your child afraid—why she cries, for example, when daddy comes to pick her up for the weekend—provide her with a lot of props to titillate her imagination. With some family dolls and play furniture, she will reveal the answer in no time. You can also get down on the floor with her and offer to re-enact a frightening situation. Use play in other ways as well. For instance, think of different ways to kill off bad monsters for life.

➤ Blow them into a balloon and let go of it or burst it.

➤ Make a witch's brew for bugs, put it into a kitchen pump bottle and spray away

➤ Chain the monster and lock him in a treasure chest, then bury him deep in the depths of the ocean

When Your Child Needs Professional Ghost Busters

Your children are as part and parcel of your being as your arm or leg. If something goes wrong, you feel personally responsible and agonize over what you did wrong. This makes it hard to admit that your child may need professional help. And who wants someone else to see your dirty emotional laundry?

But if in spite of your efforts your child shows undue anxiety or phobic avoidance that doesn't lift over time, it's best to treat these fears early before they have a chance to become entrenched into your child's psyche. Child therapy is typically short-term and fun for the child, consisting largely of play and games.

The Least You Need to Know

➤ Unresolved childhood fears can become adult phobias, panic, anxiety and depression.

➤ When fears become intense, disrupt your child's life, and stick around for more than a month, they're a cause for concern.

➤ Television and movies often portray horrifying images beyond what children can manage, and exacerbate their views of the world as scary and dangerous.

➤ The best way to be a "ghost buster" is to create a world for your child that boosts self-efficacy, internal control and trust.

Chapter 20

No More "I Don't Wanna Go to School"

In This Chapter

➤ The afraid-to-leave-home syndrome

➤ The afraid-to-go-to-school syndrome

➤ Cutting the umbilical cord before it's too late

➤ Hi-ho, hi-ho, it's off to school you *must* go

Four-year old MaryBeth starts kicking, screaming, and crying, and refuses to get out of the car when her mother drops her off at school. She begs her mother to let her stay home. Nine-year-old Andy gets a stomachache most mornings Monday through Friday, and his mother has to drag him to the school bus. In the afternoon and on weekends, he feels miraculously well.

In this chapter you will learn why children resist going to school and what parents can do to help their children overcome their school jitters.

The Monday Through Friday Tummyache

Remember your first day of school? Many people can. You may have been a little jittery, wondering if your teacher would be nice, if the children would like you. Most of you adapted rather quickly to the new situation and came to look forward to at least some aspects of school—friends, gym class, story time—if not all, and got yourself on the yellow school bus with little fuss. At times, you may have shown mild avoidance of school, especially when you were very young, or if you changed schools and had to readjust all over again.

This is not five-year-old Melanie's story, or ten-year-old Derrick's. School gives them the willies and both will feign anything to convince their mother to let them stay home. If it's not a stomachache, it's a headache, or a sore throat. Getting them dressed and on the school bus is a daily struggle.

Melanie's school refusal seems to come and go, dependent on how badly her parents fight. However, it's become every day of the three weeks since her father moved out. Melanie fears that if she leaves her mother and goes to school, her mother too might disappear and Melanie will return home from school to an empty house.

Derrick's school refusal is ongoing and everyday, and has been for three months since the beginning of the school year. Derrick is not so much afraid of leaving home as he is of being ridiculed in school. Derrick is a shy African-American child in a mostly white school and some cruel children in his class taunt him with names like "chocolate boy" and "black booty."

Although both Derrick and Melanie refuse to go to school, they do so for different reasons. Melanie fears not so much what awaits her in school, but what might await her upon returning home. She has *separation anxiety disorder*. Derrick, on the other hand, fears mostly what awaits him at school. He has *school phobia*. Although played out differently, they have similarly underlying causes. Often, though not always, they occur in excessively shy children and both are manifestations of unresolved fears.

Afraid to Leave Home

At the core of the child's separation anxiety lurks a primal fear that we never shake: abandonment. No devoted caregivers, no survival. The infant depends completely upon others for her very existence—food, warmth, care, affection, and protection. By the time a baby is one year of age, separation from the people that assure him safety, comfort, and protection evokes a deeply entrenched fear; the further from these protectors, the greater the alarm. All our lives we remain in tune, to greater and lesser degrees, to any sign that our significant other may bolt: the forgotten kiss goodbye or hello, a harsh word, or an indifferent look.

By age two or three, children can maintain a mental image of mother when she's gone and understand that she will return and separation anxiety starts to wane. By four, most children can manage the anxiety they feel about leaving you and, with little to-do, give you a quick goodbye when you drop them off at preschool and make a beeline for their best-friend-of-the-day. But a small percentage of children cannot make a smooth transition from your body to the school body. They cling and rant and rave if you try to leave them, and this behavior doesn't let up.

These children show the signs of SAD, or *Separation Anxiety Disorder* (not to be confused with seasonal affective disorder, which uses the same acronym). Children with SAD will panic at any separation—sleep, school, the babysitter's—and generally claim illness to stop you from leaving. When you take off, they become preoccupied that something will harm them or you. This protest behavior typically starts after a major stressful event: starting school for the first time; moving to a new school, and especially in a new neighborhood; illness of the child or parent; and death of a close one.

If you think your child might suffer from SAD, note how his or her behavior fits the following symptoms:

Separation Anxiety Disorder Syndrome

➤ Excessive anxiety about separating from an attachment figure, manifested in worry that the parent may be harmed or not return, or that the child may be lost, kidnapped, killed or injured

➤ Persistent reluctance or refusal to go to school, to sleep, or to be alone

➤ Headache, stomachache or nausea and intense distress with crying, pleading, clinging and tantrums when anticipating separation

➤ Excessive distress when separated, and excessive drive to return home, call home, and so on

➤ Frequent nightmares involving the theme of separation

Holding on to Mother's Apron Strings

Why do some children panic when separated from their parents? The answer lies both in nature and nurture. For those who are innately fearful, separation from caregivers makes the world scary, strange and uncertain. We see this starting at a year old, when many inhibited, shy children will go to pieces when the mother leaves, while their bold counterparts may just sit still and stare for a moment. When mothers warmly help these fear-prone children become comfortable with new people and new places and slowly ease away, the child's separation and stranger anxiety ebbs. Securely attached to their mothers, they feel as if someone is always watching over them and are confident that their mother will always return. When she does, the reunion is like that of two lost lovers. The child, arms wide open, runs to the mother, arms wide open, who then scoops him up into a warm embrace.

But if mothers are inconsistently available, they behave according to their own needs more than in response to signals from their child and may leave quickly without explanation, or they may prolong the leave taking. When she returns to pick the child up, sometimes she gives him the longed for hug, sometimes she ignores him—it depends on her mood. This inconsistency leaves children unsure of what to expect and to worry if mother will be there if they need her. When she walks out the door, the child thinks that maybe it will be forever. Separation protest is their ploy for making mom feel guilty and forcing her to stay. Says attachment theorist Patricia Crittenden, it's as if to say—"When you leave me, this is the price you pay."

Some parents are out of touch with their children and fail to pick up the pain of separating. They may get annoyed or even angry when their child protests and bolt out the door in a huff. This imparts an even more painful message to the child. "Not only will I not comfort you, but showing your hurt makes me mad." When the mother returns, there is no joyful running toward each other with open arms; instead there is hesitation, confused feelings, and sometimes indifference, as if mother and baby were two strangers. For these "avoidantly" attached children, all separations conjure up great loneliness and anxiety. Terrifically fearful of abandonment, they rarely feel comfortable and safe in the world. They cope by learning to lick their own wounds and most will stop overtly showing separation protest. Instead, they will force parental protection during times of stress by becoming ill, for instance, especially since ongoing stress has an impact on the immune system.

Angst Bulletin

When separated from their mothers, infants' hearts start to beat faster. If securely attached, the heart rate will return to normal when mother and baby are re-united. But in children with an avoidant attachment to their mothers, heart rates remain accelerated during reunion, presumably because they do not feel comforted by their mothers.

Fear of death, which is common at around age seven and when children are preteens, is another reason for separation anxiety. It emerges especially if the parent has been ill or injured. If the parent is emotionally distraught or having marital problems, and thus less emotionally available, separation fears also surface. The child might worry that the parents will argue if he's not around to prevent it or that one parent might leave. If the mother and child are locked into a dependent relationship, school phobia gets reinforced by secondary gains: the child gets to stay home with mom and may even get a few hugs to boot.

Long Separations

If you have a child who comes apart at the seams over short separations, like going to school, what happens during long separations, like when you go on vacation for a week, or if you have to be hospitalized for several days? This was a question that greatly intrigued child psychoanalyst John Bowlby, who lost his mother when he was a young child.

Bowlby discovered that children go through three distinct stages of separation:

➤ Distress: The child initially protests by crying, throwing tantrums, disobedience, clinging.

➤ Despair: When protest does nothing to bring the parent back, the child feels hopeless and becomes quiet and withdrawn—depressed.

➤ Detached: The child appears to have returned to normal functioning but, in reality, has coped with the pain of separation by becoming disengaged from the parent. When the parent returns, he resists reattachment for fear of being again rejected and abandoned. This explains why you may find that your young child greets you with a stony stare when you return from a week's vacation.

After the reunion, children whose parents are generally emotionally available will go backward through the stages—clinging for awhile and then, finally, relaxing back to a normal state of affairs. But if the parent has been inconsistently available, the child stays stuck in distress and will continue to cling at the first sign of emotional withdrawal, out of fear of the parent leaving again. If the parent has been emotionally unavailable, the child lives perpetually separated from the parent—stuck between despair and emotional detachment.

Afraid to Go to School

In the comic strip "Calvin & Hobbes," Calvin plays out a fantasy that many children share. Flying in a fighter plane, he lets guns and rockets rip and pulverizes the school building, all the while howling gleefully. Calvin, needless to say, was not wild about going to school.

Some children with separation anxiety will complain about going to school because their teacher is a witch, or the children tease or bully, or the

Terror Talk

A child who has **school phobia** refuses to go to school and may show panic reactions if forced to go.

Secret Weapons

To distinguish a school-phobic child from one who is separation-anxious, ask yourself where the child is when not in school. If the child is school-phobic, he is happy to be anywhere but in school. If separation-anxious, he is only happy if home with, or near, his mother, and becomes fearful and avoids not just school, but a slew of situations related to the theme of separation.

schoolwork is too hard or too easy. If your child has separation anxiety, these complaints are real but secondary to the fear of leaving you. But if your child has *school phobia*, what awaits him at school is the primary issue.

If you are concerned that your child may be school phobic, check his behavior against these symptoms:

School Phobia

➤ The child refuses to go to school or stay in school.

➤ If forced to go, the child may show symptoms of panic—trembling, racing heart, dizziness.

➤ The nature of the phobia may be specific, for example, fear of being harmed by a bully, or of being teased, ridiculed or criticized by teachers or other children.

Let's look more closely at the reasons why a child may fear school:

➤ Learning problems: A child may have learning problems and become easily frustrated and humiliated at his continual failure when the other children seem to come up with the answers easily.

➤ Intimidating teacher: Some very sensitive children may be frightened by an intimidating teacher who may behave harshly toward them. And though the child is well behaved—sensitive children generally are to avoid punishment—observing how other children get harshly treated is frightening.

➤ Intimidating children: Very shy or sensitive children are easily intimidated by bullies or cruel children, and are afraid to speak out and defend themselves. Even normal childhood teasing easily distresses them.

➤ Fear of failure: Taking tests, giving a speech or performing evokes fears of failure.

Hi-Ho, Hi-Ho, It's Off to School We Go

What are the secrets to getting your child happily off to school? First, be aware that separation anxiety and school phobia are complex problems that may not be resolved easily. As in overcoming childhood fears in general, the more you help boost your child's self-efficacy, inner control and trust in people (see Chapter 19) through empathy, information, gradual exposure, play and stories, the safer your child will feel anywhere in the world—school, summer camp, parties, grandma's house, or overnights. Should you too suffer from separation anxiety, you need to address your own pain in letting your child go.

It's Okay to Be Afraid

Always take your child's feelings seriously. If you validate her concerns about leaving you and reassure her—"I know you're afraid about going to school. But when you come home, I will be there. I will never leave you."—she will trust in your availability and, when she returns and finds you at home, that what you say is dependable and reliable. This will enable her to predict your comings and goings, encouraging inner control and self-efficacy. Give young children a personal possession like a photo, or a charm, to keep with them and turn to when feeling stressed. A favorite snack also helps. When you return, greet your child warmly, ask about her day, and remind her of your promise—"See, mommy told you she would be back," for example, "You can trust me." Recognize how hard it was for her to be away from you and praise her for being in school all day.

Watch It!

Some children who take forever to get dressed in the morning may be tactile-defensive and greatly bothered by the feel of clothing on their skin. Some signs: demanding removal of labels in clothing and requesting loose clothing of soft material. For more information, contact the Sensory Integration Institute and see *The Out-of-Sync Child*, by Carol Kranowitz (see Appendix B).

Disenmesh Yourself Mommy!

If you have a child who clings as you try to leave, you probably feel terrible, as if you are a bad mother to leave her all alone with twenty other children and a room full of toys. To help your child separate from you, work on letting yourself separate from her.

Often, it is the mother's need for the child and her own difficulty in separating that creates *folie à deux*—a kind of mutual delusion that can lead to an unhealthy mutual dependency. Perhaps you're in a lousy marriage and wish your child to fill in for the love you're not getting from your partner. Or perhaps you just wish to keep him "momma's boy" so he'll never leave you. Whatever the reason, enmeshment is smothering and unhealthy. If you can't separate, you make it hard for your child to separate. Give him a hug and a shove.

Secret Weapons

With preschool children, who have a poor conception of time, describe your return in terms of their activities. "When you get up from your nap, you're going to have a snack. By the time you finish your snack, mommy will come pick you up." For more information on the preschool child and negotiating separation, see *Starting School*, by Nancy Balaban.

School Information Highway

Give your child as much information as possible regarding school and your whereabouts, to help him better appraise the situation. When he goes to school, let him know if you will be home when he returns and, if not, where you will be and what time you will be home. In this way, he will feel greater predictability and control over his world.

If you are having marital difficulties, discuss these problems openly. This will dampen the child's egocentric view that she is the cause of your fights with your spouse. Reassure her that you love her and that just as brothers and sisters argue, so do grownups.

If your child is afraid of something at school, probe to discover the problem and give your child some realistic solutions. "Sticks and stones can break my bones, but words can never hurt me," has helped many a child retort to teasing. Reassure her that when she comes home she can talk to you about how much it really *did* hurt. If your child is being tormented by another child, talk to the school about the situation and see if arrangements can be made to minimize confrontation, like changing recess times, for example.

Introduce your child to a new school ahead of time. In this way, the first day won't seem so strange and he may even recognize a friendly face or two.

Work with your child on a fear pep talk that he can learn to tell himself when he becomes anxious. Statements like:

1. Jimmy is a nice boy and will play with me.
2. The principal smiles when he sees me.
3. I have my favorite little panda bear in my desk to touch.
4. If anyone bothers me, I will tell the teacher.

If your child will be starting a new school, prepare her ahead of time:

➤ Talk your child through everything—what will be different, what will be the same, what the school looks like, where he will be dropped off and picked up.

➤ Check to see if the new school offers an orientation.

One Day at a Time

If your child is afraid of going to school, expose her to school gradually.

➤ Picturing: First have her imagine school as a positive place. Talk about all the good things that happen when you go to school.

1. You can dress up and wear pretty clothes.

2. You can giggle with your friend Susie.

3. You get to play kick ball during recess time.

4. On Wednesday, you get to eat pizza.

5. If you feel frightened, you can rub your stuffed bunny or look at mommy's picture.

➤ Walking through: Take her on a tour through school.

➤ Staying there: Attend school with a young child and move slowly out of sight as she begins to settle in and gets comfortable—playing with a toy, sitting or playing next to other children. With the older child, spend a few minutes with her at the beginning and end of school and let her stay only as long as she can tolerate being in school without becoming unduly anxious. For some, that may be only an hour, for others half a day. And it may not be in the classroom, but in the principal or nurse's office. That's all right. At least she's in school. The next goal will be class attendance.

➤ Finding surrogates: Drop your child off and have someone arrange to meet her, like the teacher, school counselor, principal, or nurse, and escort her to her classroom.

➤ Increasing attendance: Gradually increase the length of time your child is able to remain at school.

Angst Bulletin

The value of play as a "catharsis" for separation anxiety struck Sigmund Freud, following an incident with his 18-month-old grandson. After his mother left, the child took a cotton reel on the end of a string and played the double game of throwing it away with an expression of "gone" and pulling it back again with a joyful "da." It was, Freud realized, as if he were staging his mother's disappearance and reappearance.

Secret Weapons

The Three Little Pigs, a classic story on the theme of separating from parents and home, is an all-time favorite and young children will ask to hear it over and over again. Like children beginning school, The Little Pigs are told to "make their way." And though it's hard and dangerous, hard work and cleverness win out against The Big Bad Wolf.

"Read All About It"

Books will expose your child to new experiences and solutions to problems like being teased, coping with bullies, family problems, and academic difficulties, thereby broadening his view.

Here are some suggestions:

1. *A Child Goes to School: A Storybook for Parents and Children Together.* Sara Bonnet Stein. (NY: Doubleday, 1978).

2. *First Grade Jitters,* Robert Quakenbush (NY: Lippincott, 1982).

3. *Ramona Quimby, Age 8.* Beverly Clearly. (NY: Morrow, 1981).

4. *Will I Have a Friend?* Miriam Cohen. (NY: Macmillan, 1976).

5. *The Runaway Bunny.* M.W. Brown (NY: Harper & Row, 1942).

6. *Mr. Grumpy's Motorcar.* J. Bumingham (NY: Crowell, 1976).

7. *Swimmy.* L. Lionni (NY: Pantheon, 1963).

8. *The Tale of Peter Rabbit.* B. Potter (London: Warne, 1902).

Play's the Thing

Encourage your children to play out in fantasy their feelings regarding separation. Provide props like mommy and daddy clothing, play cars, and school items. Playing teacher for many children is second only to playing mommy.

Back-to-School Pros

Just as parents need to go to work, it is the child's job to go to school. If your child persists in refusing to go to school, it's time to seek professional help. Separation anxiety, which can lead to agoraphobia, and school phobia, which may be an early form of social phobia, need to be nipped in the bud when the child is still young.

The Least You Need to Know

➤ Some children protest going to school primarily because they are afraid of separating from their mother.

➤ Some children protest going to school out of fear of something at school, like bullies, being teased, harsh treatment by teachers or difficulty in school work.

➤ One way of distinguishing the separation-anxious from the school-phobic is to ask where the child is when not in school. If he is happy to be anywhere but in school, he is school-phobic. If he insists on being at home with mother or with her nearby, he is primarily separation-anxious. The school-phobic child just wants to avoid going to school, while the separation-anxious becomes fearful and avoids a variety of situations related to the theme of separation.

➤ Both separation anxiety and school phobia are complex problems that often require professional help to overcome.

After It All Comes Crashing Down

In This Chapter

➤ Children too scared to cry

➤ Childhood horrors that haunt forever

➤ The signs of a traumatized child

➤ Becoming a shock absorber for your child

Five-year-old Jody is losing her mother to breast cancer. Fourteen-year-old Darlene's father has sexually abused her since she was nine. Ten-year-old Billy turned on the 6 o'clock news and witnessed his police officer father being shot to death by an assailant. Eight-year-old Bambi and 13-year-old Timmy lost their house and all their possessions to a tornado.

All these children have suffered a trauma that would tax any adult, let alone a child. While none will forget the experience, over time, some will break free of the shock's gridlock and get on with their lives. Others won't be so lucky. Their lives will be irrevocably altered and the trauma will stalk them all their days. In this chapter, you will learn what events create post-traumatic stress in children, how to recognize the symptoms of PTSD, and what you can do to help your child.

Childhood "Possessions"

Stephen King is the most well known writer of horror fiction in America today. What might "possess" someone to devote their life to writing of the macabre and the super-natural? Could his childhood have been filled with trauma of such magnitude that it would haunt him all his life? Indeed.

When he was four, his mother told him—he has no memory of the event—that he witnessed a friend run over by a freight train while playing on or crossing railroad tracks. When he came home "white as a ghost," his pants wet from having been peed in, he would not speak for the rest of the day.

Angst Bulletin

Could the stories of famous horror writers be extended post-traumatic play? Good chance, writes Dr. Lenore Terr. Fatherless at 18-months-old, Edgar Allen Poe was barely three when his mother died of tuberculosis. In his fiction, beautiful dead women assume a sleep-like state, people are buried alive or people who were once dead re-emerge. At two, Stephen King's father fled. At four, King apparently witnessed a friend run over by a train.

Of course, this one event could not entirely explain his lifelong preoccupation with the monstrous. There are other skeletons in the closet. At two, his father took off and was never heard from again. His ultra-religious mother appeared not the type to buffer these two major traumas. When his brother and he misbehaved, she confined them in an outhouse and insisted that they spend their incarceration praying. In *Too Scared to Cry*, Dr. Lenore Terr, a leading authority on childhood trauma and its aftermath, notes how his writing reflects his possession with the past and apparently serves, on a profound level, as continued post-traumatic play. In *Carrie*, you have a Bible-spouting horror-of-a-mother. In *Stand by Me*, you have children walking along the railroad tracks in search of a dead, mutilated boy.

Horrible childhood experiences can scar your mind and haunt you all your life. You as the parent are your child's best shock absorber. But sometimes you are too shocked yourself—by death, assault, the ravages of war, accidents, or natural disasters—to ease the blow. And parents themselves can perpetrate the wound, by divorce, or by sexual and physical abuse.

Even when you are available to help and support your child, you can be fooled by and may not understand the extent of their trauma. True, some immediately collapse into sobs, like an adult. But others appear merely serious and quiet, as did Stephen King, or Prince Harry and Prince Will as they followed the casket of their mother Princess Diana. How are they not falling apart, we asked ourselves, as we fought back our own tears? Other children seem unconcerned altogether that their father has died or that their house has burnt down.

Too Scared to Cry

Most of us have been struck by this baffling and incongruous behavior in children who experience trauma, how in the midst of the tragedy some seem neither sad nor look frightened. Take 15-year-old Joseph and ten-year-old Debbie. As their mother sat in shock during the wake, wrestling with her husband's untimely death in an auto accident, the two were wrestling each other on the floor, screaming and chortling.

Don't let this behavior deceive you. Inside, children feel terrified, helpless, and are scared to death about the future. They just don't show their behavior as adults do. Instead, their fear and sadness sneaks up in other ways: post-traumatic play re-enactments, sudden new fears, clinginess, moodiness, daredevil and aggressive behavior, nightmares, and sometimes night terrors and sleepwalking.

Watch It!

Following trauma, the universal falling dreams and being chased dreams, in which we awake before striking the ground or being caught, take on terrifying twists. During the fall, the child hits the ground—dead; during the chase, the bad man catches and kills the child. Often children have nightmarish dreams of actual re-enactments of the trauma.

Children retain powerful snapshot memories of traumatic events, frozen in their minds in graphic detail. Long after the original trauma, specific sights, sounds, smells, tastes and other physical sensations can trigger powerful reminders of the event in flashbacks. Suddenly, your child may become overwhelmed with a feeling of fear and imminent danger. After witnessing a friend run over by a car, a child shakes when hearing a car screech, for instance. Some children change personalities. A carefree and cheerful child may become suddenly serious and withdrawn. Or the child appears his old self but falls apart during anniversaries of the trauma.

Children behave differently from adults because they don't grasp the nature of traumas as adults do, especially if young. Lacking the coping skills or life perspective to understand that hurricanes, cancer and daddy's senseless murder are rare events, children don't know that people can grieve and then reconstruct their lives and return to normal. Instead, they are mystified and confused at what has happened, why it happened, and don't have the confidence to know that it's unlikely to happen again.

If the parent was also traumatized and has become vulnerable, or if a parent has died, the child has a double blow to overcome: The trauma itself and the loss of the parental protection that makes the child feel safe and secure in the world. Just seeing the all-powerful parent who's supposed to keep him from harm suddenly vulnerable and overwhelmed increases the child's feeling of being unsafe. If your father can't stop the hurricane from blowing your house away or prevent God from taking your mother away, then who will protect you?

Childhood Horrors

All childhoods are scathed by scary events that temporarily frighten and disorganize. Your child may have had an abscessed tooth pulled, tubes put in her ears, an arm put in a cast or a leg stitched up. She may have lost a pet or a grandparent, listened to you screaming and sobbing behind a closed door or watched you lie in bed too ill to take care of her. To help her get past the fright, you held her more, sometimes let her sneak into your bed at night (if she doesn't already sleep there), and took her on that promised trip to Disney Land; in time the hurt went away.

Trauma goes beyond the child's usual experience. It profoundly disrupts and changes children's lives and leaves them mentally and often physically unprepared to handle the ordeal. Feeling extremely helpless and unsafe, many are unable to forget, and unable to go about the business of just being a child.

Some trauma is horrific beyond imagination. Children are buried alive by kidnappers, locked away in closets by crazy mothers, and burned in their beds by demented fathers. Some witness monstrous events—their father hanging from the ceiling, their friend burned alive in a car that they were luckily thrown from, their mother slashed bloody by a burglar.

And although these events are rare, other childhood traumas are more common, like the death of a parent, life-threatening illness, sexual and physical abuse, and media events that shock the world and temporarily traumatize children, like the Challenger explosion, the Oklahoma City bombing, or the murder of JonBenet Ramsey. What baby-boomer can't tell you where he or she was when told that President Kennedy had been shot?

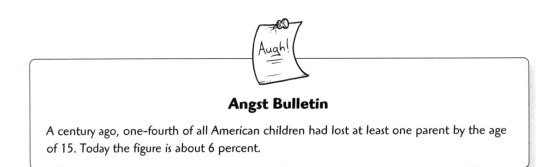

Angst Bulletin

A century ago, one-fourth of all American children had lost at least one parent by the age of 15. Today the figure is about 6 percent.

When You Lose Half Your World

When Janice was twelve, her father died of a heart attack. Now thirty-five, she still hasn't gotten over the pain and sense of longing. At every life passage—graduations, marriage, the births of her three children—joy was mixed with sorrow for the missing smiling face, proud words of praise, and tender touch on her cheek. She remembers how she longed to go to sleep, knowing she might dream of her father alive and with her. And how she dreaded awaking in the morning, knowing it was just a dream and that he wouldn't be there to greet her. Some part of her remains forever the 12-year old child whose father lay stone dead on the living room floor.

Our children see us not as mortal beings but as permanently there to love, protect, take care of and teach them. Death destabilizes their world. Since they can do nothing to bring the parent back and make it all better again, they feel a profound sense of helplessness and abandonment and need a long and gradual recovery period to restore a sense of well-being.

Secret Weapons

Should your child need help in coping with the death of a loved one, in the last 20 years or so, over 160 "bereavement centers" have opened around the country to help children express and channel their grief over the death of a parent or sibling.

But grieving can be a complicated affair, especially for young children under the age of six, who can't grasp the finality of death. You can tearfully explain to a five-year-old all the reasons why daddy won't be coming home anymore, and they solemnly nod their head. An hour later, they will ask you if daddy will still be able to read them a bedtime story.

During pre-adolescence and adolescence, when the life of a child is changing drastically and calling for continual readjustments, the burden of losing a parent hits especially hard. At 12, when Prince Harry lost his mother Princess Diana, he was caught in the middle of a developmental period: too old to break down and sob like a child and too young to behave with the greater independence of an adolescent. At 15, Prince William was dealing with the change of becoming adolescent and of losing his childhood. And both children were still in the throes of coping with the divorce of Charles and Diana.

If the death incurs trauma as well as loss, for instance if the child sees the parent mutilated or murdered, the child faces a double challenge of coping with both trauma and loss. And the grieving process cannot even begin until the child can cope with the traumatic memories; this can take time.

Daddy in the Wrong Bed: The Ultimate Betrayal

Childhood sexual abuse is unimaginable and unthinkable, a crime of hideous proportion that scars the child for life. Several reasons make it especially traumatic:

➤ It is a violation of the child's basic sense of trust and right to depend upon adults for care and protection, particularly if the parent is the molester. If you can't trust your parents, who can you trust?

➤ It blurs normal family boundaries. Fathers and mothers are supposed to sleep together and have sex with each other. Children are not supposed to have sex with adults.

➤ It is a premature introduction to sexuality. Genital arousal overstimulates the child, who doesn't know how to handle the excitation. Often, it leads to inappropriate sexual acting out.

➤ It interrupts a child's normal development. Pre-occupied with thoughts of the molestation and attendant confusing and uncomfortable feelings, the child cannot concentrate in school. Socially, the child may feel different—a freak— and be unable to relate to her peer group: if you're having sex with your father, how can you feel like other girls your age who are giggling about boys who have kissed them?

If parents become overly distraught—how could you not?—they unwittingly increase their child's fright. Plus, the child feels the additional burden of feeling responsible for the parent's pain. If the legal system gets involved and removes the child from the home and family, extensively and intrusively interviews them, or if parent or professional doubt the child's disclosures, the child is further traumatized. Should father or mother get arrested, feelings of guilt and parental rejection further complicate matters for the child. And with the case now embroiled in the legal process, which can go on for some time, the child will be unable to put the abuse behind and begin the healing process.

Bad Touch

When threatened, your child seeks closeness and protection from you. Your frightened two-year-old hides behind your skirt when a stranger approaches. Your scared eight-year-old inches a little closer to daddy when the balloon suddenly bursts. But what does a child do when a parent physically abuses the child and becomes the source of danger? Who do they turn to for protection? This is a tragic paradox because, as developmental psychologist Mary Main explains, it puts the child in a double bind: to flee from danger (the violent parent) or to come toward the haven of safety (the same protective parent).

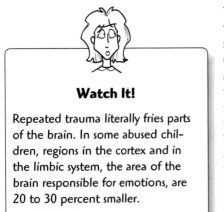

Watch It!

Repeated trauma literally fries parts of the brain. In some abused children, regions in the cortex and in the limbic system, the area of the brain responsible for emotions, are 20 to 30 percent smaller.

Young children solve it by doing both. For instance, when an irate mother slapped her three-year-old, he started crying and then tried to lay his head in her lap. Older children will rationalize the abuse as their fault and believe they deserve the beating. If their parents, who are there to love and care for them, hit them, they must be bad. To minimize further abuse and increase their chances for protection, children learn very early to behave in ways that appease the parent. This is why children often won't "squeal" on the abusive parent. Who, then, would protect them?

Repeated and severe physical abuse leads to disabling and severe chronic post-traumatic stress. Thoughts of, dreams about, or the slightest reminder of the trauma—a father walks in drunk—release stress chemicals that surge through the child's brain and reactivate the areas in the brain originally affected by the trauma. Thus, children remain on guard, their body posture stiff in anticipation of an impending attack.

When Band-Aids and a Kiss Can't Heal

Edith Wharton, an American novelist of the early part of the century, wrote some terrifically scary ghost stories in which white phantoms lurk outside of doorways and in hallways to attack their victims. At eight, while visiting a European spa with her parents, Wharton became gravely ill with typhoid fever and was isolated with a nurse in a separate wing. A masked and gowned physician came daily, paused outside her door to avoid catching the dreaded disease himself, and then went on his way. For seven or eight years after her recuperation, she felt trailed by this white ghost at the door, "forever dogging my steps, lurking and threatening." The specter of this doctor-of-death haunted her from 1870, when she recovered from the typhoid, until her death in 1937. In her last story, "All Souls," written months before her death, an old lady about to die sees her ghostly antagonist leaving the entryway of her house.

How frightening for a child to become gravely ill, whether from life-threatening illness or serious physical injury. He must cope with the physical pain, along with the needles that stick him and the medications that sicken him. But it is the psychic terror of an unsure future, of being robbed of "happily ever after," that makes the trauma so hard to bear. And unlike a one-time traumatic incidence, like a natural disaster, the trauma is ongoing. If other people were injured or died, and especially loved ones, the child will carry an additional burden of grief and survivor guilt.

Mother Nature's Wrath

Mother Nature is another wicked source of childhood trauma. When floods, tornadoes, hurricanes, earthquakes, or volcanoes unleash their wrath, or a fire strikes, they can instantly take away a house, pets, teddy bears, soft familiar beds, friends—everything that makes your child's life safe, stable, predictable and comfortable. Vulnerable and frightened, your child worries that the hurricane will return and blow him away along with the house, as it did Dorothy. Only he won't wake up in the lush Land of Oz, but in a place where he may find mommy or daddy injured or even dead. Even if you remain safe, you may feel too traumatized and vulnerable yourself to be available to help your child.

It Could Happen to Me Too: Vicarious Trauma

If your child hears about, sees, or learns from another person about terrible things that happen to other people, such as highly publicized media events like the Oklahoma City bombing, the drowning murder of Susan Smith's two children, or the gruesome killing of JonBenet Ramsey, he's likely to identify with the victims, especially if they are close in age to him. Whether the place is Oklahoma City or a luxurious Colorado mansion, the sight of injured or dead children carries the same message: children are not safe in the world. His daycare could also be bombed. You could get mad enough to dump him in the river. Or someone could sneak into his bed at night and kill him and you would be powerless to protect him. Fortunately, the effects of these "vicarious traumas" generally disappear over time.

Angst Bulletin

A month or two following the January 28, 1986 destruction of the space shuttle Challenger, Dr. Lenore Terr interviewed 149 children and adolescents. New fears and exaggerated old ones popped up in most: of airplanes, of explosions, of space exploration, or of death and dying, as well as fears related to everyday life, like house-heater explosions, scary hot-water tanks, and out-of-control cars. A year later, only a few fears lingered but the memory remained imprinted in the children's minds.

After the Fall

Following a shock, how do you recognize if your child is at risk for Post-Traumatic Stress Disorder (PTSD), especially if she seems unfazed? First, don't be fooled by her apparent lack of concern. This could be a delayed reaction and later she could develop strong fears. Look for signs of preoccupation with the trauma returning and hyper-vigilance of any sign of impending danger—sudden terror upon hearing a loud noise in the house that could intimate a break-in, for instance. Being continually "prepared" is the traumatized child's way of feeling less helpless and powerless. Also notice if the child has new fears related specifically to the trauma, like panic upon hearing the ambulance siren which might take you back to the hospital. Or if your child becomes more fearful in general of things like the dark, noises, animals, death and dying, enclosed spaces, people, and separating from you.

Don't expect your child to necessarily talk directly or coherently about the trauma—few children under the age of 12 can express uncomfortable or painful feelings. Instead, look for signs of distress in the changes that may occur in your child's behavior.

Too Young to Understand

Traumatized children under the age of two are in some ways the most tragic. Although the child may be unable to tell of, make sense of, or later recall what happened, the memories remain forever stamped into his brain and body at a cellular level. A throat that was penetrated with a penis feels constricted and the child suffers from frequent sore throats and later as an adult from TMJ (Temporomandibular Joint Problems), hyperventilation, or a raspy voice, for instance. An arm that was pulled out of the socket is unconsciously kept in the pocket for protection and the person finds himself always buying clothes with roomy pockets. Feet that were burned recoil from touch.

Here are the signs of PTSD in children under the age of two:

➤ Sleep and eating problems

➤ Being startled at loud or unusual noises

➤ Fussiness; clinginess; uncharacteristic crying

➤ Stilling in response to people or situations previously welcomed

➤ Freezing in their development; failure to learn new and expected tasks

Watch It!

Following a trauma, children may develop fears unrelated to the event itself, such as fears of the dark, of sleeping alone, of the "bogeyman," ghosts, snakes, or thunderstorms. Their timing and intensity will help you recognize if these fears are a reaction to the trauma.

If you suspect childhood sexual abuse, here are some traumatic reactions to look for under the age of two:

➤ Preoccupation with private parts

➤ Sudden, intense masturbation

➤ Inappropriate private touching of others

➤ Recoiling when the genitals are washed or touched

Old Enough to Imagine the Worst

By preschool age, your traumatized child can understand what has happened to her. But because of her egocentricity and limited view of the world, and her tendency to assume that her own behavior, thoughts, or wishes can cause events, she will distort the meaning of a traumatic event into a fictionalized true story. For instance, if a three-year-old has screamed that she wishes her baby brother would just "go back to the hospital," she will feel that she is the cause if the baby becomes ill or dies. If a four-year-old disobeys his father, and the parents divorce and the father moves out, the child will believe that his naughty behavior caused the parent's break-up.

Remember also that preschool children are poor at distinguishing fantasy from reality. For instance, a child will interpret the lightning that struck down a classmate as the response of an angry sky; should they be naughty, lightning might strike them down as well.

Angst Bulletin

Young children distort reality to fit into their magical way of thinking. For instance, in 1992, when Hurricane Andrew was fast approaching South Florida, the children listened to the news of this "huge," "fast," "dangerous" thing with "one eye," that was about to strike and hurt them. They interpreted Andrew not as a tropical storm but a terrible one-eyed monster, drawing closer and closer and threatening to take away their homes and toys.

These fantasies and distortions make it often hard to discern your child's verbal description of a traumatic experience, if she gives one. But her play, which is the child's means for mastering feelings and gaining a feeling of control, will speak volumes.

Be prepared, though. Unlike the typical "playfulness" of children's pretend play, post-traumatic play is a driven and serious repetitive reenactment of the actual trauma. The child puts the mommy "to sleep" over and over. Or, in an attempt to gain power and defeat the evil force, the child may become the aggressor and shoot the bad daddy repeatedly, or pummel the lion puppet over and over.

Watch It!

The children who appear the most undisturbed by a terrifying event are the ones most likely to act out in their play the most powerful, aggressive or scariest characters and ask to watch horror movies or to be told the scariest stories. Desperate to feel some power and control over their frightening lives, they cope by trying to convince themselves and others of their invincibility.

In the brilliant 1950 French film *Forbidden Games,* we see an extraordinary demonstration of post-traumatic play. A little girl and her parents are among a group of French refugees fleeing the Germans. A bomb kills the parents and others, and the surviving refugees bury the dead on the side of the road. The little girl is taken in by a family in a nearby village, where she begins to hunt down dead animals and insects and bury them. Soon, she kills small animals, like a bird and a rabbit, and buries them. Together with the boy of the house, they organize a secret graveyard of dead animals. In need of a cross for their cemetery, the little girl convinces the boy to climb to the top of the local church steeple and pry one off of the cross. The boy slips and falls dead to the ground. The next day, the town searches for the missing boy. They find him buried in the secret cemetery with the cross stuck up over the freshly dug grave.

Here are some signs of PTSD in the preschool child:

➤ Separation anxiety: clinginess, fussiness, refusing to separate from parents

➤ Regression: thumb-sucking, bed-wetting, refusing to go to sleep, nightmares, night terrors, or night awakening

➤ Aggressiveness: pushing, hitting, biting, scratching other children or parents, smashing, throwing, pounding toys

➤ Overt anxiety: trembling; shuddering; stuttering or stammering; stiffening when touched; refusing to eat; hiding; extreme startle response

➤ Personality changes: withdrawing or acting out, self-centeredness

➤ Physical complaints: stomachaches; headaches, and so on

➤ Magical ideas: "The flood took away our house because I was so mad." "Daddy left because I was bad."

➤ Denial of feelings: looking morose, angry, or intense while claiming to be having fun

Angst Bulletin

In *Too Scared to Cry*, Dr. Lenore Terr describes her study of the children of Chowchilla, California, who in 1976 were kidnapped at gunpoint and buried in a bus for 16 hours. A year later, 19 of the 25 exhibited some shift in personality. Others that she followed over the years continued to show distinct personality changes. A sense of "futurelessness" and a perception that the world was unsafe pervaded their lives.

If you suspect childhood sexual abuse, here are some traumatic reactions to look for in the preschool child:

➤ Unusually sexualized play with toys or other children—playing out oral sex for instance

➤ Focusing on or unusually concerned about his own or other's private parts

➤ Excessive masturbation

➤ Unusually sexualized or aggressive touching of others or sexualized relating to others

➤ Sudden, specific fear or mistrust of certain people or particular places

➤ Preoccupation with bodily concerns, complaints of pain or itching in genital area or mouth, or flinching when genitals are touched during washing or bathing

Watch It!

Various studies of sexually abused children show that from 21 to 60 percent show no behaviors indicative of sexual abuse. The most salient behavior to distinguish those traumatized by sexual abuse is age-inappropriate sexualized behavior: masturbation; need to expose genitals and attempts to sexually touch or undress, or attempts to have intercourse or oral sex with another child.

Watch It!

As if trying to tempt fate, children whose trauma involved physical harm to themselves or someone else commonly engage in daredevil behavior, show reckless disregard for their safety and are accident-prone.

Old Enough to Imagine and Understand

By school-age, your child is able to distinguish fantasy from reality and knows that he didn't cause someone's death or illness or the tornado to ravage your house. But this is not an unmitigated blessing. The "age of reason" comes with greater awareness of real threats—how frightening they can be, and that you, sometimes also terrified and vulnerable, cannot protect him against all dangers.

Don't be surprised if, after a trauma, your nine-year-old keeps to herself. She may not know how to express her feelings or she may not want to further distress you. To avoid misinterpreting this behavior as her being unscathed by the crisis, here are some signs of PTSD in the school-aged child:

➤ Regressive behavior: bed-wetting, crying jags, egocentric thinking like someone having died because they had bad thoughts about that person

➤ Self-blame: unreasonably perceiving their behavior as responsible for the trauma

➤ Reckless behavior: self-destructive behavior or irresponsible risk taking

➤ School performance: difficulty concentrating and performing in school or intensely focused on schoolwork to the exclusion of having fun

➤ Oppositional behavior: testing the rules about mealtime, bedtime, homework, or chores

➤ Change in friendships: losing interest in spending time with a best friend, for instance

➤ Sleep disturbance: nightmares, night terrors, difficulty falling asleep

If you suspect childhood sexual abuse, here are some traumatic reactions to look for in the school-aged child:

➤ A drive to repetitive and sometimes aggressive sexual rehearsal play, even when other children are disinterested, and attempts toward engaging older children or adults sexually

➤ Hints at or actual verbal descriptions of sexual misuse

➤ Excessive concerns or preoccupation with private parts and adult sexual behavior

➤ Sexualized relating to adults

➤ Sudden, specific fear or mistrust of certain people or places

➤ Age-inappropriate knowledge of adult sexual behavior

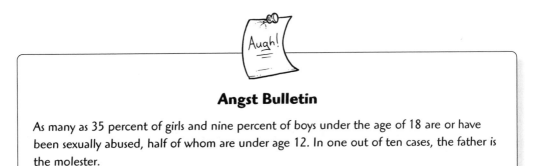

Angst Bulletin

As many as 35 percent of girls and nine percent of boys under the age of 18 are or have been sexually abused, half of whom are under age 12. In one out of ten cases, the father is the molester.

All Grown Up, but Still Scared

How do adolescents, who cry their hearts out to you one day and lock their doors the next, react to trauma? As you would expect, with mixed behavior. Because your teen is able to fully grasp the reality of the trauma, she may try to cope with the shock like a mature adult, by helping you out and by holding back her own distress. Yet, because she is still highly vulnerable and in need of your support, she may behave like a young child and become clingy, act silly, or behave recklessly.

Here are some signs of PTSD in teenagers:

➤ Emotional numbness and denial of shame, guilt, and humiliation

➤ Recklessness, risk-taking, or sexual acting out behavior

➤ Sleep disturbances and nightmares

➤ Changes in eating habits or personal cleanliness

➤ Negative self-image

➤ Acting not like him/herself

➤ Thoughts of revenge

➤ Increased self-focus and withdrawal from friends, or over involvement with friends

➤ School failure

➤ Depression

➤ Flight into premature adult behavior—early marriage, pregnancy, dropping out of school, seeking older friends

➤ Obsession with traumatic event and disturbing memories and flashbacks

➤ Rejection of parents, or neediness

If you suspect childhood sexual abuse, here are some traumatic reactions to look for in teenagers:

➤ Sexually exploitative or aggressive interactions with younger children

➤ Sexual promiscuity, or avoidance of any sexual involvement

➤ Running away from home

Helping Your Child Build a Safe Fortress

Seeing your child in pain is heartbreaking for a parent. Seeing your child traumatized, perhaps irrevocably, is devastating beyond words and pierces your very being.

What can you as a parent do to put your child on the healing path and soothe her emotional wounds? Be there to support, comfort and reassure her in every way possible. Although you can't push the erase button and make the traumatic event disappear, the more she can feel you as a protective presence—against physical attack, emotional pain, another's cruelty—the more secure she will feel. Don't hold back on holding—touch is the best elixir of all sorrow and nature's homemade security blanket. Be kind, but firm—the more consistency and structure in a child's life, the less confusion and disorganization. Take her pain and fears seriously and respect them—to feel understood and valued is one of life's greatest gifts.

Here are more suggestions:

➤ Try to remain calm in your child's presence. Children are vulnerable to the impact of their trauma on the people they love and look to their parents to discover the meaning of what has happened to them. Be mindful of how your own anxiety and reactions to the trauma might escalate your child's distress.

➤ Get your child to talk about the trauma and her feelings. If she's too young to easily describe the event or her feelings, give her the words—"You're having these scary nightmares because it was very frightening for you to see daddy die. It's okay. The bad dreams won't always be there." "I think you're afraid when we drive over the bridge because you're worried that you could fall in the water and drown like your friend Susie. But that was an unusual accident and doesn't happen very often to little children. Mommy and daddy won't let that happen to you." Explain to children that it's perfectly normal to have strong uncomfortable feelings like shame, guilt, or a wish for revenge.

➤ Encourage your child to tell you a story, draw, and play out the trauma (provide salient toy props—family dolls or puppets, houses, cars).

➤ Avoid unnecessary separations from you.

➤ Avoid exposing your child to reminders of the trauma, as well as frightening experiences like scary stories, TV programs, and movies.

➤ Maintain sleeping and eating routines—change of any kind can be unwelcome and disruptive.

➤ Don't make an issue of regressive behavior and have patience with difficult or uncharacteristic behavior, while at the same time being firm about household rules.

➤ Listen empathetically to your child's repetitious retelling of the event and expression of her fears, regardless of intensity or pervasiveness, and share her reactions. The more she can express her pain and fear, the safer she will feel with those feelings. Reassure her that the bad feelings will lessen in time.

➤ Watch his play and behavior at home and monitor his progress at school and out-of-home settings.

➤ Gently explain to your child the cause or nature of their traumas and correct their misunderstandings and distortions. "Baby Jenny didn't die because you said you wished she would. She died because she was born very, very sick and wasn't strong enough to live."

➤ Encourage any activities that are pleasurable and offer emotional release, such as dancing, sports, and games.

➤ Make every effort to provide opportunities in which your child can feel control and make choices, and feel mastery and self-esteem.

Watch It!

Parents, themselves unsure of how to cope with the trauma, may go to the extreme and either minimize or exaggerate its importance or severity for the child. Both leave the child feeling lonely and misunderstood and make it harder for the child to cope.

Secret Weapons

Physical exercise is an essential tool for children to release the muscle tension lodged in their bodies resulting from a traumatic experience and to give them positive bodily experiences. Whacking a baseball or kicking a soccer ball especially empowers a child who was physically assaulted or harmed, as does feeling your body slammed down onto a mat while wrestling or crashing down on a trampoline.

When You Need Help to Put Your Child Back Together Again

The need for professional help following trauma is common, especially if you are traumatized yourself, and should be sought if your child's behavior has not begun to return to normal within a month following the trauma. Here are the signs to indicate that your child needs professional help:

➤ Ongoing depression, reckless or aggressive behavior

➤ Frequent nightmares that don't lessen with time

➤ Persistent uncharacteristic behavior

➤ Obsession with the trauma and vivid terror in response to trauma related triggers

➤ Psychosomatic complaints that signal unexpressed underlying emotional pain

➤ Continued inability to concentrate and attend

➤ Overfocus on self-blame or need for revenge

Angst Bulletin

For more information on how to handle childhood trauma, see *Children and Trauma* by Cynthia Monahon, *Too Scared to Cry* by Lenore Terr and *The Scared Child* by Barbara Brooks and Paula Siegel.

The Least You Need to Know

➤ Following trauma, don't be deceived if your child appears unconcerned. It may just be a delayed reaction.

➤ To assess the impact of trauma on your child, look for signs of distress in the changes that may occur in your child's behavior.

➤ If not overly traumatized yourself, you can be your child's best shock absorber.

➤ If your child's behavior doesn't begin to normalize a month or so following the trauma, consider seeking professional help for your child.

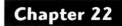

Chapter 22

Teen Terror

In This Chapter

➤ Quietly disturbed teens who fall through the cracks

➤ Normal self-consciousness versus social anxiety

➤ Warning signs of serious teen turmoil

➤ Getting help for your family and your teen

Remember being an adolescent, how self-conscious you felt about your appearance, your words, your actions? Psychologists call this the *imaginary audience* phenomenon—you imagine yourself the focus of everyone's attention. When you went to a rock concert with 20,000 people, you worried that "everyone" noticed your bad hair day—or your mother's, the dork.

For most, this self-consciousness is normal adolescent baggage that gets dumped as we mature and realize that the world has better things to worry about than our hair or our zits. But for some teens, this heightened self-consciousness is extreme and accompanied by strong fears and atypical behavior, like not wanting to go out with friends on a Saturday night or skipping school on gym days to avoid undressing in front of others. It represents not normal angst, but a deeper problem, and begs for psychological intervention before it follows them into adulthood.

In this chapter you will learn how to identify when your teen is worried well or worried sick, how you can help him and when you need to get outside help.

Watch It!

Occasional depression during adolescence is common, especially in girls. As many as 28 percent of girls report feeling depressed every day or at least a few times a week.

Secret Weapons

If you are worried that your teen may be having problems that go beyond the normal adolescent turmoil, go with your gut feeling. It's been estimated that about fifty percent of disturbed adolescents needing help go unrecognized by adults.

When No One Listens!

Sixteen-year-old Franny appeared to be your typical adolescent. Cute, energetic and bright, she seemed to enjoy school, got average grades, belonged to a clique, had a best friend, occasionally dated and was a cheerleader. But inside she felt confused, lost, empty, constantly anxious or depressed, and different from others. She was uncomfortable with males of any age, and felt ill at ease with any girls she considered smarter or prettier than herself, which were most. In their presence, she felt like she was nothing—unworthy to talk to them. To defend herself against her anxiety and reduce her discomfort, she behaved arrogantly. She became known as an "independent snob."

Since junior high, she had felt deeply in love and obsessed with Danny, one of the basketball players. Danny was clever, seductive, and cruel, and the girls swooned over him. She found every other boy dull and lived for the hope that he would fall madly in love with her, as it seemed he had done when they went steady at 13. Yet, she also believed that he never would love her, nor would any guy.

Something was very wrong. When she was with him, she felt so nervous that she would perspire profusely, quickly soaking her blouse, which deeply humiliated her. Her hands would shake uncontrollably. When he kissed her, she felt overwhelmed with sexual pleasure and at the same time, deeply ashamed and terrified of these feelings, so she would stop his hands from slipping inside her blouse or panties. Were they to go "all the way," she felt desire would overtake her and she would lose herself entirely.

Yet, she neglected the rest of her life and fantasized day and night of nothing else but the two of them making love. Her room was a mess, she was failing math, and she had to "borrow" a "brain's" report to pass biology. She refused dates from other boys and had no desire to go with her friends to any party where he might not show up; her friends were losing patience with her. Her acute anxiety showed up in other ways as well. Before a game, she became so nervous about cheerleading that she felt like throwing up. She felt the same way before public speaking.

She couldn't talk to her mother about her problems. Her mother only snapped at Franny and criticized her. Franny hated her mother, whom she felt was her personal tormentor. Nor was it easy to talk to her distant and controlling father. Yet, at times he was sympathetic. So, one day she burst into tears, blurting out to him her terrifying nervousness. Like so many parents, he dismissed her problems as a normal part of growing up. Desperate, she turned to her pediatrician, who also assured her that her problems were teen-business-as-usual, and would pass. She felt utterly alone. At 19, panic attacks began, along with severe depression. Soon, she became agoraphobic.

Teens Who Fall Through the Cracks

Franny is among a group of adolescents called the "quietly disturbed." Seemingly normal functioning, they may not be the ones with the messy green hair, and a ring through their tongue and nose but, like Franny, get good enough grades, have good enough behavior and blend in with the crowd. Some were perfect as children. Consequently, many are not brought to the attention of mental health workers and educators, and parents dismiss their fright, extreme self-consciousness, and unhappiness as a normal adolescent rite of passage.

Watch It!

The teen suicide rate has tripled in the last 25 years, ranking it as the third leading cause of death among adolescents. Even more alarming is that for every completed adolescent suicide, there are more than 60 unsuccessful suicidal attempts.

When they emerge from their silence and loneliness and stick their heads out of the sand, some put a gun to it. Others feel compelled to make little slashes with razors and knives on their arms, not to actually kill themselves, but to make visible some of their pain. Some, like Franny, have panic attacks, debilitating phobias and anxiety, and severe depression, while others have nervous breakdowns or become anorexic or bulimic. Once in a while, one gets pregnant, tells no one, and then kills her newborn and the secret she tried to hide from everyone gets revealed to the whole world in a 30-second sound bite on the six o'clock news.

Once they "come out," the perfect child can become the perfect nightmare—defiant, rebellious, and even anti-social. Now they may dye their hair purple and wear nothing but torn jeans and a T-shirt that says, "Life Sucks." Some experiment with drugs, and refuse to study, do chores, participate in school activities or get a job. Some never emerge at all but just carry their problems around like a heavy weight.

Storm and Strife Is Not the Way of All Adolescents

Why do some disturbed teens with problems fall through the cracks? The answer lies in the generally turbulent nature of adolescence itself, which makes most adolescents seem a bit crazy at times.

When puberty hits, life begins to change at a fast and profound pace—body shape, skin, and hair, as well as thinking, as teens begin to explore who they are and their place in the universe. Neither adult nor child, adolescents feel pulled in two directions. They want to separate from their parents, but desperately need them to help sort their confusion and protect them. They want to be unique but, because peer acceptance is paramount in their quest for identity, they also want to be like every other adolescent. Even if they're close to you, too much is happening inside for them to communicate all the confusion. And fearful of your disapproval and needing to take control of their lives, they don't want to share everything. Moodiness, locking themselves in their bedrooms, frequent bickering over trivialities, staying home because of a pimple, bristling when you go to kiss them—these are all things that parents expect from their teen, especially in early adolescence.

If you have a teenage daughter, you may find her especially thrown by her newly curved body. For the sake of being one of the "populars" rather than the "nerds," many teenage girls feel pressured to reach a cultural feminine ideal that, for many, is foreign to their true selves. They strive to be pretty when they're not; thin when their body type won't allow it; and not "too" bright—though boys can get away with being a "brain," smart girls are considered a threat and feel at a disadvantage.

Angst Bulletin

Adolescent girls describe themselves as sadder, lonelier, and easier to hurt than do adolescent boys. They are more ashamed of their bodies, frequently feel themselves ugly and unattractive, and are more confused, shameful, and fearful. They feel less like leaders, and are more empathic and attached to relatives and friends. For more information on the plight of adolescent girls, see *Reviving Ophelia* by Mary Pipher.

Yet, in spite of the daunting task of weaving together and growing into a new self, initial adjustment problems generally taper off as adolescents settle into high school and become at home in their new bodies. In general, psychiatrist Dr. Daniel Offer of the University of Chicago found that the average teen has a good self-image and does not see himself as having major problems, though boys tend to do better than girls. Evaluating the psychological, social and sexual functioning of adolescents, as well as their family relations and basic coping, he found the average American adolescent to be confident, generally happy, getting along with their peers, close to their parents, and hopeful of the future. Studies have found only 15 to 30 percent to be plagued with ongoing "storm and strife."

The following describes the overall behavior, attitudes, and feelings of the normal adolescent.

Normal Adolescent Profile

Psychological:

➤ Enjoys life

➤ Happy with self

➤ Generally relaxed

➤ Optimistic

Social:

➤ Does well in school or work

➤ Makes friends easily

Family:

➤ Feels warm towards family

➤ Openly communicative with parents

Sexual:

➤ Feels proud of changing body and unafraid of budding sexuality

➤ Eases into having sex

Coping:

➤ Not easily frustrated

➤ Willing to do work necessary to achieve successful outcome

➤ Enjoys challenges

➤ Looks forward to a productive future

➤ Doesn't feel overwhelmed by feelings

Angst Bulletin

Teen moodiness appears to be a fact of life. Reed Larson, a psychologist at the University of Illinois, found that at any given moment, the average adolescent feels more delight and more sadness than adults and moves from one mood to another more rapidly. For teenagers, emotional states generally last no more than 15 minutes. Reed concluded that, "The typical adolescent may be moody, but not in turmoil."

Adolescent Angst

With moodiness and self-consciousness as an adolescent norm, it's easy to see how serious emotional difficulties can get masked as normal teen behavior, as happened with Franny, and why as many as half of disturbed teens go undiagnosed.

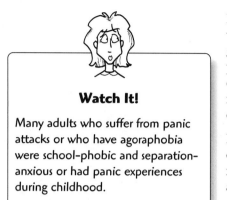

It's important that you don't let this happen to your teenager. Both social phobia (see Chapters 12–14), generalized anxiety disorder (see Chapter 16), and panic attacks (see Chapter 15) surface during adolescence. If not handled at this time, they're likely to intensify. In some cases, they turn into panic disorder or agoraphobia.

How do you know if your teen is in trouble? The quietly disturbed are more depressed, anxious, lonely, and fearful of failure and criticism than normal adolescents and have a more rigid personality style. Nor can you expect a disturbed teen to make a 180-degree turnabout and emerge from adolescence with flying colors. Instead, she will vacillate between feeling blue with sadness or red with rage. The closer she comes to young adulthood and separating from you to go off on her own, the more magnified her misery, shame, anxiety and terror of the future.

To help you assess if your teen is atypically anxious, see how much her behavior fits the general, overall behavior, attitudes, and feelings of the disturbed adolescent, as outlined below, as well as the subsequent diagnostic descriptions of social anxiety.

Disturbed Adolescent Profile

Psychological:

➤ First to put herself down, describing self as "a zero," "no talent," "no brains," or "ugly"

➤ Speaks quietly, tentatively and less articulately; when excited, chirps rapidly like a bird or is too loud

➤ Easily offended by a wayward glance, a wrong word, silence, or a frown

➤ Cry at the drop of a hat; laughter forced, overdone, or tinged with bit of hysteria

➤ Anxious, depressed, and generally miserable, but helpless to control these feelings

➤ Withdrawn and hard to read

➤ Narcissistic and self-absorbed

➤ Relentlessly combative and on the defense

Social:

➤ Reclusive

➤ Few to no friends or may choose only "losers"

➤ Falsely concerned about others or openly unconcerned

Family:

> ➤ Estranged from family members, who she doesn't feel as a source of support

> ➤ Doesn't get along with parents or share feelings with them

Sexual:

> ➤ Poor body image and discomfort with bodily changes

> ➤ Afraid of sex and will avoid it, or will act out sexually

Coping:

> ➤ Wide mood swings and bad moods that persist for long periods

> ➤ Easily frustrated and often acting impulsively

> ➤ Feels overwhelmed with negative and frightening feelings

Watch It!

Don't take lightly any expression of suicidal thoughts, fascination with death or dying, or expressions like "I wish I were dead." Seek immediate help from your teen's doctor, the school psychologist or counselor, a suicide prevention center, the community mental health center, a family service agency or an emergency room.

Saturday Night Blues Every Week

It's Saturday night and you have an extra $60 ticket to see the smash Broadway play *Ragtime.* You offer to treat your seventeen-year-old but the ingrate declines. For teens, being with their parents on a Saturday night is about the nerdiest thing imaginable.

This is what you expect of the normal adolescent. But some will not only take up your offer, but will prefer your company to going out socially with peers.

Mostly, these are shy youth who wish to be out with friends, but become too uncomfortable in the company of others to be able to relax and enjoy

Terror Talk

A **social phobia** is a persistent or recurrent fear of public embarrassment and avoidance of situations involving evaluation or performance that may occur mainly with adults, mainly with peers, or with both. The avoidance or fear of social encounters is extreme, atypical of adolescent behavior and impacts on social functioning.

themselves. Generally unassertive and lacking confidence, they worry that others won't want them as a friend; consequently, they have few or no friends. Extremely reluctant to enter situations where there is someone they don't know, they also shun parties and dating. They are the *socially anxious—the social phobics.*

Intensely self-conscious, they strongly fear potential failure and public embarrassment in a broad range of social encounters. Topping the list is speaking in front of the class or public performance of any kind: acting, singing, dancing, playing a musical instrument, or athletic performance.

The most distressing situation is getting stuck in an impromptu conversation, as while waiting for the school bus or someone stopping you in the hall at school to converse. Some feel self-conscious about eating in the cafeteria, or changing clothes and taking showers during gym time. Another big fear is test-taking, when fear of failure looms large (see Chapter 14). Some become so anxious when taking an exam that even the brightest fail.

To avoid these anxiety-provoking situations, adolescents may skip school on gym days, the day of their speech or test, or become suddenly ill in school and spend the day in the nurse's office. If school phobia becomes intense, they may skip going to school altogether. School phobia also may emerge upon entering junior high and high school, when change and strangeness become especially intimidating. Some avoid not only school, but also parties, dating, shopping, eating in public restaurants, or using public toilets. Under stress, avoidance exacerbates.

Teen Jitters

Seventeen-year-old Eddie is jittery and tense, and forever fretting and worrying. He's nervous that he will fail his zoology exam, do poorly on the college boards, not get a date for the junior prom, cause his soccer team to lose the big game of the season, and that he's a lousy kisser. He's acutely self-conscious about being too tall and having frizzy hair, and so fears bad breath and BO that his personal hygiene can take up to an hour in the morning and he's often late for school. He needs constant reassurance and asks everyone he knows for continual advice. If a girl refuses a date, he mulls over everything he said and did. He has hay fever, constant diarrhea, and frequent colds. Eddie has all the signs of general anxiety disorder (GAD) and social anxiety.

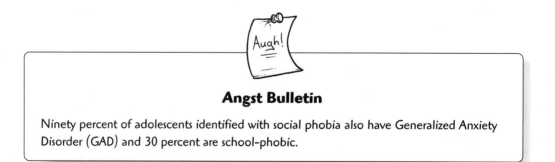

Angst Bulletin

Ninety percent of adolescents identified with social phobia also have Generalized Anxiety Disorder (GAD) and 30 percent are school-phobic.

Adolescents with GAD are worrywarts and nervous wrecks. Tense, edgy, high-strung and self-conscious, they are racked with self-doubt and in need of continual reassurance. They worry much about the future, but also dwell on something they said or did wrong in the past.

They are generally quiet and well-behaved kids from well-to-do families who feel terrific pressure to please, because they feel so displeasing, to perform flawlessly, because they feel inherently flawed, to be liked by everyone, because they feel so unlikable. Tense and under pressure, they commonly complain of physical ailments like headaches, stomach ailments, backaches, nervous bladder and the like, and sleep disturbances. Their nervousness is seen in behavior like eye-blinking, nail-biting, foot- and finger-tapping, rapid speech, hair-pulling and fidgeting. Panic attacks may strike from time to time.

It's not uncommon for those with GAD to also be socially phobic and feel anxious about dating, going to parties, or public speaking. Many tend to be depressed as well. Because of marked worry, self-consciousness, and the feeling that they invariably fall short, school is anxiety-provoking and school phobia is not uncommon. They may shun sports, music, and school government.

Fear of Fear

By adolescence, some nervous children begin to have panic attacks, especially those who are innately fear-prone. Most panic attacks occur in response to stressful events like taking a test, public speaking, or dating. Few understand what is happening to them, or why, and most will try to stay close to home and to their parents.

Watch It!

If you are concerned about your teenager and they don't fit the profile of phobia or general anxiety disorder, don't dismiss your concerns. Outgoing and seemingly easygoing children can also feel lost, lonely, frightened, anxious, and depressed.

Origins of Teen Terror

Why do some teens quietly fall apart? There are four primary risk factors:

➤ Shy temperament

➤ Insecure attachment

➤ Social ineptitude

➤ Cultural expectations

And normal adjustment is more difficult the more these risk factors are combined.

When innately inhibited children don't outgrow their shyness, it hits hard during adolescence, because peer acceptance and popularity assume extreme importance for identity formation. If your teen has been shy about friendships all along, he has not had a chance to develop good social skills, which intensifies his discomfort with peers and exacerbates his timidity. The more peers reject him, the further he retreats into his shell.

When children are insecurely attached to their parents, and particularly when avoidantly attached (see Chapter 4), they behave to please their parents. They attempt to bury bad feelings and behavior that gets a frown or look of indifference and replace them with that which gets the smile and nod of approval. In other words, they sacrifice their authentic self for parental protection. Often, they are perfect children.

And then comes puberty and all its turbulence. Suddenly, the pressure to hide their feelings, desires, and thoughts becomes too much and the tightly held false persona begins to unravel. As all the bad feelings start to seep out, earlier, unresolved fears take shape as social fears, school fears or other phobias, like a fear of burglars, and even panic attacks.

To sort out the confusion, teens turn more to their peers than to their parents and fitting into the crowd drives their behavior. But conformity has its own perils for identity, as teens feel compelled to further inhibit their true self for the sake of popularity. This is especially true for girls. Though our culture has come a long way from the *Ozzie and Harriet* scenario of the '50s, gender stereotypes still abound. The female interns on the TV program ER, for instance, look more like they could grace the cover of Cosmopolitan than Scientific American.

Angst Bulletin

Jerome Kagan and colleagues, who have been following shy children since infancy, re-tested them at ages 12 to 14 and found similar inhibited behavioral patterns. During interviews with a child psychiatrist, the inhibited children generally spoke only when spoken to, while the uninhibited ones often popped up with their own questions. The shy children were serious and somber as they slumped through the questioning, while the bold ones smiled and laughed frequently.

Angst Smashers

If your teen has an anxiety disorder, you can't go on blind faith that these problems will just work themselves out. Instead, you need to do all you can, which likely includes seeking outside help.

Mostly, you need to concentrate on building trust and opening up the channels of communication. If your teen has a good relationship with you and feels she can pour her heart out when life becomes overwhelming, you can buffer some of her extreme feelings and increase self-efficacy and inner control. As long as you don't alienate her, her behavior should begin to stabilize in time. You can't stop your teen's turmoil, especially if she is sensitive and introverted. But your thumbs-up show of support will plug the dam and save her from drowning in inner turmoil.

Here are some suggestions:

➤ *Lend a Sympathetic Ear:* Try to get him to start talking about his feelings; listen but don't judge. Ask without being accusing where he was until 3 o'clock in the morning. In this way, he will feel more able to confide in you. And the more he can openly talk to you, the better the chance that he will get painful feelings off his chest and work through his confusion and conflict.

➤ *Show your support*: If his girlfriend has dumped him, don't preach about what he may have done wrong but point out his good qualities and how special he is to you. Try to make yourself more available should he want to talk.

Secret Weapons

Work on your relationship with your teen. Positive and supportive relationships with parents help temper most adolescent difficulties, including transitions to new schools and traumatic separations, such as divorce and death.

➤ *Avoid Criticism*: Teenagers, more than anyone, are allergic to criticism. Try to view behavior like wearing torn jeans or shaving his head as a normal attempt to define himself and take it with a grain of salt. When you do criticize, it should be constructive and not a condemnation, which will only alienate him. Your tone should always reflect disapproval of his *behavior*, and not of *him*. Love is unconditional, not based on worth.

➤ *Respect Boundaries*: Be involved in her life but not intrusively so. At this age, it's normal to be close-mouthed about their private lives—to whisper when friends come over, to run to her room to take her phone calls, to close her notebook when you start peering over her shoulder. It's part of the separation and individuation process and her way of saying she wants to take control, not necessarily a rejection of you. Try to accept that her life is no longer an open book and if she tells you to get lost, don't put your head against the door when she's on the phone or look through her things for her diary. Try to express your concern for her safety and let her know you're there if she feels like talking. The more you respect her privacy, the more she will trust and open up to you.

➤ *Stay Involved*: The more interested and involved you are in your child's life, without being intrusive, the safer he will feel and the easier it will be to sort out some of the confusion. Ask specific questions like "How did your biology test go?" Offer to help with homework.

➤ *Stick to Your Guns:* Your teen may rebel against rules, claiming he's ready to make his own. However, his judgment is likely still that of a child and he needs direction and structure. Make him stick to house rules like bedtime, doing homework, chores, eating with the family, and so on.

Secret Weapons

Encourage your teen to get involved in sports as much as possible. It will help blow off excess energy and stress chemicals. It's also one of the best antidotes for depression.

➤ *Back Off*: Don't pressure your kids to succeed. The more overwhelmed your teen feels by academic or parental demands, the more stressed and anxious. Rather, concentrate on supporting him as much as possible in his efforts. This will help boost self-efficacy and your teen will become intrinsically motivated to do his best.

See the Pros!

If your teen exhibits the following on a regular basis, don't hesitate to ask your family doctor or a school counselor for a referral for psychological treatment:

➤ Bad moods that don't change with time and other indications of depression like a change in appetite or sleep habits

➤ Reclusive behavior, social withdrawal, few or no friends

➤ Noticeable drop in academic performance

➤ Avoidance of normal teen activities

➤ Poor self-esteem and frequent self-derogatory remarks

➤ Fears or anxieties that are incapacitating

➤ Stress-related illnesses like frequents colds, stomach problems, headaches, or allergies

➤ Sudden personality changes, for example, a quiet child who becomes suddenly rebellious and wild

➤ Constant bitter fighting that disrupts the everyday life of the family

➤ Alienation from the family

➤ Any sign of drug or alcohol abuse

➤ Any talk or threat of suicide

For a description of the interventions for social phobia, see Chapters 12–14; for GAD, see Chapter 16; and for panic attacks, see Chapter 15.

The Least You Need to Know

➤ Moodiness, but not turmoil, is normal adolescent behavior.

➤ About half of all teens with severe emotional problems are "quietly disturbed" and go unrecognized by the school or the parents as needing help.

➤ Both social phobia and generalized anxiety disorder surface as a problem during adolescence.

➤ If your teen shows the signs of serious emotional disturbance, seek out outside help since his problems will not go away on their own.

Glossary

Acrophobia   Fear of heights.

Agoraphobia   Fear of open places and of being in places or situations from which escape might be difficult or embarrassing, and in which help may not be available.

Angst   A Danish and German word meaning anxiety, apprehension, or insecurity.

Anxiety   A vague feeling of fear and apprehension that creates unease.

Arachnophobia   Fear of Spiders

Autonomic Nervous System   That part of the nervous system concerned with visceral activities, smooth muscles, and endocrine glands.

Aviophobia   Fear of flying.

Claustrophobia   Fear of enclosed spaces.

Cognitive therapy   A short-term psychological treatment to help overcome restrictions to everyday life by breaking the vicious cycle of negative thoughts. Fear-provoking thoughts are changed by repeatedly replacing them with positive encouragement.

EMDR (Eye Movement Desensitization and Reprocessing)   A new therapy in which a patient recalls a traumatic memory while following with their eyes the back-and-forth rhythm of the therapist's hand while it moves across her field of vision.

Fear   A state of alarm or dread that prepares you for flee, fight, or freeze.

Generalized Anxiety Disorder   Prolonged, vague, unexplained but intense fears that are chronic and felt in many different situations and in which the person is continually tense, apprehensive, and in a state of autonomic nervous system arousal.

Hormones   Substances, like cortisol, estrogen, testosterone, or growth hormones that travel through the bloodstream to tissues and organs and impact on their function or structure.

Hyperventilation   Involuntary rapid, shallow breathing that leads sometimes to excessive lowering of carbon dioxide in your bloodstream and results in light-headedness, dizziness, feeling of unreality, shortness of breath and numbness, not unlike having a panic attack.

Hypoglycemia   A condition in which blood sugar levels fall too low as a result of improper diet or stress.

Irrational Fear   A powerful feeling of peril when little or no real danger threatens.

Kava   An herb that works as a natural tranquilizer.

MAOIs (Monoamine Oxidase Inhibitors)   Antidepressants that keep the neurotransmitters serotonin, dopamine, and norepinephrine elevated by destroying enzymes that burn them up.

Meditation   The technique of relaxing through concentrating on a thought, sensation, or special word or mantra.

Mitral Valve Prolapse   A slight defect in the valve separating the upper and lower chambers of the left side of the heart in which the valve doesn't close completely and some of the blood can flow back from the lower to upper chamber, creating a slight heart murmur.

Neurotransmitters   Chemical messengers of the nervous system that make possible the movement of the nerve impulse across the synapse.

Obsessive-Compulsive Disorder (OCD)   Thinking certain unwanted repetitive thoughts (obsessions), often accompanied by repetitive rituals (compulsions).

Panic   A sudden surge of acute terror accompanied by severe agitation.

Parasympathetic Nervous System   The division of the autonomic nervous system that calms the body, conserving its energy.

Phobia   A disrupting and persistent fear aroused by a specific type of situation, such as heights, animals (snakes), or objects (open drawers) that is out of proportion to any proposed danger.

Post-Traumatic Stress Disorder (PTSD)   The development of symptoms in response to events of such severity that would cause most people stress. Symptoms often include a feeling of numbness in response to or psychological re-experience of the event in thoughts, dreams, or nightmares.

Psychoanalysis   A form of long-term therapy that utilizes Freud's therapeutic techniques of free association (saying whatever comes into your mind), dreams and transferences (the feelings for the analyst linked with other relationships, as love or hatred for a parent), that the analyst interprets and in which the patient experiences a release of previously repressed feelings.

Psychodynamic Therapy   A type of psychological treatment that utilizes psychoanalytic principles of treatment to help people gain insight into their problems by exploring their roots in childhood experiences.

Psychotherapy   A planned and emotionally charged interaction between a trained healer and a sufferer to treat and help resolve emotional and mental conflicts.

School Phobia   A condition in which the child refuses to go to school and may show panic reactions if forced to go.

SSRIs (Selective Serotonin Reuptake Inhibitors)   Antidepressants that work by interfering with the re-absorption of mainly serotonin, thereby ensuring a sufficient supply streaming through your brain. They may help in treating panic disorder, agoraphobia, social phobia, and OCD.

Serotonin   One of a group of chemical neurotransmitters that implement neural transmission across the synapse and which is thought to be involved in some types of depression and anxiety.

Sensory Defensiveness   Perceiving presumably harmless sensory stimuli as dangerous and reacting with the defensive flight-fight response.

Separation Anxiety Disorder (SAD)   Excessive and prolonged worry about separating from attachment figures, characterized by incessant clinging, refusal to go to sleep, to school, to babysitters, or to be alone.

Social Phobia   A persistent fear of one of more situations in which the person is exposed to possible scrutiny by others and worries about doing something or acting in a way that will be humiliating or embarrassing.

Sympathetic Nervous System   The division of the autonomic nervous system that arouses the body, mobilizing its energy in stressful situations.

Systematic Desensitization   A form of psychological therapy in which you associate a pleasant, relaxed state with gradually increasing anxiety-triggering stimuli.

Tranquilizers (Benzodiazepines)   A group of drugs used to decrease anxiety by depressing the activity of the central nervous system.

Tricyclics   Older antidepressants that work by boosting the brain's supply of norepinephrine and serotonin.

Further Reading and References

Stress Reduction

Benson, Herbert. *The Relaxation Response.* New York: Morrow, 1975.

———. *Beyond the Relaxation Response.* New York: Berkley Books, 1985.

Charlesworth, Edward A., and Nathan, Ronald G. *Stress Management* New York: Atheneum, 1984.

Davidson, Jeff. *The Complete Idiot's Guide to Overcoming Stress.* New York: Alpha Books, 1996.

Fahri, Donna. *The Breathing Book.* New York: Owl Books, Henry Holt, 1996.

Harp, David. *The Three Minute Meditator.* 3d ed. Oakland, CA: New Harbinger Publications, 1996.

Jacobson, Edmund. *Progressive Relaxation.* Midway Reprint, Chicago: The University of Chicago Press, 1974.

Kabat-Zinn, Jon. *Wherever You Go, There You Are.* New York: Hyperion, 1994.

LeShan, Lawrence. *How to Meditate.* New York: Bantam Books, 1974.

Mason, John. *Guide to Stress Reduction.* Berkeley, CA: Celestial Arts, 1985. Contains many good relaxation scripts.

Naranjo, Claudio, and Ornstein, Robert. *The Psychology of Meditation.* New York: The Viking Press, 1971.

Zi, Nancy, *The Art of Breathing.* Glendale, CA: Vivi Co., 1997.

Diet and Nutrition

Airola, Paavo. *Hypoglycemia: A Better Approach*. Phoenix, AR: Health Plus, 1977.

Ballentine, Rudolph. *Diet and Nutrition: A Holistic Approach*. Honesdale, PA: The Himalayan International Institute, 1982.

Cass, Hyla & McNally, Terrence. *Kava*. Rocklin, CA: Prima Health, 1998.

Colbin, Annemarie. *Food and Healing*. New York: Ballantine Books, 1986.

Crook William. *The Yeast Connection*. 3rd ed. Jackson, TN: Professional Books, 1989.

Dufty, William. *Sugar Blues*. New York: Warner Books, 1975.

Hunt, Douglas, M.D. *No More Fears*. New York: Warner Books, 1988.

Norden, Michael J. *Beyond Prozac*. New York: Regan Books, Harper Collins, 1995.

Sears, Barry. *The Zone*. New York: Regan Books, Harper Collins, 1995.

Slagle, Priscilla. *The Way UP from Down*. New York: Random House, 1987.

Anxiety Disorders

General

Andrews, Gavin, Crino, Rocco, Hunt, Caroline et al. *The Treatment of Anxiety Disorders, Clinician's Guide and Patient Manuals*. Cambridge University Press, 1994.

Barlow, David H., and M.G. Craske. *Mastery of Your Anxiety and Panic*. Albany, NY: Graywind Publications, 1988.

Bourne, Edmund J. *The Anxiety and Phobia Workbook*. Oakland, CA: New Harbinger Publications, 1995.

——. *Healing Fear*. Oakland, CA: New Harbinger Publications, 1998.

Fensterheim, Herbert, and Jean Baer. *How to Conquer Your Fears, Phobias and Anxieties*. Green Farms, CT: Wildcat, 1995. Originally published as *Stop Running Scared!*, Rawson, 1977.

Hallowell, Edward M. *Worry*. New York: Pantheon, 1997.

Peurifoy, Reneau. *Anxiety, Phobias, & Panic*. New York: Warner Books, 1995.

Ross, Jerilyn. *Triumph Over Fear*. New York: Bantam, 1994.

Trickett, Shirley. *Anxiety and Depression*. Berkely, CA: Ulysses Press, 1997.

Weekes, C. *Hope and Help for Your Nerves*. New York: Hawthorne Books, 1969.

Specific Treatments

Beck, Aaron. T., G. Emery, and R. Greenberg. *Anxiety Disorders and Phobias: A Cognitive Perspective*. New York: Basic Books, 1985.

Levinson, Harold N. *Phobia Free*. New York: M. Evans & Co., Inc., 1986.

Liberman, Jacob. *Light, the Medicine of the Future*. Sante Fe, NM: Bear & Co. 1991.

Gold, Mark S. *The Good News About Panic, Anxiety & Phobias*. New York: Villard, 1989.

Schiffer, Fredric. *Of Two Minds*. New York: Free Press, 1998.

Shapiro, Francine, and Margot Silk Forrest. *EMDR*. New York: Basic Books, 1997.

Fear of Flying

Brown, Duane. *Flying without Fear*. Oakland, CA: New Harbinger Publications, 1996.

Sternstein, E., and T. Gold. *From Takeoff to Landing: Everything You Wanted to Know About Airplanes but Had No One to Ask*. New York: Pocket Books, 1990.

Tieger, M.E., and B. Elkus. *The Fearful Flyers Resource Guide*. Cincinnati, OH: Argonaut Entertainment, 1993. To order, call toll-free 1-800-776-9800.

Obsessive Compulsive Disorder

Rapoport, Judith L. *The Boy Who Couldn't Stop Washing*. New York: E. P. Dutton, Division of NAL Penguin Inc., 1989.

Social Anxiety

Ashley, Joyce. *Overcoming Stage Fright in Everyday Life*. New York: Three Rivers Press, 1996.

Desberg, Peter. *No More Butterflies*. Oakland, CA: New Harbinger Publications, 1996.

Gabor, Don. *Talking with Confidence for the Painfully Shy*. New York: Three Rivers Press, 1997.

Markway, B.G., C. N. Carmin, et al. *Dying of Embarassment: Help for Social Anxiety and Phobias*. Oakland, CA: New Harbinger Publications, 1992.

Marshall, John R. *Social Phobia, from Shyness to Stage Fright*. New York: Basic Books, 1994.

Trauma

Colodzin, Benjamin. *How to Survive Trauma*. Barrytown, NY: Station Hill Press, 1993.

Childhood Anxiety Disorders

Balaban, Nancy, *Starting School*. New York: Teachers College Press, 1985.

Feiner, Joel, and Graham Yost. *Taming Monsters, Slaying Dragons* New York: Arbor House/Morrow, 1988.

Garber, Stephen, Marianne Daniels Garber, and Robyn Freedman Spizman. *Monsters Under the Bed.* New York: Villard, 1993.

Kranowitz, Carol Stock. *The Out-of-Sync Child.* New York: Perigee, 1998.

Monahan, Cynthia. *Children and Trauma.* New York: Lexington Books, 1993.

Pipher, Mary. *Reviving Ophelia.* New York: Grosset/Putnam, 1994.

Terr, Lenore. *Too Scared to Cry.* New York: Basic Books, 1990.

Tapes

Anxiety Disorders

Callahan, Roger. *Five-Minute Phobia Cure.* Available from: Callahan Techniques, 45-350 Vista Santa Rosa, Dept. PT, Indian Wells, CA 92210. To order, call 1-800-359-CURE. Cost: #9.96 plus $6 shipping.

Wilson, R. *Achieving Comfortable Flight.* Audio tape series available through Pathway Systems. To order, call toll free 1-800-394-2299.

——. *Don't Panic: Taking Control of Anxiety Attacks.* New York: Harper and Row, 1986. Audio tape series available through Pathway Systems. To order, call toll-free 1-800-394-2299.

Stress

Fanning, P. *Applied Relaxation Training.* Oakland, CA: New Harbinger, 1991.

——. *Progressive Relaxation and Breathing.* Oakland, CA: New Harbinger, 1987.

Kabat-Zinn, Jon. *Mindfulness Meditation.* (7 cassettes for $59.98). Order from: Living Arts, 1-800-254-8464.

McKay, M. *Time Out from Stress*, Volume One. Oakland, CA: New Harbinger, 1993.

Relaxation & Meditation with Music & Nature. Santa Monica, CA: Delta Music.

Yee, Rodney. *The Art of Breath and Relaxation.* (120 minutes on 2 audiocassettes with practice guide for $19.98). Available from: Living Arts 1-800-254-8464.

Zi, Nancy. *The Art of Breathing* Video. Available from: Vivi Company, 1-800-INHALE-8.

Organizations

Anxiety Disorders

Anxiety Disorders Association of America
6000 Executive Boulevard, Suite 513
Rockville, MD 20852
(301) 231-8368
www.cyberpsych.org/

To receive a list of mental health professionals in your area who treat anxiety disorders, along with a list of local self-help groups, call or write. (Include $3 postage and handling.)

EMDR International Association
P.O.Box 140824
Austin, TX 78714-0824

For information about qualified clinicians, call (512) 451-6944

Freedom from Fear
308 Seaview Avenue
Staten Island, NY 10305
(718) 351-1717

Provides a free newsletter on anxiety disorders and a referral list of treatment specialists.

National Anxiety Foundation
3135 Custer Drive
Lexington, KY 40517-4001
(606) 272-7166

NAF provides referrals to their members and other mental health professionals around the country. (Include $10.00 for postage and handling.)

National Panic/Anxiety Disorder News, Inc.
1718 Burgandy Place
Santa Rosa, CA 95403
(707) 527-5738
www.spiderweb.com/npadnews

Call or write for referral sources and contacts for support groups for many parts of the country.

Obsessive Compulsive Anonymous
P.O. Box 215
New Hyde Park, NY 11040
(516) 741-4901

Obsessive Compulsive Foundation
9 Depot Street
Milford, CT 06460
(203) 878-5669
http://pages.prodigy.com/alwillen/ocf.html

Call or write for a list of mental health practitioners in your area who specialize in treating OCD.

Sensory Defensiveness
Sensory Integration International
1602 Cabrillo Avenue
Torrance, CA 90501-2819
(310) 320-9987

Index

347

U-V